TURNING EMOTION INSIDE OUT

Northwestern University
Studies in Phenomenology
and
Existential Philosophy

General Editor Anthony J. Steinbock

TURNING EMOTION INSIDE OUT

Affective Life beyond the Subject

Edward S. Casey

Northwestern University Press
Evanston, Illinois

Northwestern University Press
www.nupress.northwestern.edu

Printed in the United States of America

10 9 8 7 6 5 4 3 2 1

Library of Congress Cataloging-in-Publication Data

Names: Casey, Edward S., 1939– author.
Title: Turning emotion inside out : affective life beyond the subject / Edward S Casey.
Other titles: Studies in phenomenology and existential philosophy.
Description: Evanston, Illinois : Northwestern University Press, 2022. | Series: Northwestern University studies in phenomenology and existential philosophy | Includes index.
Identifiers: LCCN 2021021674 | ISBN 9780810144330 (paperback) | ISBN 9780810144347 (cloth) | ISBN 9780810144354 (ebook)
Subjects: LCSH: Emotions (Philosophy) | Affect (Psychology)
Classification: LCC B815 .C37 2022 | DDC 128.37—dc23
LC record available at https://lccn.loc.gov/2021021674

To Chris Ebele, my Nigerian asylee friend, whose courageous struggles embody those of the dispossessed everywhere at this perilous moment: impoverished, homeless, incarcerated, held in detention, seeking asylum, trying to avoid violence, fleeing climate change, attempting to escape the dark legacy of colonialism by creating a life in which affirmation and fulfillment can once again become possible.

And to the person who has brought me to realize much more fully the plight of Chris and others in comparable circumstances, who has inspired me and many others to act in response to their deep emotional distress and ongoing suffering, someone with extraordinary communitarian vision and abundant moral courage: Mary Watkins.

Contents

Prologue

As I finish writing this book in January 2021, the human population on earth is still caught up in the coronavirus pandemic. This has brought forth stark emotions ranging from anxiety and depression to outright fear and dismay—as well as wild hope for vanquishing the virus. It has brought millions down psychologically and economically while wreaking havoc on racial and ethnic minorities. Intensely felt emotions have spread everywhere in the darkened atmosphere of illness and death despite the recent announcement of effective vaccines for COVID-19. Grief for those who have already succumbed is widespread, and intense empathy is keenly felt: anger at one level becomes chagrin at another, apprehension threatens to turn into panic, while medical salvation beckons from a still uncertain future. Virtually everyone on earth is submerged in a dense stew of conflicting emotions. In the midst of this engulfing global health crisis, the murder of George Floyd last Memorial Day gave rise to widespread protests and demonstrations against police brutality and racial injustice and inequality. This long-standing crisis in another domain has engendered a different range of emotions, going from outrage and despair to chagrin and sadness. Demands for racial justice in this country and abroad have arisen in a tidal wave of highly charged affect.

Given that intensely felt emotions are rife at this historical moment across a wide spectrum of contexts, this book raises the question: Just where are they located? Where do they show themselves? It is customary to say that emotions are *felt within us*, and certainly this is true if we mean that we register them in our minds and resonate with them in our bodies. A widely held view maintains that we carry emotions inside us—wholly contained in an interiority that is regarded as their proper home—and experience them from there. This view, first proposed in the seventeenth century and now buttressed by neurological studies, has come to be taken for granted as a rarely questioned assumption. But what if it is only partially true, if not deeply misguided?

In this study I seek to contest the view that emotions belong to our interiority, that they are *inside us* somewhere, somehow: inside our minds, brains, hearts, or body. I argue that emotions—including those experienced in a historical moment of extreme turmoil, such as the present time—have their own locations between us as well as beyond us. I shall maintain that they originate and are received from outside us far more than is usually acknowledged. Being so often amorphous and transient, emotions are difficult to pin down, or even to define and name accurately. Thanks to their protean character, they do not fall into easily identifiable "kinds." Where is the boundary between anger and rage, emotions so prominent at present? Is the latter an intensification of the former, or a separate emotion? How can we determine this boundary except by arbitrary decree? Given these challenges, it becomes tempting to contain and sequester emotions in "inner selves," where we imagine we can better identify and control them.

Due in considerable part to emotion's elusiveness and indeterminacy, this book has been a long time coming. For at least a decade I have been teaching classes in which emotion figured as a topic, directly or indirectly, and I have started several earlier writing projects on the subject. My efforts to come to terms with emotion as a teachable subject have been continually frustrated, impelling me to realize that there are no "bare" emotions, no emotional essences, or even persisting paradigmatic cases. Emotions are so closely embroiled with our continually changing lives that no reliable classifications, or certain predictabilities, obtain. When I came to realize that describing emotions by eidetic "type" is a losing game, I began to seek a basis in careful phenomenological description. As a consequence, I came to see clearly that emotions are as much displayed *around* us as they are *in* us: indeed, more decisively and impactfully so. Acknowledging that they are often exhibited in various distinctive locations beyond our determinate bodies and minds gives us a more expansive way of construing them, thereby redeeming efforts to come to terms with them in our personal and collective lives.

This book seeks to anchor emotion in a way that does not depend on recourse to the felt interiority of sentient beings. This anchor is found in the placement of many emotions in the world around us. Such placement is not fixed, but neither is it simply ephemeral. Though stabilizing, it is not itself fully stable. It is a matter of what the British psychoanalyst D. W. Winnicott called "transitional space"—a space that orients without requiring exact positioning, that locates without being reducible to anything like "simple location," to use Whitehead's term. Many of the most significant emotions are situated beyond the confines of our subjectivity: how to make sense of this claim constitutes the challenge of this book.

This book is complementary to my recent book *The World on Edge*, published in 2017, not only because each bears on our tumultuous times—far more so than I had originally imagined—but also insofar as each offers a distinctive way of understanding these times. The earlier book considered what it means to be "on the edge" psychologically and in many other ways. Just as I was finishing it in November 2016, Donald Trump was elected to the presidency; my preface noted that he was likely to take us to precarious edges in our collective life. Not only did his election portend missteps and miseries to come, but it brought to the fore the issue of the public expression of emotion, especially in such forms as chagrin and outrage, which are difficult to contain. By the time of Trump's inauguration, I could not contain my troubled emotions and found myself transported onto the streets of New York City, marching and chanting in the impassioned company of hundreds of thousands of others in the Women's March of January 21, 2017. Participating in that event, my emotions were not merely *in me* as something privately held, but were much more significantly located *outside me*—outside any privatized self that holds strong feelings and thoughts within; I was quite literally *beside myself* in sharing emotions with others in this fateful circumstance. By "outside me" I mean not only that which exceeds and surrounds my conscious anticipation or control, but especially the ways in which emotions emerge as coming from somewhere other than in my body and/or mind. Emotions appear in this surrounding space construed as a scene of manifestation. In this way, they present themselves as situated elsewhere than in me, an elsewhere of several sorts which I explore in parts 2 and 3 of this book.

If Trump's election led me to rethink my whole approach to emotion, the sudden onset of the coronavirus during the final stages of this book's completion made the question of where emotion is located still more urgent. The general atmosphere of fear and anxiety was only heightened by the forced isolation of being sheltered in place. A dense mixture of difficult emotions came to be experienced by millions across every continent, further contributing to my conviction that emotion is capable of showing itself in settings that are decidedly extra-personal. The emotions elicited by the virus have come to inhabit a cloud of foreboding that encircles the planet. If such despair and grief are not felt only within ourselves as isolated individuals, then where are they located?

The inauguration of a new president has just occurred as I complete this book. This has brought with it high hopes on the part of many, including myself. Here I ask: Where is this "high"? How are we to situate it? This new political turn, together with the ongoing pandemic as well as massive unrest over racial justice, have brought us to an extremity in which issues of emotion and its location are paramount and unavoidable. If we cannot specify where emotions present themselves to us, how can we hope to understand them adequately, much less redirect them? How might we learn how they can become part of a less destructive era than we have known recently? Emotions "hang in the air" at this fateful moment—soaring high but also descending low. How are we to comprehend the full force of this irrefutable fact?

Note to the Reader: If you wish to get to the heart of my contention, then go straight to parts 2 and 3 as well as the epilogue. Part 1 provides conceptual and historical background.

Acknowledgments

This book, the third in a series of periphenomenological studies, is the work of many hands. It began in an undergraduate course at Stony Brook University that explored affect and emotion, and was further pursued in several graduate-level courses on the same subject matter. I am deeply indebted to the students in these courses, who led me to clarify my scattered thoughts and to have distinctly new ones. Along the way, I met several fellow travelers who encouraged me to restate my position in light of their own original research. Just as emotion takes us out of ourselves, so I have gone outside my home discipline of philosophy to other fields, where I have learned much from thinkers as diverse as the psychologist Eugene Gendlin, the poet George Quasha, and the architect Kent Bloomer. Intense discussions with each of these three thinkers helped to confirm my thematization of the edges of emotion as giving special access to their operative intentionality.

Closer to home, I have benefited greatly from discussions with Fred Evans, who reminded me of the discursive dimensions of emotion, and with Anthony Steinbock, himself a master theorist of emotion in its broader and deeper moral dimensions. Megan Craig is a fearless thinker who breaks inspiring new ground in everything she writes. Robert Crease is exemplary as department chair while remaining a leading scholar in his areas of specialty. Robert Harvey has shown me the importance of devising one's own original paradigms for thinking through a given subject. Anne O'Byrne has exemplified the need to reach out to other fields in order to deepen one's own research in philosophy. Others who contributed directly or indirectly to the completion of this work are Asad Naqvi, Harvey Cormier, Lee Miller, Lorenzo Simpson, Alissa Betz, Mary Rawlinson, Roy Ben-Shai, Gary Mar, Allegra de Laurentiis, Bob Stone, Adam Blair, Oli Stephano, Lisa-Beth Platania, Martin Benson, Peter Carravetta,

Kurt Goerwitz, Drew Leder, Hannah Bacon, John Protevi, Alina Feld, and Jeff Edwards. Judith Lochhead, of the music department, is an intrepid pioneer in the pursuit of a nuanced understanding of the relationship between music and philosophy.

An early version of this book was first presented at the Collegium Phaenomenologicum in Italy in July 2017. I am indebted to Bret Davis for the invitation and to the students and faculty in attendance who witnessed my first groping steps in all their awkward turns and misturns. Later presentations occurred at meetings of SPEP and the Merleau-Ponty Circle, as well as at several other venues.

I owe a special debt to my first dissertation student, Glen Mazis, whose early book *Emotion and Embodiment: Fragile Ontology* (1993) staked out common ground, and with whom I have had many energizing discussions over the years. Another former student, David Abram, has explored dimensions of emotion that converge with my own emphasis in this book.

Grant Nagai made an essential contribution by his astute readings of later chapters of this book, suggesting new directions and invoking invaluable references. His influence has been profound. Lissa McCullough, my indefatigable long-term friend and scrupulous close reader, saved me from many imprecisions in the evolving manuscript.

Thanks to his immense erudition and equally immense generosity, Eric Casey once again kept me honest in my treatment of ancient texts.

Cynthia Willett and Gary Shapiro, official readers invited by Northwestern University Press, both made astute and valuable comments that have influenced the final draft. Trevor Perri, former senior acquisitions editor at this press, was invariably encouraging and supportive ever since I first discussed the possibility of this book with him several years ago. I also thank Anne Gendler, Patrick Samuel, and Paul Mendelson for their invaluable assistance at later stages of the book's production.

It is to Mary Watkins that I owe the largest debt of all. Without her inspiration—intellectual, moral, and political—this book would never have seen the light of day. Her life is exemplary both for its creative scholarship and for its committed teaching of many populations of students, including those in prisons, and for assisting those held in forced detention. She does not just speculate on the nature of emotion, but instills a sure sense of hope and a return of joy in those who have suffered unjustly in today's otherwise cruel and indifferent world.

TURNING EMOTION INSIDE OUT

The Extraversion of Emotion

> Nothing determines me from the outside, not that nothing
> solicits me [from there], but, rather because I am immediately
> outside of myself and open to the world.
> —Merleau-Ponty, *Phenomenology of Perception* (483)

What then if emotions are not subjective—contained *in us*—but are somehow outside and around us, belonging to places and spaces that are essentially public, rather than to our private mind or unique bodily being? What if emotions are not only or mainly an indication of subjectivity—as is often presumed—but an expression of something extra-subjective? What if emotion is more *out there* than *in here*? What difference would that make? This book explores the thesis that the experiential locales of many (even if not all) emotions are to be found in the circumambient world—on the edges of the lives of individual human subjects, as well as in between these same subjects.

This is to propose a quite different view than is found in the common assumption that emotional life is the exclusive property of corporeal or psychical subjectivity. This assumption holds especially in modernist Western views of the human subject, and prototypically in Descartes. But crucial traces of it persist down to our day in the common idea that experiencing emotion "within" is what matters; that we feel it (or should feel it) "in our hearts," that it is something *heart-felt*. This view is further reinforced by the widespread recent recourse to neurophysiological accounts of particular emotions, suggesting that the proper place of emotions is inside the brain's circuitry, which in turn is literally inside the individual subject as its critical core.[1] But what if an attentive phenomenology of emotion turns out to yield a very different view—what if many emotions, among them the most significant ones, have their proper locus somewhere other than in the brain, body, and conscious psyche of the subject, and are occurring "entirely outside of myself"?[2]

I

This book is less about emotion as such, its essence, than about where it *shows up* experientially in human life, its distinctive places-of-presentation. Instead of concentrating on the causation of emotion and its presumptive residency within the human subject, I explore ways in which emotion presents itself beyond the interiority of this same subject; that is to say, where it appears and is configured in various circumambient settings. Some basic distinctions underlie the two different approaches to emotion that I designate as *endogeny/exogeny*, on the one hand, and *periphany* on the other. In overview, endogeny and exogeny concern the *how* of emotions, how a given emotion results from a nexus of internal and external causes; while periphany has to do with the *where* of emotions, where they appear in a space surrounding and exceeding the feeling subject. (I discuss "periphany" in the next section just below.)

The terms "endogeny" and "exogeny" designate approaches that trace out the *genesis* of emotion (as indicated by the root *-gen*, meaning "birth," "origin"): in the case of endogeny, from within, that is, in internally generated psychophysical happenings; and in the case of exogeny, from without, in the guise of the impingements of the natural and social environment. Either way, the emphasis is on a model of generation in which a closely concatenated matrix evolves that is composed of causally related successive events: a matrix that gives rise to specific emotions such as anger, fear, depression, joy, or chagrin.

Consider "endogenous depression," for example, the revealing clinical name for an overwhelming sense of hopelessness, feeling feckless and unmotivated to do anything effective or fully intentional. When depressed, I feel *down*—lacking energy, aim, ambition, and in many cases self-esteem. In depression of an endogenous kind, one finds oneself taken over by and literally *sub-jected* ("thrown under") by this dark mood, which is presumed to stem from somewhere within one's psyche or soma, though often the depressed person does not know exactly where, why, or why just then. Nevertheless, the depressed person feels certain that the condition has emerged from a dense configuration of factors that are closely concatenated—so closely that one is convinced there is no escape from this massive meshwork, which seems to leave no way out: *endogeny* has triumphed.

Contrast this with *exogeny*, in which emotion has an identifiable precipitating cause that is external. One example among many: I get angry with a friend who fails to show up for a meeting we had carefully planned in advance. "No wonder I'm upset," I say, "he didn't show up even though he promised to be here." I am unable to imagine any circumstances that would explain or justify my friend's behavior. Indeed, I know of no good reason for me to have thought that my friend would *not* show up. In this way, I leave no room for the possibility that my friend might have been diverted by an urgency that neither he nor I foresaw. Even if my anger may turn to forgiveness on learning that he had rushed his aging mother to the emergency room, in my present angry response I am caught up in a determinative matrix from which there seems to be no exit. I justify my anger by reference to the external structure of the event, where there are no obvious gaps and few evident ambiguities. At such a moment I am subscribing to an exogenous model of the genesis of my anger, where the *ex-* of exogeny refers to the externality of the precipitating cause. The no-show of my friend happens *to* me, releasing that which now happens *in* me (my anger). The externality, something other-than-me, unleashes an anger I feel as *mine*, as part of my psychic and personal being.

Though a given emotion can be analyzed by reference to both its exogenous and endogenous causation, there is no simple parity here. It is tempting to think of the exogenous factor as comparatively superficial— what "got me angry"—in contrast with an endogenous activity within me as the generative core of a depression that I undergo. In this line of thinking, endogeny emerges as the more basic process. Either a given emotion such as depression takes place largely, if not entirely, in the internality of the subject, or else, if it starts elsewhere with a single external event (real or imagined), it quickly becomes an internal event: it is literally *incorporated* as *my emotion*: as the anger I feel welling up within me. It is not surprising, then, that most if not all emotions are described in terms of their genesis and development within the subject. Indeed, endogenous models of emotional emergence have prevailed in the modernist West since the middle of the seventeenth century, contributing to the view that it is in the human subject that emotion finds its proper locus, its indigenous home-place.

Despite this subjectivist proclivity, endogenous and exogenous models exhibit a basic commonality Both are founded on a conception of emotionality as stemming from a congeries of causes—closely interacting causes that Aristotle would have designated as "efficient." Even if other kinds of causes are at play in this model—material, final, formal, and perhaps others—the preoccupation of endogenous and exogenous accounts alike is to explain how a given emotion arises, whether we have consciously anticipated it or not, and whether its ostensible cause lies in what I have encountered in my current or recent experience (for example, my friend's no-show) or in what derives from inside me, say, a deep-seated and recurrent depression. Both endogenous and exogenous models attempt to account for the *generation* of a given emotion, its coming-into-existence.

II

Matters are very different when it comes to a *periphanous* model of emotion. In this case, what counts is not the internal or external genesis of a given emotion by means of causal interactions, but how the emotion *shows itself* to me and others, and *from where*. Hence the suffix *-phanous*, which I derive from *phainesthai*, a verb that in the middle voice means "to appear" and the verbal root invoked by Heidegger in his initial discussion of phenomenology in *Being and Time*.[3] With the periphanous, the emphasis is on the presentation of emotion rather than on its causal generation, whether from within or from without. Such generation need not be denied, but if acknowledged, it is not allowed to dominate our understanding of emotion; what matters most is the *scene* of the showing of emotion itself: where it emerges in our experience, where it presents itself as coming from.[4]

The key terms at stake in emotional periphaneity are threefold: the showing, the scene of showing, and the showing itself:

1. The showing refers to *what* I witness, the sheer appearing—what exhibits itself as belonging to a scene before or around me. However striking and powerful it may be, this showing is not valorized as a discrete precipitating cause, even if it may be impactful in various ways (as when it is entirely unexpected). It is a matter of a whole set of sights (a "vista") or a more or less coherent group of sounds (a "soundscape"), or else an "atmosphere" or a complete "environment" considered in and for itself, independently of its causal efficacy.

2. The scene of showing is *where* what is shown is witnessed; it is what I call the emotion's *place-of-presentation*. Such a place can matter considerably in the experience of a given emotion. The fact that the emotion stems from a scene in which you as my friend were expected to figure, rather than from some random setting, can make all the difference: your nonappearance in the empty scene of my waiting has everything to do with the emergence of my anger. It is not your nonappearance just anywhere but precisely *here*, in this place where I was anticipating your showing up, that is critical to the birth of my anger. The fact that this specific here-space is empty is a telling component in the emergence of my anger.

3. The showing itself refers to the way that what is shown is not mediated by representations or codifications of various kinds but is given as such, presented *in propria persona* as it were. It is not experienced as part of a distinct causal nexus—even if subsequent analysis may attribute a forceful influence to such a nexus. Rather, it appears on its own terms as *self-shown, shown as itself*. It is a matter of what philosophers sometimes call *ipseity*: the very itselfness of something that is shown, whether exhibited as present or as absent.

All three of the factors I have just singled out are often operative in public space, the space I share with others in fact or in principle. Such shared space figures in the minimal form first proposed by Heidegger in his notion of *Mitsein,* "being-with-others," and is given a more detailed description in Jean-Luc Nancy's *Being Singular Plural* (1996). Such space contrasts both with the external, indifferent space of exogeny (in which a single isolated item can precipitate the generation of an entire emotion) and with the internal, privatized space of endogeny (where everything is held to happen within the bodily or psychical space of my organism). The open space that is the proper home of periphanetically presented emotions is neither indifferent to human experience, nor is it altogether "mine": it is decidedly *not* "mine to be, in one way or another," in Heidegger's telling words from the opening pages of *Being and Time.*[5] No such egoic exclusivity or personal possessiveness—no such solipsism—is at stake in the periphanous presentation of emotion, nor does existential uniqueness figure, as is implied in the phrase "mine alone." Certain emotions may well be associated with me as characteristic or typical of myself, but in periphanous space they *do not belong to me alone.* We enter here a transmissive emotional arena whose operations and configurations call out to be described.

The word "emotion" points in the direction in which a periphanetic account of emotion takes us: a movement outward, as "*e*-motion" (literally, moving out) signifies. This is a familiar movement that we travel every day of our conscious life, even though endogenous and exogenous accounts alike studiously ignore this basic outwardizing directionality. The seductive rigor of such accounts often takes the place of what I have come to identify as a *periphenomenological* approach, in which the emphasis is on the showing of emotion from somewhere outside us that is beyond our individuated psyche and soma. I use the term *peri*-phenomenological to emphasize that we are talking about the peripheral dimensions of emotions that are displayed in scenes *around* (*peri-*) us and thereby deliver them *to* us.[6]

III

Urgent times call for a reexamination of human emotional life, a life that we tend to take for granted in more halcyon moments. As Edmund Burke wrote, "these waters must be [experienced as] troubled before they can exert their virtues."[7] Philosophy, and phenomenology in particular, should have something to say—indeed, something insightful to say, given their nuanced descriptive procedures—about our emotional bearings or their lack in our own *dürftiger Zeit*, a time of crisis and urgent need. A comparable emotional turmoil, though much more highly intensified, was experienced in much of Europe in the Nazi period, although few philosophers rose to the challenge—most notably *not* Martin Heidegger. As the premier thinker of emotion in the early stages of the phenomenological movement, Max Scheler, had he lived into the 1930s, would have had a lot to say about the *Nazi-Zeit*.[8] I am hoping that the study of emotion as presented in this book will be of value to those living through our own version of what Hannah Arendt called "dark times"—and will extend insight into the inherent emotionality of our own current tumult. In particular, my emphasis on the public face of emotion should help to illuminate aspects of our immediate period that might otherwise remain concealed. This may not lead to direct alleviation of the suffering endured in this time, but it will allow us to better understand how it operates and how it impinges on us in the emotional sphere.

My aim in this book is mainly a descriptive one—that is to say, to arrive at a more precise sense of the emergence of emotion in terms of where it comes from, not as construed causally but as *undergone experientially*. Accordingly, I shall pursue the paths of the multiple manifestations of emotion, how they are shown to oneself and to others. Rather than being an inner experience only, we shall see that much emotion emerges from a scene of manifestation in which we witness as happening outside us what we all too often consider to be happening inside of us. In that scene, emotions are not only accessible; they are there, *out there*, before us rather than in us. Their appearing—their periphanous being—occurs in a space beyond the privatized psyche, a space situated around us, located in front of us, and above and beneath us.

If the life of emotion is all too often a Trail of Tears, this is because we suffer from who we are: ineluctably emotional creatures who have no unemotional way out: no exit from our own and others' emotions, being subject to them even if they are not located in us as separate subjects. Each of us, in our own distinctive way, walks the demanding and urgent path of emotions that are often beyond our private province or personal control. They take us out into the world where, as Sartre wrote just before the German occupation of Paris, human intentionality always takes us— hurling us "into the dry dust of the world, onto the rough earth, among things"—onto the *via dolorosa* of a forced migration in our affective experience. Being on this road (and there is no other) amounts to living with the consequences of the manifestation of emotions, their periphaneity.[9]

IV

In this book, then, the guiding questions will be: Where is emotion? How does it show itself? I shall maintain that I do not experience emotion primarily, much less only, within myself—in a strictly subjective domain—but somewhere beside or beyond me, in a charged space that is at once expressive and demanding. How can this be? How can emotions that I often feel intensely as *mine* be situated somewhere *other than in me*—located somewhere *outside*? Just where is this outside, and how can we better understand it? The title of this book, *Turning Emotion Inside Out: Affective Life beyond the Subject*, points to the felt spatiality that is characteristic of various emotional states: how some emotions present themselves as expansive, others as contractive, still others as uncomfortably uneven, and all situated beyond the narrow compass of subjective experience. Emotions have their own distinctive placements—the characteristic scenes in which they appear, by which we not only identify them but through which we feel them intensely. They often emerge at the outer edges of our experience, as when they are presented in certain gestures in which our faces and voices, along with body language, carry emotion outward to others (and just as often back to ourselves). Other such scenes of emotional presentation are found in places that modern philosophy has conspicuously neglected: in crowd behavior, entire atmospheres, and various environments. A primary goal of this book is to offer a periphenomenological description of the more important of these places as they present themselves in human experience.

The phrase "turning emotion inside out" denotes the effort to understand emotion by way of its literal "extra-version"—relocating it *outside* rather than *inside*, where "inside" signifies being contained within the subject, where feelings fester and emotions remain "cabined, cribbed, and confined" in interior regions. The temptation in modernity has been to take them there and to keep them there despite all the counter-evidence provided by the intentionality and expressivity of emotion—which wants to make itself known outwardly, both to oneself and to others, and which is not only generated in the company of other humans but also in other-than-human settings. Though this extraverted directionality is always already happening, when acknowledged at all it has been misconstrued and literally misplaced—interred in the innards of the self of modernity, whether this self is understood as the Cartesian *cogito* or as the Kantian *Gemüt*. How can we show that the ongoing self is turned inside out in its emotional life, this self continuously turning to what is outside it so as to be better attuned to it? This is the primary challenge undertaken in this book.

A comparable question has been raised by certain contemporary thinkers, albeit in different contexts. Andy Fisher, in *Radical Ecopsychology* (2013), speaks of "turning the psyche inside out" in an effort to make mind continuous with the natural world.[10] Similarly, in *The Spell of the Sensuous* (1996), David Abram urges us to "turn inside-out, loosening the psyche from its confinement within a strictly psychical sphere, freeing sentience to return to the visible world that contains us."[11] In parallel with these declarations, my own task is to *free emotion* from its confinement within the human subject—from its imprisonment in the "inner man"—and in doing so I follow Merleau-Ponty's dictum: "There is no 'inner man,' man is in and toward the world, and it is in the world that he knows himself."[12] Merleau-Ponty only briefly pursues his own emphasis on outering with regard to its implications for emotion, and the same is true for Abram and Fisher.[13] In my conception, the relevant outsideness is at once social-political as well as environmental, while existing in still other formats such as the artistic and the therapeutic.

V

The structure of the argument. Part 1 of this book, "Understanding Emotion: Ancient to Modern Views," offers a close reading of selected ancient and modern conceptions of emotion. The first chapter considers early Greek views of emotion, especially anger—most notably as conceived by Plato and Aristotle—in order to indicate that these Greek thinkers converged on a conviction that emotion is a largely public concern: if not always expressly so, then certainly by its direct consequences. I link this emphasis to the rise of democracy in ancient Athens. In contrast with most early modern thinkers, ancient Greek philosophers already took a major step toward the notion that emotion is primarily located in public space, beyond the shutters of the self-enclosed subject, thus anticipating views that more recent authors have come to for their own reasons, explored later in the book.

A second chapter begins by considering Seneca's detailed analysis of anger, a scrutiny that looks both backward in its appeal to deliberative reason and at the same time forward to modern subjectivism. In the same chapter, I examine Descartes's theory that emotions are the private property of individual minds and bodies, generated endogenously within the human subject. I take this as emblematic of early modern views of emotion as inherently subjectivist. Chapter 3 explores the starkly contrasting position of Spinoza, who forcefully extricates emotion from the toils of subjectivity. He brings emotion *out*, far enough out to appeal to the likes of Gilles Deleuze, the self-proclaimed philosopher of the Outside (*le Dehors*), who developed his own take on affect as an active force that *comes to* the human subject much more than *coming from* this same subject.[14]

The fourth and final chapter of part 1 takes up the intriguing but elusive experience of sublimity in relation to the question of the location of emotion. When we experience what we consider sublime, is it something generated from within our mind, or is it somehow found in the very scene that has elicited this experience? Kant is the focus here both because of his detailed treatment of the experience of the sublime in the *Critique of Judgment* and because of his assiduous effort to restrict its proper location to the machinations of mind when one is confronted with a sublime spectacle. I argue instead that emotions associated with the sublime are situated in entire placescapes, which captivate us by their sheer force and outreach. This suggests that the emotionality of the sublime in its several avatars (awe, wonder, being overwhelmed) is inextricable from the vistas that present this emotionality to the human subject.

Part 2, "Emotional Placescapes: The Interpersonal Dynamics of Emotion," opens with a detailed discussion, in chapter 5, of Merleau-Ponty's insistence that emotion is not located in individuals but *between* them; the anger I feel is not merely mine but something that arises in my interaction with you. This inter-personalist view was anticipated by Max Scheler, who traces out several of its main variants that I examine in the same chapter. Starting from the same basic premise of emotion as intersubjective, the contemporary philosopher Sara Ahmed gives this view nuanced focus by situating it in concrete racial and political contexts, an analysis discussed in chapter 6. The seventh chapter starts with the work of Daniel Stern on affective attunement between mother and infant, and then turns to Gustav Le Bon's pioneering work on crowd psychology, focusing on suggestibility in the generation of emotional contagion. To this I add a discussion of incipient fascism as an instance of such contagion in an extremely destructive modality. Chapter 8 discusses the distinctive contribution of Sigmund Freud, who (unlike Le Bon) explored leader–follower psychodynamics in terms of the primary and secondary identifications that underlie what he designates as "emotional ties." Freud also posits unconscious emotions that are situated *under* the conscious ego. Notably, neither Stern nor Le Bon nor Freud locates emotion squarely in individual conscious subjects, but mainly in the intense and intimate interactions between these subjects.

Part 3, "Toward a Prospective Periphenomenology of Emotion," offers a panoramic view of my own construal of emotion. In chapter 9, I start by discerning the distinctive edges of emotional states, and then spell out the basic role of the lived body in the course of emotional experience, with an emphasis on interembodiment in groups and crowds. In so doing I carry forward my recent work on the neglected importance of edges in human experience.[15]

Chapter 10 presents the thesis that emotion is elastic in such a way as to be inherently transmissible rather than being contained in separate subjects. Building upon the pioneering work of Teresa Brennan and Cynthia Willett, I explore the specific means by which emotions are conveyed to us from others, including other species, as well as from the particular places where we experience them. The recent research of Marjolein Oele on the "e-co-affectivity" of environmental interfaces offers further support for a broadly based notion of affective transmissibility, as does the idea of "ecoproprioception" as proposed by George Quasha. To claim all this and to demonstrate how such transmissibility obtains for entire affective fields is to make a strong case for the extra-subjective locus of emotion. I make a more complete statement of this approach in chapter 11, which considers ways in which emotion comes to us from beyond ourselves by way of entire atmospheres, and can be regarded as "airborne" in this respect. I argue that much emotion belongs first and finally to the environments which surround us and of which we are integral parts. In pursuing this direction, I seek to understand how affective force fields deliver emotions to us from sundry regional placements, each of which constitutes a distinctive mode of emotional presentation.

The epilogue insists that we pursue emotion in vain if we look for it as situated only within ourselves. We need to look for it in the diverse placescapes of its emergence and full appearance, acknowledging its temporal and gesticular edges—the poignant peripheries of emotional experience. An appendix, "Art and Affect in the Wake of the Holocaust," compares the presentation of emotionality in the work of two contemporary painters, Anselm Kiefer and Gerhard Richter—each of whom invokes the Holocaust in haunting and instructively different ways.

A note on terminology. The word *emotion* will be employed quite generically to designate virtually any and all ways that an experience or a situation *moves* us with sufficient intensity to act in certain concerted ways, whether by verbal utterances and/or in making various bodily movements. "Emotionality" names the overall state of being emotional. There are several main ways of undergoing emotion—feeling, mood, affect, and affectivity—which can be considered not so much as determinate species but rather as coordinate dimensions of emotionality:

1. I take *feeling* to refer to the subjective state in which I receive and register emotions; in my usage, the word has a much more limited range of meaning than is found in, say, Whitehead's, Collingwood's, or Langer's

uses of the term. (See especially chapter 9 and the epilogue for a discussion of specific ways that feeling differs from emotion in my assessment.)

2. *Mood* refers to an emotional state in which I (and often others) are caught up; it is notably diffuse and indeterminate, but even if a given mood lacks definite shape or precise definition, it can be quite captivating (see chapter 11 for more detail).

3. *Affect* refers to the way that emotions impinge on us—by direct impaction, as it were: as in Spinoza's concept of *affectus* and as indicated in the ordinary English expression "I was *affected* right away by what she said." (On Spinoza's sense of affect, see especially chapter 3; on affect in art, see the epilogue.) With affect, the emphasis is on the moment of incidence when the outer edges of an emotion first reach us, rather than on factors of history and understanding that may come to figure as ingredient in the full scope of emotion. In this respect, an affect is comparatively "abstract" in that it does not call for interpretation at the time of its arrival: the arrival itself is the whole show.

4. *Affectivity* refers to a matrix of several affective states, closely connected with each other so as to create the equivalent of what I call "atmosphere." (This is a central thread in chapter 10.)[16]

My effort in this book is to make a convincing case that emotion comes at us and to us from different directions, emerging from within disparate scenes of manifestation. These scenes cannot be adequately analyzed in terms of endogenous or exogenous causation, for they are arenas of periphanous presentation that do not lie within us but are arrayed before and around us.

Part 1

Understanding Emotion

Ancient to Modern Views

1

Ancient Anger: Plato, Aristotle, and Early Democracy

This opening chapter traces a long thread of considerations of anger stretching between two otherwise unconnected starting points, one historically recent, the other ancient. The recent one is the singular experience that first led me to write this book: outrage over the election of Donald Trump, which found one of its first public expressions in the Women's March in January 2017 in New York City. Participating in that march not only expressed the dismay I felt at Trump's inauguration the day before, but also brought home to me the importance not just of expressing my anger, but the experience of *feeling angry together with others*. This massive political protest included marching side-by-side down a major metropolitan avenue, carrying signs, chanting slogans, and so on, but more significantly, it was a *performing* of anger in the company of others in a particular location (in this case, along Fifth Avenue in Manhattan heading north toward Trump Tower). Having an effective place-for-protest and a shared activity in that place are two factors that took my anger beyond the merely personal and allowed it to find a genuinely *interpersonal* manifestation. *My* anger became *our* anger.

The second starting point—the "other beginning," in Heidegger's phrase—is the commencement of Western philosophy in ancient Athens in the period of its early public theater and the rise of political oratory, that is, in the sixth and fifth centuries B.C. This theater was the very place that Plato regretted as a scene of undue emotional outbursts, one that he considered obscene. Soon after, Aristotle carefully analyzed political speeches with respect to their rhetorical force. This chapter and the next will draw on writings that feature anger as a major theme stretching from Plato onward, a theme that by the time of Roman writers such as Seneca filled entire treatises.[1]

Contributing to this emphasis on anger was the turbulence of life in ancient Greece and Rome, when wars were so frequent that peace never lasted long—generating intense frustration on all sides of those conflicts and struggles, a frustration that gave rise to widespread collective anger. Another factor was the increasing prominence of public debate, which was often fraught with pitched passions; open forums, often focused on war and violence, easily turned vehement as speakers vented their views and tried to convince others of their truth. Given the frequency of such discussions, along with the uneasy circumstances of Athens and Rome at any given moment, it is not surprising that anger figured prominently in the writings of those who reflected on the nature of public life. This is a topic to which we shall return later in this chapter.

What Merleau-Ponty writes of anger that arises in the presence of others is pertinent here: "The location of my anger is in the space we both share—in which we exchange arguments instead of blows—and not in me."[2] Merleau-Ponty affirms that "the space we both share" is where emotion emerges in whole cloth. For us at this beginning point, the question becomes: How does anger figure in ancient accounts of its origin and purpose, and how does this bear on the issue of the location of this emotion? In particular, is anger situated inside human subjects, or is it somehow emergent between them—and to this extent outside each individual party?

|

Imagine yourself in a semicircular outdoor amphitheater on the outskirts of Athens in the sixth century B.C. watching a dramatic production: a play conveyed through bodily actions, gestures, and words, accompanied by the music of flutes and lyres. People around you are attentive and silent at first, but as the evening progresses they become increasingly demonstrative: laughing, crying, sometimes screaming at high volume. Their voices are high-pitched and high-energy—to the point that your body seems reduced to a sounding board for them. So boisterous are the voices rising around you that before long you can barely hear what the actors on stage are saying. This kind of scenario, familiar to us in our contemporary world of rock concerts and soccer games, was not a usual thing for Athenians; it was an extraordinary circumstance, unprecedented. In the ancient Greek world, audiences were expected to remain attentive and observe silence at theatrical events. The practice of absorbed listening obtained both for the verbal performance and for the music that was a prominent feature of such events. In the *Laws*, after recounting the main types of songs played at public theater in the Athens of his era—namely, hymns, laments, paeans, dithyrambs, and nomes—Plato remarks that these were originally subject to regulations and standards:

> People of taste and education made it a rule to listen to the performance
> with silent attention right through to the end. . . . Such was the rigor

with which the mass of the people was prepared to be controlled in the theater, and to refrain from passing judgment by shouting. Later, as time went on, composers arose who started to set a fashion of breaking the rules and offending good taste. They did have a natural artistic talent, but they were ignorant of the correct and legitimate standards laid down by the Muse. Gripped by a frenzied and excessive lust for pleasure, they jumbled together laments and hymns, mixed paeans and dithyrambs, and even imitated pipe tunes on the lyre. The result was a total confusion of styles. . . . [Composers came to claim] that in music there are no standards of right and wrong at all, but that the most "correct" criterion is the pleasure of a man who enjoyed the performance, whether he is a good man or not.[3]

Plato here invokes a tradition of the strict control of musical standards that had evolved over a considerable period of time in the context of popular theater. He does not tell us just when and how these standards were established—dodging these questions by alluding to "the Muse" as their source—but underlines how they were regretfully eroded and finally undermined by renegade composers who were more interested in engendering pleasure in the audience than in observing the standards themselves. What R. G. Collingwood calls "art as entertainment" arose and spread rapidly.[4] This is a familiar story in the history of music, of course. What is accepted as canonical in an early generation gives way, sometimes quite suddenly, to music that not only breaks the accepted rules of given genres, but does so by aiming at vociferous approval by the audience that goes beyond receptive attention and quiet admiration.

But something still more momentous was happening in the case of the history recounted by Plato. The change he lamented was not only about the evolution of a musical genre and its mode of reception in popular theater; it signaled a deeper *political* change that had major consequences. At stake was nothing less than the *birth of democracy*. Remarking that the new musicians accompanied their composition "with propaganda to the same effect," Plato goes on to say:

Consequently they gave the ordinary man not only a taste for breaking the laws of music but the arrogance to set himself up as a capable judge. The audiences, once silent, began to use their tongues; they claimed to know what was good and bad in music, and instead of a "musical meritocracy," a sort of vicious "theatocracy" arose. But if this democracy had been limited to gentlemen and had applied only to music, no great harm would have been done; in the event, however, music proved to be the starting-point of everyone's conviction that he was an authority on everything, and of a general disregard for the law. Complete license was not

> far behind. . . . First people grow unwilling to submit to the authorities, then they refuse to obey the admonitions of their fathers and mothers and elders. As they hurtle along towards the end of this primrose path, they try to escape the authority of the laws.[5]

In these reproving words, we note the striking linking of the term "democracy" to "theatocracy"—that is to say, to spontaneous and uninhibited responses on the part of auditors, accompanied by an overbearing confidence that they are the best judges of the quality or value of what is heard, manifesting a willingness to disavow any or all existing standards. This downward spiral threatens to end in something closer to anarchy than to constitutional democracy. Plato is so disturbed by these unruly "democratic vistas" (in Walt Whitman's phrase) that he seems to conflate these two different forms of political life, as if to suggest that democracy is inherently anarchic.

Common to these currents traced out by Plato—the degeneration of musical genres and the emergence of a vociferous and uncontrolled reception by audiences—is the *expression of emotion*. As Plato puts it later in the *Laws*: "When faced with good or vicious musical representations, and the emotions [*pathémata*] aroused by them, they [i.e., discerning members of the audience] may be able to select the works based on good presentation and reject those based on bad."[6] Leaving aside the question of how to distinguish between "good" and "bad" representations, let us agree that emotions are an intrinsic part of listening to music—at least music that is moving or stirring in ways that go beyond questions of its sheer classification, cognition, and perception. But just how is this so? And how is this emotionality related to the emergence of democratic institutions in the West? A fuller story of this emergence is traced in the groundbreaking work of Travis Holloway, especially in his recent essay "How to Perform a Democracy: A Genealogy of Bare Voices."[7] Rather than review the history he relates so convincingly, I shall focus here on the issue of how emotional display was integral to the evolution of the first full form of democracy in the West.

The crux is this: when people's voices are at once *proffered* and just as spontaneously *heard* by others, two material conditions for the emergence of democracy have been met. Voices are raised—by whatever means and however situated—and are taken in by others who hear them. When these two circumstances conjoin in the context of the expression of emotion, the transaction between proffering and hearing is augmented and intensified. It is given the kind of directly felt authenticity that no preexisting law of genre or codified tradition can deliver in and by itself—not without the animating force of emotion.

II

In order to bear this out, we need to discern three dimensions of any proto-democratic circumstance such as that which took place in early Athenian popular theater: showing emotion *to others*, *for others*, and *with others*. These dimensions are closely related but are not the same thing. When I show emotion *to others*, I manifest it outright, not necessarily intending it to be noticed but bringing this manifestation to a point where others can easily take it in, for I bring it out in *a space shared* with these same others. In contrast, when I show emotion *for others*, I direct it to them with full conscious intention; I make clear for whom it is intended: namely, those others who now surround me and witness my emotional display. Finally, I show emotion *with others* in circumstances where I and others are emotional *together*; emotional expressiveness is not being directed to a certain subset of the surrounding others, or merely manifested as if indifferent to these others. Instead, I and my companions are engaging in a joint display of emotion that we experience together, as happened at the Women's March in 2017. Though I need not attend in any concerted way to how others are being emotionally moved, I am well aware that emotionality is happening and that it is happening *now*. Each participant has a conscious share in this intertwined emotional circumstance, albeit only at the edges of the auditory fabric that is being woven by the intermodulation of the voices I hear, mine and others, joining forces at the same time, constituting a scene of synchronous speaking and listening.

Together, these three modes of showing—especially the third— constitute the germinal state of democracy, its material preconditions as it were, though of course it is not yet a matter of democracy as a developed form of government "of the people, by the people, for the people." This comes later, if it comes at all, as a consequence of these preconditions being met. In the case of ancient Athens as reconstructed by Holloway, genuine participatory democracy arose less than a decade after the crowds became clamorous in popular theatrical events. I would like to propose that this happened because the situation of showing emotion *with* others at public events—not just *to* them or *for* them—effectively prepared the way for the creation of a kind of government in which the people's voices were listened to and valued as making coherent collective sense. By providing a place for such mutual showing, the popular theater prepared the path for the emergence of democracy as an institutional form of government. It showed that people can be emotional together in ways that are responsive to what they are seeing and hearing on the stage—a medley of bodily movements and music, mediated by voices—but not necessarily in the disruptive or incoherent ways regretted by Plato; it showed that theatoc-racy can evolve into democracy.

In short, instead of signaling the emergence of anarchy as Plato feared, the relaxing of formal rules of established genres on the part of musicians in popular theater performances may well have opened the space for the open discourse that is essential to democracy. In this sce-nario, people began to listen to each other in public spaces, not just vent unconsidered personal feelings. Such mutual listening set the stage for the onset of democracy, in which the voice of the people, *vox populi*, was heard and valued. The collective voices first released in the setting of popular theater proved to be an essential ingredient in the formation of democratic institutions in ancient Greece and later elsewhere.

III

There are three stages in the process just traced: gaining freedom from fixed patterns in musical performance in a public theater; intense and un-rehearsed displays of emotion on the part of the audience in this theater; and the germination of democracy. Threading though all three is the basic factor of emotional display in public settings. This display is not always articulate or easily identifiable, nor need it be as vociferous as it was in ancient Athens; it can be quite subtle and more like a *basso profundo* than an insistent melody (as with the low howl that coursed through the crowd at the Women's March). But in whatever form it occurs, it congeals what is otherwise an anarchic and incoherent scene of the sort Plato re-grets in the popular theater. The collective expression of emotion pro-vided social-political connective tissue that was to issue in the emergence of ancient democracy. The fact that democracy itself was regarded with suspicion by Plato—as governing in a way that sanctioned freedom to pursue personal pleasure—does not diminish the historical importance of this emergence itself.

The place-of-presentation for emotion is of critical importance in this process: not just the bare fact of such a place, but the special charac-ter of the *particular* place where the emotion arose and was taken in. With regard to the reconstructed history just traced out, it is far from trivial that this history took place first in a public theater. The stage where the performance occurred was contiguous with the space where the audience was seated and where the overt expression of emotion took place so tell-ingly, and the rows of seats in the amphitheater put members of the audi-ence close to each other as they listened to the music and the words—and to each other. Early philosophical debates concerning democracy, by notable contrast, occurred in the agora, a public arena in which certain tacit rules privileging reasoned discussion prevailed—however impassioned these debates may sometimes have become. The open theater gave way to a decisive relocation of the scene of emotional expression: from a place where its clamorous display was permitted to a scene of more disciplined political activity in which the manifestation of emotion became a subsidiary presence. But this change of place and tenor of voice must not lead us to overlook the continuing role of emotion in the generation of the kind of democracy that was debated in the agora, and to consign it (as did Plato) to unruly crowd behavior rather than to the emergence of an unprecedented form of governmental institution.

In the *Republic* Plato, the self-proclaimed philosopher of reason (*nous*), locates emotion in the middle and lower parts of his tripartite model of human being—in the chest and gut, as if to contain it *under* reason located in the head. Not surprisingly, he also argues for strict enforcement of the rules of genre in music, especially in early education, so that malleable minds can be appropriately molded by listening to formally structured and adroitly performed music. An integral intent of such education is to limit, if not eliminate altogether, emotional displays: "Good literature, therefore, and good music, beauty of form and good rhythm all depend on goodness of character . . . a mind and character truly well and fairly formed. . . . And ugliness of form and bad rhythm and disharmony are akin to poor-quality expression and character. . . . We must issue . . . orders to all artists and craftsmen, and prevent them from portraying bad character, ill-discipline, meanness, or ugliness."[8] Here emotion is absorbed into the domain of "character" (*ethos*). The unstated assumption is that the undue or undisciplined exhibition of emotion—as occurred so dramatically in the public amphitheater in Athens—is a sign of "bad character" (*kakoetheia*). The further inference is that people with "good character" (those who are known for their virtuous conduct) have their emotional life under control, that is to say, under "self-control" (*sophrosyne*).[9] Rather than affirming the integrity and validity of emotional life, this is to limit if not to suppress it: to put it "under the bar," as Lacan says happens when ideas or words are repressed into the unconscious. Even when Plato more fully recognized the importance of emotion in its own right—as in its formative role in artistic inspiration in the *Ion* and its place in the genesis of love in the *Phaedrus* and the *Symposium*—he considers it a "dark horse" in comparison with the noble steed of reason.[10]

IV

Everywhere in early Greek culture, the life of emotions presents a drama—sometimes a melodrama—of the constrained versus the unconstrained. We have just seen how Plato was preoccupied with emotion in popular theater and models of early education, with the latter considered as instilling a constraint on the former. A similar treatment pertains with respect to *anger* in Greek culture, a theme I shall now pursue more systematically. Whereas Plato tried to pin down anger by locating it in the chest (*thumos*), which he conceived as the seat of anger as well as of the moral virtue of courage, his successors attempted to confront anger on its own terms. Especially notable among these efforts was that of Aristotle, whose treatment of anger proceeds in three stages: as it is exhibited in the psyche, in ethical conduct, and in rhetorical contexts. We can regard these as steps in the progressive outwardizing of anger from being positioned in the soul into its embodiment, then to the interpersonal world of interaction with others in the ethical domain, and finally to the political world of persuasion by rhetorical means.

In book 1 of Aristotle's *De anima* (*On the Soul*), we find no fewer than seven passages that deal directly with anger, and each time it appears it is inseparable from bodily manifestations, however much we may feel anger psychically. Here is a characteristic passage: "It is clear that the affections [of the soul] are principles [*logoi*] involving matter. Hence their definitions are such as 'Being angry is a particular movement of a body of such and such a kind, or a part or potentiality of it, as a result of this thing and for the sake of that.' . . . [Such] affections of the soul [as anger] are . . . inseparable . . . from the natural matter of the animals in which they occur."[11] Two points emerge here. First, far from being blind or dumb, affections (*pathémata*, also translatable as "emotions") direct bodily movements as their specific principles (*logoi*) from a justifiable and ultimately stateable motive. Second, there is no understanding of any such state of soul without a grasp of its bodily being, its "natural matter."

Here is another revealing passage: "To say that the soul is angry is as if one were to say that the soul weaves or builds. For it is surely better not to say that the soul [by itself] pities, learns, or thinks, but that the man does these *with* his soul; and this not because the movement takes place in [the soul], but because sometimes [the soul] reaches as far as [the body] or at other times comes from [the body]."[12] This passage points to the close dialectical interchange between body and soul, with the initiative sometimes coming from one, and sometimes from the other: from the soul in the case of affections and thoughts, and from the body in the case of sensations. Not only do affections of the soul provide *logoi* (reasons, accounts) and the basis for movement, but "the soul weaves or builds" by means of its affections: that is, the latter help it to have effects that cannot be reduced to efficient causality because they exercise an inherent creativity in which the effect exceeds what the cause alone might predict. This anticipates a point that has been reaffirmed by emotion theorists quite recently: namely, that anger is not only explosive or destructive but is often constructive as well; it can tell us where we are going and not just where we have come from, thereby revealing the deeper intentionality of our emotional life.[13]

Consider also a passage that forms the conclusion to chapter 4 of *De anima*: "Thinking and loving or hating are not affections of [the body alone], but of the individual thing which has [a body] . . . for these [affections] do not belong to [the body alone] but to the composite thing" (408b 26–30).[14] Here Aristotle draws together the parts into which he has divided the emotional subject—that is, soul-parts and body-parts—to argue that the "individual thing" or "composite thing" is the true subject, the very seat, of emotions. Here analysis is succeeded by synthesis, as if to say that in order to understand emotions we have to distinguish the respective roles of soul and body to begin with, but that finally it is the *whole person* who is emotional. In *De anima*, then, Aristotle seeks to *embed* affection or emotion in its differential sources and carriers—namely, soul and body—and to show the intricacy with which these relate to each other. This amounts to a concerted attempt to address the question "Where is emotion to be found?" His response is that it is located in soul and body alike, albeit differentially, and especially in their intimate interactions within the embrace of the whole human being who feels and emotes, as well as thinks and moves from place to place.

There is one limit to this assessment, ingenious and resourceful though it is. By Aristotle's own admission, his analysis is limited to that of the single person—the "individual thing." As if recognizing this limitation, in the *Nichomachean Ethics* he proceeds to assess the role of emotions as they play out *between* individuals, and thereby to offer a genuinely *intersubjective* account of the operation of given emotions. This is an important step in the direction I am pursuing in this book overall: the direction of de-subjectification, which I hold to be essential for a deeper understanding of the origin and fate of the emotional life of human beings.

V

Anger plays a pivotal role in the second phase of Aristotle's treatment of emotion, and an entire section of the *Ethics* (book 4, chapter 5) is devoted to it. Here Aristotle seeks to establish the "mean" of anger as it is situated midway between the extremes of irascibility and an inability to get angry at all. The mean he seeks—being "even-tempered"—is determined by how it relates to a set of variables that define the full circumstance of anger. It is here that other people figure expressly, especially those *with whom* one gets angry: "There is praise for someone who gets angry at the right things and *with the right people*, as well as in the right way, at the right time, and for the right length of time. This, then, will be the even-tempered person, since it is his even temper that is praised."[15] The same set of variables applies to those who have a deficiency of anger—who are "in-irascible"—as well as those who exhibit an excess of anger: "The deficiency . . . is blamed, because people who do not get angry at things that they ought to get angry at are thought to be foolish, as are those who do so in the wrong way, at the wrong time, and with the wrong people. . . . The excess occurs in all these respects—in getting angry with the wrong people, for the wrong reasons, as well to a greater degree, more quickly, and for a longer time than is right."[16] Aristotle here anticipates the skeptic who wonders if anger can be sorted out quite so elegantly and formulaically as his variables suggest:

> It is not easy to determine how, with whom, at what, and how long one should be angry, and the limits of acting rightly and missing the mark. . . . [Nor is it] easy to articulate how far a person has to go in getting angry, and in what way, before he is liable to blame; such things depend on the particular circumstances, and judgment lies in perception. But so much at least is clear, that the mean state—in virtue of which we get angry with the right people, at the right things, in the right way, and so on—is praiseworthy, while the excesses and deficiencies are to be blamed. . . . Obviously, then, we should keep close to the mean state.[17]

All told, anger engages at least seven factors: things, people, manner ("way"), timing, length of time, degree, and reasons. Not only are these factors not easily quantifiable, but they can be difficult to determine with precision on any given occasion; to repeat Aristotle's phrase, they vary with "particular circumstances," which by definition are changing all the time—just as we as emotional subjects are ourselves altering continually. Precisely in view of the difficulty of determining the quantity of each factor, Aristotle advocates aiming for the mean, which possesses latitude and allows for variation—so much so that we can even say that often "the mean is nameless."[18]

Thanks to Aristotle's insights into the interpersonal dimensions of an emotion such as anger, we can add an important nuance to my earlier allusion (in the introduction) to emotion's places-of-presentation. In virtually any case we can imagine, the place-of-presentation of our anger is a scene of disharmony: a loss of equipoise. A shared space that might be well-attuned has become discordant. When angry we are caught up in an interpersonal matrix, a dense cat's cradle of human actions—one that includes failed or missing actions, and circumstances that we ourselves have played a role in engendering—which has brought about the anger-inducing situation. This matrix is not *in me* by any means; instead, I find myself *in it*—caught up in and overdetermined by it—and my anger is a response to this circumambient circumstance.

The dimensions of anger, we can conclude, are intersubjectively configured, directly or indirectly—such as *when* it happens, for how long it persists, the manner in which it happens, the degree of its vehemence, and even our justifying reasons for it. If we find ourselves in stifling, painful, frustrating, obstructed circumstances and become angry about this, our anger has arisen from a state of affairs that is almost always interpersonally determined and overdetermined. Our anger emerges in an intersubjective nexus of which we are part. This is not only because we tend to get angry with people more than with physical things, but because the encompassing situation in which we get angry is so often precipitated by the actions of others. Even if we don't direct our anger at given persons, the "particular circumstances" that are angrifying have often been brought about by misdirection or bad intentions on the part of others (though certainly sometimes ourselves), and if not recently, then some time ago.[19]

VI

Aristotle's treatment of anger has taken us from the soul to the body, and from the composite individual to an intersubjective scene of conjoint causation. In a third and final step, Aristotle locates anger (and other poignant emotions) in an open public space, a specifically political arena. He does this in his *Art of Rhetoric*, a text that reflects on the advent of democracy in Athens a century earlier when, by 460 B.C., public speaking had become a prominent feature of public life, especially in the Assembly (*ekklesia*) and the Council (*boulé*), arenas in which open discussion flourished. Aristotle reflects on the nature and purpose of the public speeches delivered in these settings and other more casual ones. The purpose of rhetoric—here construed as equivalent to "oratory" and "public speech"—is not simply to induce agreement but to generate discourse that, by its accessibility and inherent logical force, leads listeners to be swayed by the "persuasive aspects" of the speaker's take on a given topic. Rhetoric is defined as "the detection of the persuasive aspects of each matter" or "the given" in the topic of discussion; it is "the power to observe the persuasiveness of which any particular matter consists."[20] The rhetorician has two means of persuasion at his disposal: concrete examples ("induction") and enthymemes, that is, syllogisms that omit mention of one or more premises, since it would be tedious to state each and every premise in a given speech.[21] Either way, the "proof" that is offered in rhetoric is always a "demonstration" of the truth or the desirability of a given line of thought, and thus to advocate for it as the undeniably preferable way to consider a given topic.

In the midst of a rather elaborate analysis of three basic styles of rhetorical speech—"deliberative," "forensic," and "display"—Aristotle suddenly remarks that "the rhetorician needs to know much about emotion."[22] Why so? Here we need to realize that rhetorical speech has three basic dimensions: the character of the speaker (it is this that is on "display" for the audience), the nature of the speech itself (whether it leans primarily on examples or enthymemes), and the "disposition" of the audience that listens. Instead of emphasizing the hermeneutical aspect of the audience's listening—as has become so thematic in the wake of Schleiermacher—Aristotle singles out the emotional state of the audience as most pertinent. He states straightforwardly that the disposition of anyone listening to a public speech is "induced by the speech into an emotional state."[23] It follows that the effective orator needs to know "what, and of what kind, each of the emotions is and also from what and how they are engendered."[24]

This last observation sets the stage for section 6 of the *Art of Rhetoric*, in which Aristotle moves to a detailed discussion of emotion that is especially pertinent for our purposes. He begins by stating explicitly that "emotions are those things by the alteration of which men differ with regard to those judgments which pain and pleasure accompany, such as anger, pity, fear, and all other such and their opposites."[25] Precisely as alterable, emotions are subject to the influence of effective oratory; when they change, so do the "judgments which pain and pleasure accompany." This is to say that people's judgments on the topics addressed by an effective orator will be modified in accordance with the degree and kind of pain and pleasure that such modification entails. In this model, the speaker and his listeners constitute a close-knit circle in which a successful speech elicits emotions that eventuate in judgments that affirm what the speaker recommends (or disrecommends). They affirm it not only at the level of belief or opinion (*doxa*), but in terms of the action to which it leads.

Aristotle proceeds to argue that any given emotion can be analyzed into three factors: "*what state* men are in when they are [emotional in a particular way], *with what people* they are accustomed to be [emotional in this way], and *in what circumstances* [such an emotion emerges]."[26] These factors are, in effect, the psychological state of the emotion as it is felt by the human subject, the social aspect of sharing this same emotion with others, and being cognizant of the situation in which this emotion arises. We can take this to imply that there are three roles human beings assume in the generation of emotions in political space: being moved emotionally oneself upon listening to rhetorical utterances; experiencing such emotions alongside others; and being aware of the overall situation in which such emotionality arises. Even if Aristotle doesn't invoke the four causes that he considered capable of illuminating any given subject matter, we see here his characteristic effort to sort things out in terms of the most relevant parameters of what he is investigating.[27]

Anger is, strikingly, Aristotle's first and leading example of an emotion characteristic of this threefold rhetorical circumstance. He defines anger as "desire, accompanied by pain, for revenge for an obvious belittlement [*oligoria*] of oneself or one of one's dependents, the belittlement being uncalled for."[28] At first glance, this way of stating the essence of anger may seem to diminish its scope by confining it to the interaction between the person belittling and the person belittled: the same kind of person-to-person that was so characteristic of his treatment of emotion in the *Nicomachean Ethics*. Strikingly, Aristotle maintains that the angry person "must always be angry with a *particular person* (for example, with Cleon, but not with mankind)."[29] And it limits the motive of the angry person to "revenge," regarding which he adds that it brings a particular pleasure.[30] This analysis is expanded, however, when he adds that there are at least three sorts of belittlement: "contempt, spite, and insult."[31] If belittlement itself thus takes several forms, the orator only needs to convince his auditors that they have been taken advantage of in one way or another to induce (or increase) anger in them: a familiar ploy in political speeches down to this day.

One of the notable points in the *Art of Rhetoric* is that belittlement as a cause of anger is intensified when those who commit the anger-inducing belittling take the belittled to be "inferior to them by birth, by power, and by virtue and in general by whatever it is in which they much excel; for instance, with money, the rich have this attitude to the poor."[32] The sting of anger cuts all the more deeply when there is a claimed or felt discrepancy in economic or social station between the belittler and the belittled. Strikingly, a comparable discrepancy can arise when a public speaker feigns superiority to "those who cannot speak."[33] Although Aristotle is talking about given situations in the public life of his time, and despite his own conservative leanings, we can sense here the germ of a critique of coloniality, in which those who cannot speak—who speak another language or are not allowed to speak at all—are belittled by the colonizers, who regard them as "inferior to them by birth." The importance of this factor is further evident in Aristotle's remark that when people are "sick, or poor, or in love, or thirsty or in general in a state of unrequited desire, they are hot-tempered and easily provoked, especially toward those who belittle their current predicament, as the sick man is angry with those who attach little importance to his illness, the poor man who does this to his poverty, . . . for each [person] is *guided towards his peculiar anger by his present suffering*."[34] Even if we balk at regarding such remarks as presciently decolonial, we can at least grant that here Aristotle strikes at an especially powerful root of anger—namely, human vulnerability, which obtains with special force for those who are disadvantaged by illness or poverty, and are thus especially susceptible when insult is added to injury.

Aristotle's treatment of anger in the *Rhetoric* is quite comprehensive and for the most part convincing, though it contains ambiguities that call for clarification. One of these concerns the ultimate aim of the orator: is it to incite the audience to action or to calm them down? There is a manifest tension in Aristotle's account between the oratorical aim of stirring up anger in the audience over their belittlement, and the quite different aim of bringing the audience to a calmer state. He makes clear that calm is the contrary of anger—its "suspension and placation"—but he complicates rather than clarifies this tension when he writes that "those who wish to calm the audience down . . . [should bring them] into the appropriate condition and [make] out those with whom they are angry to be either fearsome or worthy of respect or having done favors or acting involuntarily or being excessively pained at their deeds."[35] By both acknowledging the angrifying effect of certain figures *and* what might exonerate those same figures, Aristotle only complicates the question of whether the purpose of public speaking is to generate anger in listeners (by underlining their belittlement) or to induce tranquility in them (as those who have done the belittling are exculpated). In a complex example such as this one, we are left uncertain as to what the primary purpose of political rhetoric is: inducing inaction by pacifying the speaker's audience or inciting this audience to take action—or a complex combination of both aims.

A second area of ambiguity is found in Aristotle's insistence that the only emotions at stake in political rhetoric are those of the audience. This leads us to wonder: what about the speaker's own emotions—those that are overt and contribute directly to the efficacy of the oratory, as well as those which are not fully manifest yet are still motivational? Instead of treating the role of emotions in the speaker, he addresses only the speaker's *character*. But if this character is indeed on "display" (in Aristotle's own preferred term), will it not have its own emotional tenor? Is not character often, and sometimes even mainly, revealed through its emotional manifestations? Indeed, certain of Aristotle's successors who write on rhetoric insist on the importance of emotionality in the speaker. Cicero, for example, presents a strong case for taking emotionality into account in his treatise "On the Orator," in which the figure Antonius argues that "orators, like actors and even playwrights, are able to arouse emotions in their audiences only insofar as they feel those same emotions even more strongly themselves."[36]

Whatever the ambiguities in his analysis of anger, we must credit Aristotle with giving us the most detailed treatment of this emotion to be found in the ancient Greek world.[37] He makes emotion integral not just to intersubjective life, but to the specifically ethical and political reaches of that life. By resolutely relocating it in those reaches and bringing out its constitutive importance there, he takes a major step forward in the history of the philosophical assessment of emotion. This is not to say that he advocated being emotional for its own sake or even for the sake of what it expresses. Rather, he wants his readers to appreciate that emotion is a very active component of ethical and political life that must be singled out, assessed, understood, and in certain cases acted upon. Ordinary individuals and public speakers alike must be savvy in their assessment of emotions if they are to move others in the direction they embody or advocate. This effort is not reducible to manipulating emotions, but in the best of cases is a matter of respecting them—taking their irreducible import seriously—for emotions *bear judgment forward*. Emotions function as animators of human action, whether by ethical example or by overt political persuasion, and they help gauge with sensitivity the particular value at stake in a given ethical action or political judgment. Aristotle makes clear that emotions *carry value judgments* not only to the brink of action, but into action itself, and do so in the ethical as well as the political domain.

VI

The issue I raised in opening this chapter remains unaddressed: Why was anger so often thematized by writers in the ancient world? Why is it that Cicero, though ultimately skeptical of the value of anger in public life, in his "Tusculan Disputations" (book 4) nevertheless "concentrates disproportionately on anger, in keeping with the importance of that emotion in the philosophical and literary tradition [of the ancient Greco-Roman world]"?[38] A clue to begin to answer these questions is found in the very first word of the *Iliad*—*ménis*, "wrath"—and above all in Achilles's wrath, an anger famously excessive and violent.[39] *Ménis*, a very ancient and rich word, derives from the Indo-European root **men-*, which means "to activate the mind." Another derivative of this same root is the Vedic Sanskrit word *manyû*, zeal, desire, anger. In the *Rig Veda* two hymns dedicated to the god Manyû were, according to Leonard Muellner's classic study *The Anger of Achilles*, "actually recited to foment the lust for battle in warriors. . . . [Thus] the [main] frame of reference for *manyû* is the world of the warrior."[40] From this clue we may infer that anger is paradigmatic for a vigorously active frame of mind: it both initiates and exemplifies dynamic mental activity, albeit with an aggressive edge that manifests itself most dramatically in the person of a warrior—of which Achilles was an archetypal exemplar in the Homeric world.

In this construal, anger is not reducible to mindless or impulsive bodily reaction, but is characterized by an energized psychical component that is suggested in the English word "wit," with its cognate "to outwit" being the frequent aim of warriors in battle—and the continual accomplishment of Achilles himself. Soldiers in combat need to channel their anger into dexterous and skillful maneuvers on the battlefield. There was an important ritual aspect to the anger, moreover, that was evoked in the reciting of hymns addressed to Manyû before battle. Muellner argues that the placement of the word *ménis* at the very beginning of the *Iliad* is a sign of the performative basis of the epic, which was recited aloud in repetitive patterns in which the use of particular epithets was crucial. The epithets were not only for the sake of identifying certain major figures, but for establishing insistent repeated patterns in the oral recitation. Here Muellner builds on the pioneering work of Albert Lord and Millman Perry, which demonstrated that the Homeric epics involved a situation in which "the process of composition takes place *in* performance" and nowhere else.[41]

This thesis is pertinent to the thematization of anger as a central topic in ancient philosophy and literature. Anger was regarded as a singular emotion not just for inducing dramatic demonstrative gestures on the part of individuals carried away by it, but more importantly for its role in the rituals of public life, and especially in areas of public life that bore upon warfare, actual or threatened. In a situation of impending war, a given emotion is valorized not for its effects in self-enclosed individual psyches—the "feeling" of anger as internally experienced—but for what its incitement enables on the battlefield. Ritualistic rehearsals of anger such as occurred in the oral recitation of the *Iliad* have the advantage of being at once dynamic and expressive—in keeping with the *men-* root of anger—yet not such as to call for literal violence, as if the ritual performance at once absorbed and sublimated the vitriol of anger itself. It is a matter of invoking war by way of verbal performance rather than calling for literal military engagement.

A more complete form of this ritual is revealing in this respect: "While murmuring these two hymns to Manyû, a diviner would stand between two opposing armies and set fire . . . to a special bundle of branches. The side that drew the smoke from the burning bundle was declared the loser."[42] In this way, a ritual dedicated to the god of anger, Manyû, in effect pre-occupied the space of what might have become an actual bloody battle between two armies: this space was preempted by murmured words and burning branches. The invocation of Manyû in a ritual space averted destructive violence in the space of battle. This pacifying ritual space was the converse of a public space in which a warmongering orator might try to whip up enthusiasm for going to war on the part of his audience. The ritual of Manyû and the recitation of the *Iliad* can both be regarded as ways to avoid the brutality of actual warfare by the indirection furnished by ritualized and poetic performances.

Even if the figure of Achilles was mythical, the familiar phrase "the wrath of Achilles" sounded the first chord in a long-standing obsession with anger in the ancient world—arguably lasting for at least 800 years, and probably longer. Two assumptions prevailed throughout the early Greek period: that anger cannot be altogether hidden, and that it must be controlled. William Harris, who takes up these assumptions in *Restraining Rage*, distinguishes between four stages in ancient thinking about anger: reining in angry actions and speech; eliminating angry actions and speech; reining in angry feelings; and eliminating angry feelings. Harris does not intend this list of stages to imply a straightforward historical progression, but to offer a tetrad of ways of dealing with anger by moderating its expression and if possible preventing its emergence altogether. Ancient authors take different stances with regard to how to realize such goals, with Plato and Aristotle largely in favor of holding anger in check (e.g., seeking a mean between extremes) and the later Stoics arguing for its suppression altogether wherever possible.

This long-standing concern with restraining anger shows the fascination—verging on a dynamics of awe in the case of Achilles—that anger held for ancient thinkers. Anger was regarded as something so powerful that it threatened not just the composure but the very integrity of the human subject—as something "dreadful, [potentially] fatal, in its effects and so . . . to be feared and avoided."[43] Among early Greeks of the Archaic period, prototypes of the kind of destructive anger that is in play in *ménis* were found in certain gods and their behavior, most notably in Zeus and Hera, Poseidon and Mars. Even when anger was located more squarely in human beings, it was regarded as something to be moderated and, if possible, removed.[44] It is a tribute to the detrimental force of anger that so many literary and philosophical writers were preoccupied with its control. Indeed, Harris maintains (and his lengthy tome attempts to demonstrate) that "anger control as a doctrine [has] had a longer and more intense history than attempts to control any other emotion."[45]

VII

At this late point, several strands in the appraisal of emotion in the ancient Greek world begin to come together. The origins of democracy in popular theater represented a moment when unrestrained emotions, including but not limited to anger, came to the fore and were openly expressed in public. It was a moment of "open mic"—albeit without an actual microphone. In Fred Evans's phrase, a "multivoiced body" emerged, activating an open space for expressive speech in which emotions ran high and were freely voiced without the constraints of decorum and tradition.[46] This occurred in the early sixth century B.C. By the end of the ensuing century, democratic institutions had arisen in Athens—along with supporting practices such as public discussions on the agora and in the Assembly—and, concurrently, widespread public speaking of the sort addressed by Aristotle in his *Art of Rhetoric*. Such governmental institutions and speech-making practices brought with them the prospect of the advance of civil society in Athens and elsewhere. Civil society was not just a matter of law and order; it also entailed "civil cooperation and decency" at various levels of the city-state and thus the control of unbridled emotion.[47]

A new concern with restraining anger emerged in this context. Aristotle's effort in his *Ethics* to advise against the extreme of "irascibility" reflected a preoccupation which had been building for the previous century and a half. During that time, uncontrolled anger such as the wrath of Achilles was increasingly seen as inimical to political processes in a civil society. Demosthenes, who was not above instilling in his audiences a sense of righteous indignation, nevertheless averred that an "honorable citizen" should manage his affairs "in an even-tempered and moderate fashion."[48] Isocrates advised his listeners to "practice self-control [*enkrateia*] in all the things by which it is shameful for the soul to be uncontrolled—gain, anger [*orgé*], pleasure, and pain."[49] Not surprisingly, Plato followed suit by criticizing Thrasymachus of Chalcedon for making "tearful speeches aimed at arousing pity for old age and poverty . . . he is [all too] clever . . . at arousing the masses to anger."[50]

Anger control became insistent at a public level from about 450 B.C. onward; that is to say, in the aftermath of the early experimentation with democracy a half-century earlier. As Harris remarks, "the Athenians seem to a large extent to have internalized the notion that their [democratic] freedom would only survive if they were able to limit the action of their own passions, including especially their own anger."[51] The irony in all this is that (in Holloway's hypothesis) democracy arose in its first fully recognizable form in the West from the unrestrained expression of passions at public theatrical events. The further irony is that democracy came to be excoriated by a thinker like Plato, whose view that it inevitably leads to anarchic confusion in the name of "freedom"—thus preparing the way for tyranny—spares no scorn for it.[52] The uninhibited expression of anger, charges Plato, is likely to lead to "terrible civil conflict."[53] The very expressivity that had made democracy possible in the first place—unfettered speech in audiences at outdoor theater events—is now what must be placed under constraint.

Despite variations in their treatment of anger, the Greeks were consistent in their avowal of the *publicity* of emotion itself. Far from confining emotion to the inner privacy of feeling human subjects, they insisted that it belongs primarily in the public sphere, in which it was to be valued in three basic ways: as integral to the origin of democracy in popular theater (despite Plato's objections to such theater in the *Laws*); as intersubjectively dynamic (e.g., in the triangulations of Aristotle's *Ethics*); and as effective in political discourse (as in Aristotle's account of the nature and purpose of public speaking in the *Art of Rhetoric*). Despite having recognized the power and scope of emotion in these diverse contexts, Greek authors from the fifth to third centuries B.C. also insisted on methods of constraining emotion that amounted to its virtual suppression, with anger a leading case in point. These two main directions—overt expression of emotion versus its ethical-political restraint—though ostensibly at odds, are coherent in the end: the Greeks' very recognition of the force and efficacy of emotion in its controlled public presentation was what led to elaborate efforts to contain its uninhibited manifestation. The containment, however, was not aimed at consigning emotion to a private subjectivity—such as we find in Descartes and other early modernist models—but amounted rather to finding ways to moderate the *public expression* of emotion, above all on certain occasions.[54]

* * *

A premise of almost everything argued about emotions thus far is that they find their proper telos in being *expressed*—in being brought out into the public space, outside the individual subject. Anger is exhibit A for this premise, given its highly demonstrative character, its proclivity for announcing itself in conspicuous gestures and words, its intention to make itself known, and in all these ways showing its inherently *public* face. Even when an angry person bites her lip to hold anger back, the very effort to restrain it reveals it. I take this ordinary occurrence to confirm a major direction advocated in this book: demonstrating the extent to which emotions emerge and show themselves in social and political settings—which is to say, intersubjectively. In ancient Greece it was the public display of excessive anger—its overt expression rather than its reasons for existing—that was found objectionable and made subject to structures of control in the wake of Homer, Plato, and Aristotle. This suggests that what was most threatening was the immoderate exhibition of anger, not its content or cause or justification. The tradition traced by Harris from the fifth century B.C. onward sought to suppress such brazen manifestation as much as possible—as if there were something inherently repugnant about the overt, unvarnished expression of anger.

This leads to a further question: Is it possible that such a critique of anger epitomized what is unacceptable about many other emotions as well: namely, their deep tendency to intrude into people's lives, their tendency to display themselves in public—in a word, by exophany, their sheer showing-forth? If so, this suggests that anger is not just a striking and exceptional emotion whose complexity calls for our sustained attention, but is emblematic of many other emotions with regard to their confrontational and demanding dimensions. And if this is the case, it might help to explain why there was such a strong temptation to relocate emotions inside the human subject in early modernity: to stuff them into the subject and keep them there, as if this would relieve or at least reduce the distraction and embarrassment of their intrusive public presentations. Something like this, I believe, may have motivated Descartes to bury emotions in the human subject. Yet we need not wait for Descartes to witness a concerted effort to interiorize emotions; a parallel move can be seen emerging in a thinker belonging to the ancient Roman world, Seneca, who anticipated the Cartesian effort in a telling way that we must now consider.

2

Turning Emotion Outside-In: From Seneca to Descartes

Anger often comes to us, but we more often go to it . . . other passions are visible, but anger makes itself obvious.
—Seneca, *De ira*

Seneca's essay on anger, *De ira* (written in A.D. 49 or 50), is the most extensive extant ancient treatment of anger. It is also the first treatise focused on any single emotion to be written in Latin. While various thinkers have had plenty to say about anger—from Aristotle's discussions of anger in several different settings to Spinoza's brief but insightful observations (addressed in chapter 3)—Seneca pursues the highways and byways of this emotion in considerable detail. He offers incisive observations such as those in the above epigraph. He was perhaps the first Western author to propose a specific therapy for anger—carried out mainly by angry persons themselves rather than by a priest or therapist.[1]

Seneca cautioned against judges condemning defendants on the basis of anger alone, rather than on an effort to understand the full circumstances of an imputed criminal action.[2] His presumption is that if we can understand and deal with anger, we can handle other emotions, no matter how different they might appear to be from anger itself. For him, anger is *prismatic* of other emotions—which are somehow condensed and reflected in it, albeit often at the price of their considerable distortion.

Before going into the details of Seneca's own analysis, let me again underscore the prominence of this emotion in the works of ancient Greek and Roman thinkers—a prominence that is not merely striking, but also instructive for our own historical moment. These ancient thinkers take up situations analogous to circumstances in our own vexed era, when policy decisions and political actions taken at the highest levels of government have proven to be highly contentious. We have much to learn from precedents in earlier troubled times, especially when it comes to collectively shared anger and affiliated emotional states such as outrage, fury, chagrin, dismay, desire for retribution, and the like. Also spurring my continuing emphasis on anger in this first part of the book is the reality that anger, the thing itself as a phenomenon, is far from unambiguous in its origin, appearance, and fate. We witness this ambiguity in the sheer fact that several Greek words are conventionally translated as "anger," such as *ménis, orgé, chole, thumos*. This raises the question of whether anger is a single thing, or rather a cluster of related phenomena that are distinguishable. Yet some familial relatedness allows such a disparate nomenclature to possess coherence, even if it is difficult to spell out this coherence with any exactitude. The coherence of the anger syndrome is like an invisible magnet that holds together the different aspects and kinds of anger that in English we designate as ire, wrath, rage, outrage, fury, and more. When a stripped-down definition is attempted—as with Aristotle's attempt to reduce anger to the two factors of belittlement (*oligoria*) and revenge (*timoria*)—we find ourselves somewhat suspicious, sensing that he has given us a rather reductive take on what is in fact a complex congeries of related phenomena. Perhaps this explains why Seneca avoids attempting a single definition of anger in his extensive treatise. He talks around the topic as if hoping the reader will come away with a better sense of what anger is *like* even if the author himself stops short of saying exactly what it *is*.

I

Now we enter Seneca's remarkable text, approaching it from several perspectives. The first of these is related to the very elusiveness of anger just emphasized. In the opening pages of *De ira* he makes clear that anger is not easily, and perhaps never fully, conquerable. As if to rebuke the sustained attempt to find effective ways to control anger (which was of major concern to Aristotle before him, and Spinoza long after him), he makes four observations. First, if we attempt to control anger as directed toward others, we shall only succeed in turning it back on ourselves: "How witless a thing do you reckon anger to be, seeing that it turns against itself when it cannot burst out against another as quickly as it wants?"[3] Second, it is far better not to feel anger at all or at least to cut it off at its root than to have to devise methods of controlling it: "It's easier to keep harmful agents [like anger] out and not admit them [into our ongoing life] than to direct and control them once they've been admitted."[4] Third, "if it allows itself to be [severely] limited, it should be called by some other

name: it has ceased to be anger."[5] Fourth, and most decisively, anger itself
is such that it *cannot be controlled*: "it has this particular evil trait: it's unwill-
ing to be controlled."[6] In short, we could avoid all the fuss over learning
how to effectively master, direct, or eliminate anger if only we can avoid
experiencing it in the first place. It is a matter of staying out of harm's way.

Early on in *De ira* Seneca distances himself from both Plato and
Aristotle. Unlike Aristotle, he does not consider anger something intrinsic to intersubjective human life; he denies that it is ever of use in the
pursuit of courage, as Plato argued in the *Republic*, or of justice, as Aristotle contends in the *Art of Rhetoric*. It is never admirable, and is "not characteristic of freedom or nobility."[7] Quite to the contrary! Seneca goes to
special pains to underline the ignoble and ignominious aspects of anger.
These include his claim that it is "soulless and frenzied" and is in fact a
form of "madness"; it is ugly and "deformed and bloated."[8] To engage in it
comes at a high price: "no pestilence has been more costly for the human
race."[9] The very idea of righteous indignation, which many of us might
be tempted to invoke as justifying feeling angry when witnessing cruelty
or injustice, is beside the point for Seneca, who can find no good or right
occasion for letting ourselves get carried away by it. Aristotle's effort to
promote a minimal irascibility is futile, as is the search for a golden mean.
In the end, Seneca paints such an unremittingly negative picture of anger
that it is irredeemable in his view. It is as if, having recounted its undeniable negativities, he challenges us as readers to identify or at least try to
imagine something positive about an emotion to which no honor is due.

Seneca argues that in our basic nature, "human life is constituted
by the harmonious exchange of benefits, and is held fast in a pact of
mutual benefits not by fear but by mutual affection."[10] In such a pact,
amounting to a kind of pre-given social contract of the emotional life,
"humans are born to give and receive assistance [to one another]"; hence
there is no place in such a contract for anger, which is disruptive and
seeks harm and gets humans into danger and disharmony.[11] Anger is not
anything "natural"; it does not belong to human nature and is ultimately
useless, something at once gratuitous and regrettable. Seneca's proto-
Rousseauian premise is that we are "born to form a social union."[12] Because anger thrives in disunion, it is contranatural.[13] Anger is of no value
in engendering harmonious relations—quite the contrary. As inherently
"unbridled and untamed," it does not contribute to helping others, and is
ultimately "self-destructive" insofar as it often turns upon itself in frustration over being ineffective in its own destructive pursuits.[14] There is no
way to win with anger, in other words, because it is harmful to others,
destructive of oneself, and finally self-defeating.

De ira also describes the basic process by which all the "passions" are generated. For Seneca, passions (which I take to be equivalent to what I am calling generically "emotions") emerge from a sequence that consists of two involuntary moments between which there is an (at least partially) voluntary moment of "deliberation." The three moments (or "movements," as Seneca prefers to call them) are as follows:

> To make plain how passions begin or grow or get carried away: there's [1] the initial involuntary movement—a preparation for the passion, as it were, and a kind of threatening signal; there's [2] a second movement accompanied by an expression of will not stubbornly resolved, to the effect that "I should be avenged, since I've been harmed" or "this man should be punished, since he committed a crime." [3] The third movement is already out of control, it desires vengeance not if it's appropriate but come what may, having overthrown reason. We cannot avoid that first mental jolt with reason's help, just as we cannot avoid the other movements that . . . befall our bodies. . . . Reason cannot overcome those movements, though perhaps their force can be lessened if we become used to them and constantly keep a watch [out] for them.[15]

The first and third moments are externalized and externalizing in relation to the subject: receptive and active respectively, they bear on the situation we find ourselves in. The second moment, quasi-voluntary, occurs within the human subject, whose considerations can make a difference in the outcome, though not in any wholly autonomous way. Let us look at each moment in more detail:

1. In the first moment, we receive impressions from our interaction with others that literally and figuratively get "under our skin." This is the moment of perceived insult or hurt, especially to oneself, but also to others whom we see being injured by someone's actions or words. We *take in* such perceptions of misconduct—absorbing them into our perceptual system.

2. In the second moment, my "will" intervenes in the form of a wish or thought that I or others should be avenged. This moment is crucial precisely because it is not altogether determinate: my will is not yet "stubbornly resolved." Anger is rising in an "intentional movement" that has "not only taken in the impression [of being harmed] but affirmed it—this is anger [that we feel burgeoning in ourselves], the arousal of a mind that moves willingly and deliberately toward the goal of vengeance."[16] Full-fledged anger occurs only in and through the unfolding of the whole process; but the critical moment, the potential turn-around moment, is the second, for only this moment is intentional in the sense that the outcome can happen differently, depending on our response to the perceived

harm that initiated the process. It is *quasi*-voluntary insofar as there is not yet a fully committed or resolute act of will that has made up its mind to take revenge; we are still able to project a different course of action.

3. The bodily action whereby anger is realized, actual revenge, only occurs in the third moment—when I have given in to my inclination and deliberation, and have begun to pursue vengeance in a dedicated way that knows few if any checks.

If the first moment is passive as receptive, the third moment is active in involving express bodily movements. The second moment, reflecting its midway position, can be characterized by Husserl's celebrated phrase: "activity in passivity."[17] In this instance, I hesitate just long enough to assess the situation and decide whether I should act on it, with the result that volition emerges, whether as a will-to-do or a decision not-to-do. Such volition does not occur in the form of a determinate bodily action: it consists in something more like allowing or not-allowing such an action to happen based on a desire to take revenge or not; it can still go either way. When revenge does occur as a concrete action, we enter into the third and final moment in Seneca's tripartite sequence.

In the sweep of this whole process, the second phase is clearly pivotal, for it is the phase that decides whether anger will become fully real—not only as *felt*, rising within ourselves, but as something that moves us to take action. A critical factor in the second stage is a certain form of deliberative reason. Such reason does not act as a superior force as if it were an impartial judge; in any case, there is not adequate time to consult any such tribunal; for the act of deliberation occurs quickly, even if it comes from a place that is distinct from the original scene of the perceived injury or insult—a place in which we consider what action, if any, to take in response to such insult or injury. There is no imperative to act hovering here, either hypothetical or categorical; there is only an emerging sense of what is best to do, which action we should take, in the circumstance.

We might designate this second moment of emotional process singled out by Seneca as the "indeterminate matrix of possible action." Preceding it are the initial impressions of felt or observed hurt or harm; these often stem from a scene of "belittlement," in Aristotle's apt term. But instead of responding immediately, or merely reactively (as when, in impulsive anger, we "fly off the handle"), there is a pause in which our response percolates, so to speak. Rather than deliberative reason as a separate voice, what we might call its sotto voce presence is brought to bear, momentarily taking the place of any direct or mindless reaction. This is the pivotal moment of the indeterminate matrix, from which explicit bodily action (by gesture or word) may issue—or, alternately, no such action. In the latter case we have "thought better" than to undertake a mindless, purely reactive counteraction. Seneca adds that "the second movement, which is born from deliberation, is [itself] eradicated by deliberation."[18] That is, deliberation can be self-liquidating insofar as it seeks a solution that does not require any further thought—a solution that speaks for itself, as it were.

II

Not only is Seneca's three-part schema an ingenious analysis of what happens in the generation of anger, but it presents a model for the emergence of *all* passions—any emotional experience—and as such it has implications for a broader understanding of emotion in general. The emphasis falls on the *making explicit* of emotion, its being brought out into a public domain, rather than its sealed-in fate within the subject. Just as Aristotle focuses on the genesis of emotion as it emerges in shared spaces, Seneca sees emotion as likewise arising from an interpersonal situation of being hurt or harmed by others. This occurs in the intimate interactions of my bodily existence with that of others: their words or physical blows are emitted from their lips or hands, both of which happen in the common corporeal space of interpersonal relationships. Coming from their bodily extremities, they affect my own extremities, bringing us edge-to-edge in emotionally charged relationships.

What I later emphasize in parts 2 and 3—the overt *expression of emotion* in open places—is anticipated by Seneca's insistence that what matters in the end is whether the subject acts on whatever emotion is felt, and how this emotion is expressed in word or deed, "pressed out" into common space. This is to say that an emotion, in being directly lived and then thought through in deliberation, must reach some degree of explicitation. If it is checked in midcourse—as Seneca hopes anger will be, in keeping with Stoicism—it will never become the full-fledged emotion that renders it efficacious in action or even recognizable as such. It is not that it happens only in part or only halfway; it does not happen at all. An emotion requires some significant degree of explicitation—what I shall call "front-loading" much later in this book—to be that very emotion. It follows that there is nothing that can yet be accurately labeled "anger" in the first and second stages of its evolution: there is only the sense of being aggressed upon (insulted, dealt with unfairly, and so on), followed by a moment of consideration about how to read the aggression and what to do about it in response. Only if there is a movement to the third stage is there fully actual anger: identifiable, manifest, discussable—explicitly and expressly recognizable *as* anger, which is anger that has become itself, realizing its own telos, as it were.

As if anticipating a skeptic's concern with the ostensibly "subjective" character of the second movement as a stage of deliberation, Seneca introduces the factor of deliberative *reason* (*ratio*)—which, even if it is invoked and acted on by the individual subject, represents an extrapersonal and impersonal power whose origins cannot be confined to the vagaries of the individual subject. Seneca's notion of reason may not possess the objectivity of Kant's "pure practical reason," but it does give access to rules of reasonability that imply a certain consistency across different human subjects, each of whom has access to what such rules would suggest, however imperfectly they may be apprehended or acted on. Reason as providing criteria of evaluation for the rightness of deliberation is the very source of Seneca's conviction that anger itself is counternatural: reasoned reflection (including his own, as the author of *De ira*) shows anger to be a force that disrupts the natural order and threatens to tear apart the social fabric. Anger's full enactment in its third phase, when it is no longer controllable, runs contrary to the inherent rationality of the human social order. The restraining effect of rationality is part of our natural endowment—part of *human nature*—and to this extent we can trust it as a reliable guide to action (or nonaction). It oversees the deliberation that is the most distinctive feature of the second phase of Seneca's model of emotion. Indeed, Seneca claims that following reason's dictates will ensure that human relations will be self-sustaining: "reason suffices, in and of itself, not only for planning ahead but also for the conduct of [human] affairs."[19] In such prudential conduct, guided by reason, there is no room for the explicit expression of anger, much less for letting it get out of control.

Seneca's invocation of reason can be regarded as a valiant move to rescue emotion from a merely idiosyncratic, and thus wholly unreliable and unstable, fate. Even so, he fails to provide a *critique* of reason, taking for granted its quasi-universal status, as if it were the same in all human beings no matter what their station in history, culture, socioeconomic class, or gender. The voice of reason as he invokes it comes off (to anyone with ears to hear) as fiercely masculine, as if underwriting his own unabashed chauvinism: "A good man will follow up his obligations undisturbed and undeterred, and in doing the things worthy of a good man he will do nothing unworthy of a man."[20] And "[anger is] the mark of a lethargic and sterile mind, aware of its own feebleness, given to chronic distress, like sore and sickly bodies that groan at the lightest touch. In this respect anger is an especially womanish and childish vice."[21] In keeping with an entire misogynist culture, he is drawing on its idea of reason as impartial, impersonal, unemotional, and as "masculine" in essence: an essence invidiously predetermined by factors of political and social power as played out in privilege and prejudice.

To invoke reason *tout court* in order to save an unremittingly individualist and masculinist model of the generation of emotion is seriously flawed. Whatever its merits and temptations, this is neither a fair nor an effective way to save emotion, including anger, from subjectivism, individualism, and misogyny. The way forward is rather to be found by emphasizing the gestures, actions, and words by which the expression of anger and other emotions can be both apperceived and judged on an inherently *inter*personal basis that is capable of animating the interactive potentialities of human emotional life.

We must also acknowledge the transmissive powers that allow emotionality to be apprehended by others and understood in its variegated import in the context of places-of-presentation that are *essentially*, not just accidentally, shared with other human beings of the most diverse descriptions. In this way, emotionality can be invoked and understood in its lived synchronism and interrelationality, not confined to what is true of an isolated and separated life, however deliberative and reasonable that life may claim to be. Seneca hints at this sort of exterocentric direction when he writes strikingly that "the mind is not sequestered."[22] This would include not being self-sequestered, confined to its own domain of experience—as in Milton's revealing statement in *Paradise Lost* (an exemplary early modern text) that "the mind is its own place." Thanks to his Stoicism, Seneca looks beyond the self-confinement that is characteristic of seventeenth-century views to come. Yet an uncritical recourse to "reason" cannot get us far beyond an endogenous model, given that reason itself is culturally overdetermined and possesses only a dubious and contestable universality.

The most questionable aspect of Seneca's model of emotion, in my view, is his insistence on the second phase of the process. Though arguably the most ingenious feature of his contribution, it is also the most problematic. Not only does it posit an interiority in which deliberation occurs, it also implies that the resolution is almost altogether *individual*. Just I, or just you, determine the outcome of an emerging emotion from an indeterminate matrix that features differential directionalities. This anticipates Descartes's idea that the individual will has everything to do with the vicissitudes of emotions whose antecedents arise from the impingement of perceptual representations ("sensations") on the physiological substrate of the self-standing subject. The key difference is that in Seneca's Stoic model the role of the individual is tied to conscious deliberation, whereas in the Cartesian schema emotions run their own course along preestablished pathways.

Despite his intellectual origins in the ancient Greek world with its emphasis on the public status of emotions and on the powers of reason, Seneca is protomodern, anticipating what will become a full-blown theory sixteen centuries later. Otherwise put, the early modern tendency to encapsulate emotional experience within the individual subject first raised its problematic head with Seneca, albeit only in a preliminary form rather than in the detailed psychophysiological model that we find in Descartes. Confronted with the recently posited prospect of infinite cosmic space, Descartes thrust the subject into an incisive interiority. Even if this interiority does not include an identifiable phase of conscious deliberation, what matters most is that the origin and fate of a given emotion are confined to the individual subject.[23] This is to obscure—if not to eliminate altogether—the role of others in the genesis of a given emotion, such as anger. Descartes in effect gives the individual subject its own quasi-autonomy, as if in a compensatory move intended to protect and empower this subject as it faces up to the threatening vista of an infinite physical universe.

Of course, there were other ancient precedents for the modern internalization of emotion: for example, Saint Augustine, who advised humans to "turn within; for truth dwells in the inner man" (a statement cited by Husserl in his aptly named *Cartesian Meditations*). But our brief engagement with Seneca as a forerunner prepares us for the paradigmatic early modern view of emotion as having no place to exist except in the mind and body of the individual human subject, with Descartes as the primary proponent of this view. Julia Kristeva could be talking of Seneca when she discusses the move to an interior psychic self in the modern world—an "*inside*, an internal life, to be contrasted with the *outside*"—which produced the isolation of the modern self at the same time as seventeenth-century science was moving triumphantly toward "the conquest of the *outside* . . . of nature."[24] This was to overlook another sort of outside—that of periphanously presented emotion.

III

Descartes's resolutely endogenous model of emotion concentrates on the interiority of the subject, even as it acknowledges a factor of exogeny in the form of incoming sensations. The master thinker of matter as extension, *res extensa*, focused on the inscape of the mind in relation to the internal physiology of the body in order to do justice to emotion as he conceived it; yet in the end we shall find that he permits *no space* for emotion.

It is telling that Descartes only began to focus on emotion at the end of his career: "The Passions of the Soul" (1649) was the last treatise he finished, and he did not live to see it published. It was almost as if he withheld it from the public until the last minute, dithering over details of its formulation, as revealed in his correspondence of the time. We may wonder whether the delay in writing this work may also reflect his sense that emotions pose a special threat to his otherwise pristinely partitioned model of human experience. We should note that by speaking of *les passions* Descartes denotes whatever is felt in the soul, and is passively undergone by the "patient" subject, including perceptions and sensations as well as emotions and feelings. On the lookout for conceptual elegance and economy, Descartes became determined to confine emotions inside the human subject, where their workings could be more easily identified, simplified, and the mental versus physical dimensions strictly segregated from each other.

But emotions are notoriously messy and intrusive, and in particular they have mental and bodily dimensions that are not easy to sort out. In my rage, for example, at the peremptory deportation by Immigration and Customs Enforcement of Mexican Americans whose only "crime" may have been a traffic ticket that dates back ten years, my body enters in as I identify corporeally with the pain of families riven apart, children forcibly separated from parents. It is my body as well that takes me to protests, where my outrage becomes bodily manifest to others, while physically picking up on and connecting with their anger in solidarity. In truth, I cannot even distinguish body from mind in the full experience of my chagrin at these inhumane practices—a chagrin that suffuses my entire being: how can these travesties be happening in our time? Both of these dimensions, body and mind, qualify the emotion I feel *in* me—but just *where* in me? In beginning to search for an answer to this question in "The Passions of the Soul," it is striking that the first four paragraphs of part 1 feature an emphatic use of the preposition "in." Here are three of the passages in question:

1. "This topic [the passions], about which knowledge has always been keenly sought, does not seem to be one of the more difficult to investigate since everyone *feels passions in himself* and so has no need to look elsewhere for observations to establish their nature."[25] This prefatory sentence not only situates passions *in* the subject but argues that, because they are located therein, each subject can trust her own self-observations without having to "look elsewhere"; to be situated within one's soul is to assure

access to them, Descartes presumes. In the very idea of immediate access
we hear the rumbling of Saint Augustine's insistence that we turn within
ourselves. Descartes's assumption is that to be conscious at all is ipso facto
to be a reliable source of self-knowledge: it is to be able to draw upon what
is immediately self-evident. If there is unclarity in thought, it is not due
to any inherent opacity in the act of thinking, but rather to the "close alliance between soul and body."[26] This alliance is the disturbing force that
is manifestly operative in the case of the passions (a comprehensive term
that for Descartes includes perceptions, sensations, feelings, and emotions), and it is all the more active in the case of insistent emotions, given
their tendency to "agitate and disturb."[27] In short, if emotions—passions
in "a restricted sense"[28]—trouble us, this is due largely to the interference
or intrusion of the body as it joins forces with the soul.

2. "What is a passion in the soul is usually an action in the body."[29]
This is in effect a claim to *double internalization*: emotions are in the soul
and in the body, both at once, and nowhere else. Despite their diremptive
metaphysical difference as two kinds of substance, body and soul collude
to hold emotions *in*: even if they don't coincide, they overlap, and in their
alliance they literally *co-operate* in an action of double inwardizing. If the
mental consciousness of *res cogitans* (the cognizing subject) can be said to
possess a primary insideness, the body possesses a secondary insideness—
secondary because the body, while housing emotion in our physiological
interiority, also brings it into the world, enacting it there. In short, this
is a mode of "being-in" that Heidegger would label "categorial" rather
than "existential," for it is a matter of sheer containment: of one thing in
another.[30] In this account, not only is emotion boxed in twice—by mind
and by body—but this occurs by means of modes of containment that
are more suitable to the being of the ready-to-hand (like being literally
contained *in* a box) than to human being. We are reminded of Aristotle's
container model of place, for which to be in place is to be contained in a
determinate space, and we can only infer that Descartes denies that there
is anything unique about distinctively human implacement, starting with
the way that emotions are situated in the living subject.[31]

3. "Thus, because we have no conception of the body as thinking
in any way at all, we have reason to believe that every kind of thought
present in us *belongs to the soul*."[32] Beyond reinforcing the rigidity and exclusivity of mind–body dualism, this statement confirms that all acts of
thinking are not only located in the soul but, as belonging to the soul, are
its own property, its own aspects or attributes. Thus, anything that counts
as thinking (including emotions, memories, and various cogitations) has
no other place to be than in the soul. The unacknowledged premise is that
if such thinking exists, it has to be *somewhere*. This follows from what I call

the Archytian axiom: *to be is to be in place.*[33] In keeping with this axiom, to say that emotions as a form of thinking belong to the soul means that they have their proper place *in* the soul: the soul is the proper place of and for emotions. This is to reinforce the thesis that emotions are stationed inside us, and occur as episodes of conscious life. But by the same token, they also have their proper place in the body that subtends soul even as it differs from it as a separate kind of substance: *res extensa* (as distinguished from *res cogitans*). For Descartes, emotions are generated physiologically in the body—there and nowhere else—and it follows once again that emotions are insiders twice over: *in* soul as consciously experienced and *in* body as physiologically existent.

IV

From these revealing opening moves in "The Passions of the Soul," we can infer the following concerning Descartes's basic view of emotion: to be an emotion is to be located in a human subject; in particular, it is to be positioned in the soul of this subject, a thinking soul that can scan the content of each of its cogitations; but the same emotion also resides in this subject's body as materially subjacent to the cogitational aspects of the emotion. Thus emotion is contained in body and soul alike, albeit differentially. But to assert this is to leave two essential questions unanswered. First, if emotion is contained in body and soul differentially, just how do they differ? Second, how are these two factors—each a distinct form of substance—related to each other in the generation and experience of emotion? Descartes's answer to the second question is infamous: it is by *animal spirits* that soul and body communicate with each other; and yet this purported solution only solves one problem by giving rise to another: how can animal spirits, which are not themselves any separate kind of substance, succeed in relating *res cogitans* in the form of conscious minds with *res extensa* in the form of physical bodies? In short, how is emotion contained in soul and body when considered in tandem?

When we take animal spirits—or any such medium—into account, more than bilocation is at stake. A given emotion such as anger can now be said to be *trilocated.* It's in the mind, in the body, and in the in-between, that is, in the animal spirits that connect the two. Moreover, it's in all three of these places as contained *within the subject*: for each of these three factors is interior to the subject, ensconced there without any effective exit. The Cartesian scenario thus features a fiercely overdetermined internality. We can appreciate the grip of such enforced internality by considering a single emotion as discussed by Descartes: this is *terror*, the very emotion that Edmund Burke identified as precipitating the experience of the sublime. For Burke, terror is what the terrified subject feels when confronted with an overwhelmingly threatening scene. But Burke took little interest in tracing out its internal dynamics, whereas this is just what Descartes considers both imperative and sufficient.

Descartes begins by remarking that "the principal effect of all the human passions is that they move and dispose the soul to want the things for which they prepare the body. Thus the feeling of terror moves the soul to want to flee, that of courage to want to fight, and similarly with the others."[34] The passions, located squarely in the soul, motivate us to do certain things by way of bodily action: thus to flee in the case of terror. Yet the soul cannot by itself move the body to flee; it can only (in Descartes's own word) "*prepare*" it to do so. But just how is fleeing itself brought about? A second passage suggests Descartes's answer: "Just as the course which the spirits take to the nerves of the heart suffices to induce a movement in the [pineal] gland through which terror enters the soul, so too the mere fact that some spirits at the same time proceed to the nerves which serve to move the legs in flight causes another movement in the [pineal] gland through which the soul feels and perceives this action."[35] Suddenly we have a rather complex model in which the animal spirits, in keeping with their status as conveyors, operate both to affect the soul via the "nerves of the heart" (and thus to assure that terror is felt there) as well as to stimulate the body to action by way of their impact upon nerves that connect directly with the legs (hence to precipitate literal flight). "Nerves" here act as physical messengers of a given emotion that belong exclusively to the body, whether passing through the heart or the legs or any intermediate organs. In the case of the legs—the basis for running away—there is a direct activation; in the case of the heart, the nerves allow the perception of, say, a fearsome animal to "enter the soul," where the emotion of terror is felt as such.

Thus, it is not enough to speak of "the body" when trying to understand how an emotion induces action; we must acknowledge that the specificity of bodily action is conveyed through nerve fibers of the sort that had been hypothesized only recently in early seventeenth-century anatomical investigations, in some of which Descartes himself participated. The striking asymmetry is that there are no corresponding "soul fibers" that are the equivalent of physical nerves; as with the English expression, "heartstrings," we have to regard such fibers as imaginary compared with anatomically actual afferent and efferent nerves. Notice that now the threefold structure of soul/animal spirits/body has suddenly become fourfold:

SOUL (feels emotions)///animal spirits//physical nerves/// BODY
(effects movement)

In this model, we have two polar terms—body and soul—and two intermediate terms, animal spirits and physical nerves. We cannot but feel
uneasy as we become caught up in the rather elaborate machinery posited
by Descartes here; from it there is no escape, only an increasing proliferation of explanatory pathways inside a subject from whom there is no
effective egress. Like Theseus in the labyrinth constructed by Daedalus,
we seek a way out—but we fail to find anything like Ariadne's thread to
liberate us from entrapment.

As one follows Descartes's treatment of terror, the entrapment only
increases as he invokes additional factors that crop up inside the human
subject: for example, memory and reason, two means of coping with terror from within.[36] This is to augment further the enchainment of internal factors at play in emotion. For Descartes now proposes three factors
belonging to soul (emotions, reason, memory) and two to body (physical
nerves, actual movement), with animal spirits stationed in the middle
between these two groupings. We find ourselves drawn still deeper into
the labyrinthine mechanics of human subjectivity. Descartes's treatment
of an emotion such as terror points to a complexity of structure that may
surprise us if we were anticipating an analysis straightforwardly reducible
to a mind–body dualism. In light of particular cases such as this, the ease
with which we condemn him as rabidly reductive and dualist needs to
be nuanced.

It remains the case that Descartes's basic understanding of emotion remains stubbornly subjectivist; everything emotional happens
within, deep inside, the human subject: in the soul, in the body, among
the animal spirits, along the physical nerves, and in memory and reason,
themselves located in the human subject. All remains caught up and contained in a bipolar model of subjectivity in which the epicenters of mind
and body remain regnant despite the positing of tertiary intermediaries
that at once complicate and relieve an otherwise bare and simplistic
dualism.[37]

V

Let us step back for a moment and ask: Is it so ill-conceived to speak of
emotions as being contained within the subject? Could it be that emotions
truly *are* "internal to the soul," in Descartes's phrase, as well as internal to

the bodily apparatus that accompanies them?[38] We do speak of "harboring" feelings and emotions; for example, when we "harbor resentment" toward someone but do not express the resentment overtly. So let us grant that we do experience, and can often articulate, the distinct sense that certain feelings and emotions are held within us phenomenologically in at least three ways:

1. By employing the verb "harbor," we imply that the full life of the feeling/emotion has not yet been reached; that there are phases to come when the harbored emotion will attain full expression, will come forth in explicit words, gestures, or actions, not unlike the way a ship launches out to sea from the harbor where it was docked. Let us call this the *exteriorizing effort* of harbored emotion. When this nisus is held back indefinitely, not only is frustration likely to ensue, but often serious consequences: as when long-smoldering resentment bursts forth in physical violence.

2. It is natural to say that we harbor a certain *feeling* because it suggests there is a tacit alliance between feeling and interior positioning, as when I say generically "I *feel* angry" versus "I *am* angry." The former emphasizes that I *sense my anger*, I experience it as situated within the bounds of my own subjectivity. Whereas in saying outright that *I am angry*, I imply that distinctions between interior and exterior, harboring and releasing are secondary: I am consumed with anger; all of me is angry.

3. Most significantly, the metaphor of "harbor" is place-language. A harbored feeling or emotion is held in a kind of subjective redoubt that is both personal and private. It is not held just anywhere; it is situated *in me*, and to be situated there, there must be some kind of receptive space for it. I take this as a sign that emotions and feelings are never entirely detached meanderings in a virtual *nowhere*. They take place in a certain *somewhere*. Even as held within, they call for a certain inner lodging. This helps to explain the way in which we speak of an emotion such as resentment as "pre*occupy*ing me," or as "mostly contained," or as "seeping out." These common locutions, all spatially specific, suggest distinctive modes of emotional implacement.

By following out the common usage of a phrase such as "harboring" with reference to emotion, we are thus led to consider how "the spaces of feeling" are at stake in any comprehensive account of emotion. That it is tempting to speak of certain emotions as stemming from inside the human subject must be conceded, even if the key emphasis in this book takes us in quite another direction: toward emotions as situated outside. We should note that Descartes himself is not oblivious to the outside dimension of emotions. At one point in "The Passions of the Soul" he alludes to "the external signs of this passion." These signs, he claims, "differ according to different personal temperaments and the various other passions composing it or joined to it. Thus we see some grow pale or tremble when they become angry, and others become flushed or even weep."[39] This is a rare moment when Descartes takes the outward manifestation of emotion seriously: its showing-forth rather than its being contained. He then adds this observation: "We can distinguish two kinds of anger. One flares up quickly and is quite evident in external behavior, but it has little effect and is easy to assuage. The other is not so apparent at first, but gnaws more at one's heart and has effects that are more dangerous."[40] Thus anger has both an outward and an inward situatedness.

While Descartes does recognize such things as expressions conveyed by the eyes and the way the face changes color when experiencing various emotions, it is revealing that he considers all of these things as merely "external."[41] As such, they are not integral to the subjective matrix that is the very cradle of emotion; they are adventitious and secondary. Descartes's recognition of such manifestations takes him beyond the strict bounds imposed by the exclusively psychophysiological terms within which his official account of the generation of emotion—its endogeny—is couched. But these manifestations are not allowed any further significance; in the end, they are merely signs, contingent accompaniments of the generation of emotion within the Cartesian subject. What matters most in this generation are the psychical and physiological dimensions of the human subject as emotional. In relation to these dimensions, gestural and verbal expressions count as mere epiphenomena.

The true *phenomena*—those that matter most in the Cartesian schema—are located in the twin domains of body and mind, which together with animal spirits and other intermediary factors act to generate emotions and keep them tightly bound within the confines of the human subject. From this enclosure there is no effective way out except through sporadic outbursts of gesture and word. These outbursts are external to the only two realms of legitimate being allowed by Cartesian metaphysics: extension and thought. They are "compromise formations" (in Freud's term) and are themselves composed of the only two things that count, matter and mind. We can consider them compromises from without—momentary conjunctions between two kinds of substance that have no common meeting ground. No wonder they are so fleeting and often so unreliable.

If for Descartes, expressivity is a contingent and literally superficial feature of emotions as we live them, I maintain that expressivity is altogether essential to emotional life and not a contingent feature of it.[42] Thanks to their expressiveness, emotions exist as much outside us as inside us, indeed more so—as the very word *ex*-pressive signifies. To hold this view impels us to acknowledge the scene in which emotions appear—

the space in which they show themselves to us: a space that is decisively other than the inert space the physical body occupies or the inner realm belonging to the soul. It is a genuinely interpersonal space, in which emotional manifestation is an integral feature.

VI

If emotions require an expressive space in which to show themselves, Descartes's philosophy falls short given that his sole model for space of any kind is *res extensa*, sheer extended substance. Such a space has no capacity for directly presenting the emotions that his dualism keeps contained within the emotional subject. By rendering emotions placeless, he literally *subjectifies* them. When, in *Principles of Philosophy*, Descartes suggestively distinguishes between "external" and "internal" space, one might hope that internal space would approximate to an expressive space. But for Descartes, such space is sheer "volume" whose parameters are "size" and "shape," while external space is strictly "positional," that is, a matter of how a given spatial position relates to other such positions.[43] Both of these highly abstract modalities of space are unable to provide emotions with the kind of *residency* they call for—places in which they can emerge and exfoliate and be expressive. Worse yet, the idea of space as extension (*extensio*) reduces it to a collection of separate parts in a *partes extra partes* arrangement that fails to reflect the ways in which emotions weave together in nonpartitive, holistic, and quasi-organic patterns.

Space considered as space (*res extensa*) for Descartes is identical with physical body. A given body not only takes up a certain amount of space, it *is* that space. If "all places are full of bodies,"[44] it follows that there is no room for the life and death of emotions: no "transitional space" (in Winnicott's term once again) in which emotions can effervesce in all their complexity and subtlety. Space for Descartes is utterly inelastic, fiercely inorganic, and totally rigid. It is a premier instance of what Deleuze and Guattari designate as "striated," which they contrast with "smooth" space, a space that is at once directional and heterogeneous, able to hold a diversity of intensive affects in an expressive assemblage.[45] In contrast, Cartesian space provides no place for events that are as diverse, intermittent, and processual as the expressive presentation of emotions. Indeed, there is no place for place itself in the realm of *res extensa*. If "internal place [volume] is exactly the same as space,"[46] this means there is no such thing as inherent place, a place that has its own standing, its own bearing. If the body whose place is determined by its magnitude and figure moves elsewhere, its previous place evaporates: *nothing of it remains except empty space*. Place becomes a phantom of space, a creature of momentary occupation by a body. In any case, emotions are not bodies, chunks of matter, even if they do require a body for their enactment as well as a place in which to become manifest.

The philosophy of Descartes lacks the smooth space that affective life requires. Such space is animated by singular and specific places-of-presentation that exhibit and sustain affective events. As we shall see, even the most ordinary landscape contains such affectively active presentational places. Landscapes in the form of seascapes, mountainscapes, any form of wildscape—but also certain kinds of cityscapes—are uniquely capable of inspiring and supporting emotions such as awe and wonder. We need a more comprehensive and generous paradigm for places-of-presentation that would fit many, if not all, kinds of emotional experience. Any such paradigm, I wish to suggest, must include the dimension that Elisabeth Ströker calls "attuned space." Such space must be an "expressive totality" in her phrase, and it must be pervaded by an affective tonality that answers to the emotion felt by a given subject or subjects.[47] It is this tonality that links the human subject and space, infusing them both, coexisting in and with them.[48] "Here," Ströker writes, "lived experience means a unique communication of the living-experiencing [self] . . . with an expressively animated space."[49] Ingredient in this experience is a "pre-reflective orientation" on the part of the subject that accomplishes an "immediate affinity with the world" through a shared emotionality.[50]

Ströker's idea of attuned space provides a vivid sense of what is notably lacking in the Cartesian paradigm of extended space. She provides *room* for emotion, where emotion can flourish and be expressed, as Descartes decidedly does not. I would like to regard her thinking as furnishing the broad strokes—the "affective a priori," in Mikel Dufrenne's sense[51]—for what an adequate model of a place-of-presentation for emotions must include, even if different emotions will call for significant variations on such a model, reflecting the differentiated ways in which emotions are qualified and made accessible.

* * *

If we are to turn emotion inside out, we must wrest it from the maw of subjectivity and return it to the open world of otherness from which it stems and to which it belongs first and last. Only one major thinker in early modernity devised a model of emotion that allows for such key features as attunement and expressivity by focusing on its essentially outgoing directionality: that thinker was Benedict Spinoza. In the next chapter the

Cartesian model, as just discussed, is contrasted with Spinoza's radically periphanous view—with affect impinging on the subject from outside.

Descartes and Spinoza, concerned as they were with so many fundamental matters in philosophy (and in Descartes's case with natural science as well), both gave sustained attention to emotion under the heading of "the passions." Just why did each of them take emotion so seriously and give it a central place in their mature philosophies—philosophies that favor reason and intellect above all else? The brief answer is that emotions as passions occur at, and *as*, critical pivots in their philosophical ruminations: for Descartes, in the mind–body relation; and for Spinoza, in the mode-to-mode relation within the compass of Nature. Spinoza, as the architect of the most systematic metaphysical treatise of the early modern era, managed to secure room for emotion in a model that is at once radically impersonal and resolutely interactionist (emphasizing the contiguity of finite substances), yet which also accommodates personal feeling. His thinking about emotion is strikingly contemporary in the way he makes space for its fundamental role in human experience. Given that Spinoza's model sets the stage for the views laid out more fully in parts 2 and 3, it behooves us to take a closer look at it.

3

Emotion Everywhere: Spinoza

> Each person regulates everything in accordance with his emotion.
>
> —Spinoza, *Ethics*, part 3, proposition 2, scholium

Spinoza's treatment of emotion in his *Ethics* was completed only twenty-five years after the publication of Descartes's "Passions of the Soul," but what a vastly different take on emotion Spinoza gives us—as though anxious to critique and improve upon the French philosopher's views on emotion at every turn. One way he tries to do so is to argue that instead of six primal emotions, as Descartes had held (wonder, love, hatred, desire, joy, and sadness), there are only three: pleasure, pain, and desire. This is a significant streamlining of the Cartesian schema. Moreover, whereas Descartes regarded all emotions as "passions"—implying that we are passive subjects in their presence—Spinoza recognizes genuinely *active* emotions: those of which we have gained an adequate idea and which thereby empower us. This is to put emotions on a very different footing than we find in Descartes, and it is to already imply that emotions cannot be contained in the interiority of the human subject—in what Spinoza calls "an empire within an empire"—given that for Spinoza, action of any significant sort is *action in the world* and more especially *interaction* therein.[1]

From the very start, then, Spinoza thinks of emotion as occurring somewhere other than in a separate self, and thus as not the exclusive property of the human subject. Emotions belong to, and are inseparable from, entire systems of interrelated modes; the subject is only one coherent cluster among others, an "assemblage," in Deleuze's preferred term for this cluster.[2] As contrasted with the atomized state of things in the Cartesian world picture, in which insular individuals ("dividuals" would be a more appropriate term) are privileged, for Spinoza any given thing or event is what it is as a function of its relationship with all that impinges on it and its own impingement on them. The divisory predilection of

Cartesianism so evident in the gulf between *res extensa* and *res cogitans* is superseded in Spinoza by a deeply concatenative, relational vision.

Noting this basic difference helps to explain why Spinoza chose the term *affectus* to designate what in English would be called "emotion." What matters for Spinoza is how modes *affect* or influence each other in the generation of matrices that are produced by intermodal interactions. A primary issue becomes whether a given affect or emotion (using these terms more or less interchangeably) can be said to act on its own initiative or is determined by other entities in that system. As Spinoza characterizes this difference: the question is whether the idea associated with a given emotion is *adequate*, in which case the emotion counts as "active," or whether the idea is *inadequate*: that is, when the emotion is a "passion." Affects as emotions are integral components of a vast interstitial complex that is finally coterminous with Nature as a whole.

As George Eliot remarks in her novel *Daniel Deronda*: "There is a great deal of unmapped territory within us that would have to be taken into account in explanation of our gusts and storms."[3] It is tempting to take this striking statement in the direction of Freud, for whom the "unmapped territory within us" would be that of the unconscious as the realm of the repressed.[4] But another, very different reading would take us straight to Spinoza, who would advise us to attend to the "unmapped territory" that is outside and beyond us. Since virtually no significant sense of "inside" remains for him, to follow in Spinoza's footsteps is to begin with the all-encompassing surround, that is, the full nexus of modes that impinge upon and reflect the status of any one mode.[5] Stating this in my own preferred nomenclature, it is a matter of entering into the comprehensive *layout of places* that manifest emotional activity or passivity. Although this is not Spinoza's way of putting it, it provides the underlying framework for my interpretation of him, as for my critical reading of Descartes.

A measure of the distance between Descartes and Spinoza is found in the fact that the latter's philosophy eliminates all outright mind–body dualism. The body is not isolated from what the mind thinks, nor vice versa, for extension and thought are not two separate substances, as in Descartes, but are reconceived as coeval attributes of one monistic substance, Nature or God. Given that these two attributes of substance are covalent, mind and body are unified for Spinoza by the fact that what is conceived under the attribute of thought (a given memory, for example) can *also* be considered under the attribute of extension: "The order, i.e., the interconnection of [all] things is one, whether Nature is conceived under this or that attribute, and consequently . . . the order of the actions and passions of our body is simultaneous in nature with the order of the actions and passions of the mind."[6] Otherwise stated, "the mind involves the actual existence of the body."[7] This works both ways; for, as Deleuze comments: "What is an action in the mind is necessarily an action in the body as well, and what is a passion in the body is necessarily a passion in the mind."[8]

Part 3 of the *Ethics* defines emotions as "the affections of the body by which the body's power of acting is increased or diminished, helped or hindered, and *at the same time* the ideas of these affections."[9] Although "body" and "ideas" are certainly distinguishable, their actions are not discrete, for any bodily experience comes with an ideational component, and vice versa. The agent is neither mind nor body taken separately but is something more like "bodymind" in the Zen Buddhist term. This becomes clear when we realize that by action, being "active," Spinoza designates the situation in which our bodymind is the adequate cause, at once corporeal and ideational, of our emotion; by passion, being "passive," he designates that we are an inadequate such cause. An adequate cause is one whose effect "can be clearly and distinctly perceived through itself," that is, through its own idea of that effect; to be an inadequate cause, by contrast, is to fail to grasp that effect by way of its idea.[10] Already, then, this means that for Spinoza emotions are not limited to Cartesian "passions," since passions are only one outcome of emotional causation—thanks to our having only inadequate, incompletely formed ideas of them. For if we ourselves are the causal agents of a given emotion—by having an adequate idea of it and thereby contributing to its effectiveness as a force of its own—then that emotion is not merely the effect of a prior causal matrix but is *itself an action.* This is to lend to emotion an inherent dynamism that is altogether missing in Descartes and in many subsequent modern and late modern accounts that present the emotional life as primarily if not entirely passive.

|

We need to pause and appreciate the radicality of this model of emotion, which is far distant from an endogenous paradigm such as Descartes offers, even if we are also a long way from an exogenous model whereby what is within us is determined by what is without. What matters in Spinoza is not whether the effective action is external to a given agent, or is generated wholly within that agent; for the agent is not an isolated substance, but an integral part of a dense intermodal matrix and is an active or passive force only from within that matrix. Not only are our emotions not merely the outcome of a chain of causes—as if they were the end point of that chain—but we ourselves have an active hand in their generation; and this is so thanks to the activity of mind (by way of its adequate ideas) *and* of body (by its performative capacity, its *potentia agendi*), both acting closely in tandem. Our emotions are passive products of our environment only to the extent that we fail to be fully agentive in a given setting—that is, we fail to embrace agency because of having correspondingly inadequate ideas of our body in its engagement with other bodies.[11]

Already it is evident that we have entered a very different way of construing emotion. Instead of the disparities that populated Descartes's "Passions of the Soul"—with its diremption between body and mind requiring the invocation of animal spirits and other mediating forces to bring them together in a highly tenuous manner—we are given a picture in which connection and interrelation prevail over difference, synopsis over analysis, and unified agency over divided subjectivity. Instead of a dichotomous psychophysical mechanics of emotion, we venture into an emotional dynamics viewed up close and set within a contextualism of other forces and ideas. For we are in a realm where, as Spinoza states emphatically, Nature is one:

> Nature is always the same and everywhere is one, and its virtue and
> power of acting is the same. That is, the laws of Nature and the rules
> in accordance with which all things happen and are changed from one
> form into another are everywhere and always the same; and therefore
> there must also be one and the same way of understanding the nature of
> things of any kind—namely, by the universal laws and rules of Nature.
> Therefore, the emotions of hatred, anger, envy, etc., considered in them-
> selves, follow from the same necessity and virtue of Nature as do all other
> particular things.[12]

Rather than regarding emotions as idiosyncratic outbursts of sequestered souls and bodies, they are envisioned as part and parcel of a panpervasive natural world that everywhere operates by the same general laws and principles. Emotions are not merely episodic or exceptional occurrences, but are integral components of a vast fabric of interactive modes of Nature—two of whose infinite attributes, extension and thought, are intertwined and inseparable right down to the concrete bodily motions and attendant ideas that make up what we in late modernity have come to call the "person," with all the vicissitudes of her or his emotional life. These vicissitudes differentiate one embodied life from another insofar as *conatus*, or the power of persisting, is a principle of differentiation by way of interaction; but all human and nonhuman entities follow the basic rules of natural action and interaction in the transactional complexes to which they belong.

More radically than Descartes, Spinoza takes seventeenth-century science to heart, embracing its universalism of law, a universalism so conspicuously present in Newtonian physics, and he brings it right into the ostensible singularity of emotional experience, as characterizing your experience and my experience alike despite all their differences. In Spinoza's model of clusters of intermodal interaction we can detect premonitions of Kant's idea of a *sensus communis* in which independent judgments—about an artwork, for example—converge in a communal consensus. This model also anticipates Hegel's idea of the "concrete universal" and Husserl's notion of an "eidetic singularity."[13] Yet Spinoza avoids reducing individual experience to a general principle—a strong temptation for Kant, Hegel, and Husserl alike—by recognizing two levels: the level of the infinite attributes, of which there are innumerably many but only two of which, extension and thought, have particular relevance in the world as we know it; and the level of finite modes, which character ize particular actions and interactions, including all the ideations and emotions of human beings and other finite beings. Taken together and allowing for all their intimate interrelations, these two levels obtain for all that exists. So as to avoid Cartesian-style dualism, however, Spinoza insists that infinite attributes and finite modes alike belong to Nature or God, whose unlimited substance pervades all and ensures that the universe is indeed *uni-versum*: "turning as one." All that is discrete and singular is encompassed in one single monistic substance that is altogether natural and altogether deific, both at once and eternally.

This all-embracing cosmic model includes emotions—which in many respects provide a litmus test for this universalist metaphysics. For what could be more unique, more "individual," more *mine* than, for example, my dismay at former Attorney General Jeff Sessions's proposal several years ago to toughen sentencing for drug offenders long after it had been shown not only that incarceration on the basis of drug charges is futile, expensive, and racially biased to an extreme degree, but worse yet, that drug-possession charges are often brought on the basis of planted evidence or no evidence whatsoever as part of a concerted effort to keep prisons (many owned by for-profit enterprises) well populated. In trying to understand my strongly felt emotion in this instance, it is tempting to adopt a bifurcated model in which there is an offensive object or action as one pole (in this case, a particular stance by Sessions) and an affected subject or subjects as the other pole (all those at stake in his proposal, and primarily African Americans). Because the subjects are individu ated and individuating, their emotional responses to Sessions's proposal, along with my reaction, must be just so many *individual* responses—or so the story goes. The language with which we routinely describe such individualizing tendencies is possessive: *my* dismay, *their* outrage. It is also separative: even if you and I both detest Sessions's stance, *my* dismay cannot be lumped together with *your* dismay. Our individuated emotional responses, as felt by those aware of the situation I describe, pullulate like swarms of ants, each response differing from the next, even if only with regard to minor distinctions. Soon we reach a point where there are just "too many emotions," as Spinoza puts it, to do justice to each, given all the shades of manifestation of any single emotion.[14] Difference ends in indifference. You and I may both be feeling intense dismay, but the exact *way* I feel my dismay differs from yours at a micro-level of our respective experiences. This means that each of us is regarded as isolated in the minutiae of our subjective feelings, divided into "dividuals," and denied the emotive power of solidarity by the regnant philosophy of isolated subjectivity.

II

Spinoza's treatment of emotion adroitly avoids getting caught up in such fruitless microphysics of individuated emotion: emotion determined wholly *from within*—felt from within the differential subjectivities of yours vs. mine. Thanks to his conviction that at every level of being much more is shared than not, he searches for what experiences of emotion have in common insofar as they are determined *from without*.[15] He looks for what characterizes emotions at the level of *how they work*—how they originate, transpire, and eventually vanish. He describes these generic features in terms such as "action" and "passion," "affection" and "affect," "adequate ideas" and "inadequate ideas."[16] These terms name ongoing dimensions of the life of any given emotion, and in this respect point to an immense network of intermodal connectivity that constitutes the vast meshwork of Nature or God. This meshwork ensures that whatever the specificity of a given experience of a particular emotion, it is a matter of *individuation from without*. It is on the basis of this periphanous generation that the idiosyncrasies of individual permutations of an emotion emerge, and not the other way around. This is the very converse of an endogenous exfoliation from inside the subject. In the example of Sessions's proposal, the differentiated emotional responses should be analyzed not just in terms of what one person versus another subjectively feels about it, but in view of its concrete consequences—its impingements—on those affected by it (here primarily African Americans); our personal and opinionated reactions are secondary.

Emotions constitute a *band* or *zone* within the Spinozist system. They are situated midway between the vast scope of *Deus sive Natura* and the particular ways that given emotions are generated and manifested. In this respect, emotions constitute a cohesive stratum in the system—a space cleared for the emergence of discrete emotional experiences in the delimited specific forms that you and I undergo them. Such forms are consistent and recognizable enough for us to identify a given emotion as, say, "dismay." This identifying name is a porous genus that loosely gathers all the variations and modulations of the emotion that individuals as finite assemblages experience, though the variations themselves are so occasion-bound as to resist any strict generalization. This is why Spinoza's (and for that matter Descartes's) descriptions of individual emotions strike us as rather quaint and culturally overdetermined. Were Spinoza with us today, he might well agree with this perception, yet exonerate himself by saying that he is most of all concerned with emotions as they occupy a middle zone in the overall architectonic of the *Ethics*: an interim space between vapid generality and idiosyncratic singularity.

Spinoza's preoccupation with emotion at the level of this middle zone contrasts strikingly with what we have found in Descartes. The French thinker also situates emotion in an interim position, but for him this position only ever exists between *my* mind and *my* body, or between *your* mind and *your* body, as something that I or you alone, separately, experience. Like Spinoza, he ties emotion to substance, but only to substance as belonging to me, or you, or someone else, and with an exclusive choice to be made between the two major substances of mind and body. This represents a concerted effort to analyze emotion by recourse to finite factors: *this* body, *this* mind, both utterly discrete. Beyond this, there is only the emptiness of open space (extension) where emotions have no proper place. The Cartesian model is not unlike a shell game wherein emotions are inside the subject, and thereby also inside a body and a mind that have no internal or intrinsic relationship with each other. These same bisected subjects exist in splendid isolation from each other and from all other subjects—in dramatic difference from the close integration and metaphysical union they display in Spinoza's account.

Spinoza embeds emotion, along with all the finitude of its causation and personal history, within a dynamic space that pervades the human subject: the infinite attribute of extension is not an abstract marker or a vast empty volume, but something that is embodied *everywhere*—in one concretion after another—and which everywhere includes human and nonhuman bodies who exist in and through it. Embodied human subjects, far from being isolated from other embodied subjects, are contiguous with and interacting with each other at every moment due to the dense multi-modal meshwork that links them at all times, uniquely so at any given moment. The bodies and minds of such subjects are in continuous communication, since every bodily movement is accompanied by an ideational component that is integral to its enactment. At every level, then, Spinoza contests the separatism of which Descartes is the primary proponent in early modern thought: separatism not just in the form of mind–body dualism, but in the form of self and other and, at the most general level, of finite and infinite being. If for Descartes everything is estranged and disjointed, for Spinoza all is conjoined and intertangled—from top to bottom and back up again, and in every which way as well.

Against the backdrop of Spinoza's immanent universalism—his propensity to perceive things *sub specie aeternitatis*[17]—it might seem that emotions are, or should be, quite problematic. In their contingency and multiplicity, in their proclivity to assume highly differentiated individual variations, emotions pose a special challenge to a system of thought that proceeds *more geometrico*. In the face of this challenge, however, Spinoza is unfazed. As he puts it himself in the preface to part 3: "I shall discuss the nature and strength of the emotions . . . by the same method as that by which I discussed God and the mind [in parts 1 and 2], and [this means that] I shall discuss human actions and appetites just as if the inquiry concerned lines, planes, or bodies."[18] But of course emotions are *not* "lines, planes, or [physical] bodies," as Spinoza knew very well. But just how do they figure for a philosopher of the emerging scientific age, a systematic metaphysician, and a dedicated theologian? No wonder Spinoza felt that he had to devote two full parts, two-fifths of the *Ethics*, to the emotions—twice as much text as he spent analyzing God and the mind!

III

Let us now examine in more detail what Spinoza says about emotion. Critical here is the distinction between *affectio* and *affectus*. The former, literally translated as "affection," is the direct result of finite modes interacting with each other. A finite mode is a particular thing; for example, Socrates considered as a finite coalescence of extension and thought.[19] *Affectio* is what happens to a given mode when it bears the traces of another mode that has impinged upon it, impacting it. These traces take the form of "images" that represent how the impinging mode has left a mark on the mode impinged upon. The traces also take the form of "ideas" that capture the relationship between the two modes at a conceptual level. Each of these intermediate terms—image and idea—is comparatively static. Each is the residuum of the interaction of modes, yet each is also embedded in transitions between modes, and thus in dynamic durational spans. As Deleuze describes the situation: "From one state to another, from one image or idea to another, there are transitions, passages that are experienced, durations through which we pass to a greater or a lesser perfection. Furthermore, these states, these affections, images or ideas are not separable from the duration that attaches them to the preceding state and makes them tend towards the next state."[20]

In this reading, affections are *processual* rather than *reific*. They are how durational or transitional states *feel* to the subject who experiences them. Feelings at this immanent level resist quantification even if they are passages to greater or lesser perfection; the passage has no measurable units, and thus resists spatialization of any kind, including the animal spirits that convey emotion according to Descartes. In this reading, Spinoza is already on the way to something analogous to the *durée réelle* of Bergson, even if the way he thematizes duration is quite different from the way Bergson does.

If affections are the residual traces of the interaction of finite modes in the form of ideas and images that make up durational time at the level of feeling, affects (*affectus*), by contrast, can be considered full-fledged *emotions*. Affects as emotions belong to durational flow, but they have an integrity and being of their own. They are actions rather than ideas or images; and they cannot be reduced to feelings. What I have just called the "stratum" or "band" of emotion is an entire level of experience that is not beholden to the epistemology of representation—markedly unlike the Cartesian model of emotions as cogitational, belonging to *res cogitans* as felt even if they are generated by a body that is itself spatial. Indeed, Spinoza's conception of affect or emotion forms a significant exception to what Heidegger has dubbed "the era of representation," a representation that takes the general form of "the world as image" (*Weltbild*). Rather than anything ideational or imagistic, emotions belong to the stream of the body's becoming.[21]

Emotions emerge from a nonsubjective, nonintensive, and literally *ex-tensive* realm that is the proper province of the body. This becomes evident in what Spinoza calls "the power of acting" regarded as an intrinsic aspect of emotions. As Spinoza asserts straightforwardly: "by emotion [*affectus*] I understand the affections [*affectio*] of the body by which the body's power of acting is increased or diminished, helped or hindered."[22] "Affections of the body" are what ensue from the interaction of modes, their impact on each other, which is tantamount to what is always happening to the human being when regarded as a mode exposed to other modes.[23]

From this deep base in the interaction of modes, emotions are a matter of how the body's power of acting is increased or diminished.

Increase occurs by having adequate ideas to the point that an emotion can be considered "active"; it is "passive" when lacking such ideas, and is in that case quite literally a "passion." To the extent that increase in power occurs, we have to do with a joyous encounter; decrease in power, by contrast, means heading into negative emotions such as anger, hatred, or shame. The power of acting becomes actual empowerment when adequate ideas are formed of affections in terms of how various other modes influence our itineraries in the world. Thanks to such empowerment, the body can be said to become more active and thereby to gain more "reality."

For Spinoza, the "power of acting" is equivalent to the "force of existing." Such a force is at stake when we speak of "the form of the emotion" as affirming "something of the body, which genuinely involves more or less reality than before."[24] So the form an emotion takes—its shape and structure: its very being—has everything to do with the force with which it exists, and this force is what constitutes the reality at stake in a given emotion. Such force is what enables the emotion to impinge on other modes: as when one person's tears moves others to tears. The tears have their own effective force as an emotional reality, and they give rise to real effects in ourselves and others. Emotional reality has its own integrity— the tears streaming down my face are an undeniable feature of my own being in the mode of perceptible and perceived extension that induces an emotional reality, a real event, in those who are witnessing me. This *realizing* thrust of emotion is in effect a coming-out of an emotion by way of the body regarded as its privileged bearer or vehicle. This is to allow "emotion" to live out and live up to its name: to be genuine *e-motion*.

Emotions are "becomings," as Deleuze and Guattari call them—or events, as I would prefer to say.[25] It is from within the immanent durational domain of affection—the realm of images and ideas and more generally of feeling—that emotion delivers us to the actual world which surrounds us in the form of a vast and dense Indra's net, and to which we are subject as beings who inhabit manifold experiential worlds. Thanks to emotion (as well as perception), we are members-at-large of these worlds, even if never quite full-fledged citizens thereof. We are all in forced migration in these worlds, forever on the move and seeking our bearings wherever we can manage to find our way.

Now we come to understand more fully why Spinoza insists that emotions reflect the body's "power of acting": they do so insofar as they engage us in "more or less reality," depending on whether the emotion is active or not.[26] Reality, no longer reducible to its representation, enters here in two ways: by way of the body as the primary agent of emotion, and in terms of the world to which this body gives access. Spinoza's insistence on "reality" (*realitas*) is emphatic—a word based on the Late Latin term *realis*, meaning "real existence, all that is real" (a usage dating from ca.

1640). The ultimate root of the word "reality" is *res* (matter, thing), and thus something that exists "out there": *that thing, that event.* Our body is no exception: it is out there as experienced by others and exists as real in our interaction with them. The same is true of the emotions borne by bodies directly into the interpersonal worlds of shared experience: others see, hear, and even touch the emotions that our bodies bring to bear in these worlds. These emotions are *active*: they carry forward the force of existing into the surrounding milieu, where they affect others. They are, in Deleuze's suggestive word, "transitive"; they carry *across* various modal interactions, and they make a difference to whatever they encounter.[27]

Emotions, then, take us to things in their circumambience by way of sensitive bodies that possess the power of acting, and are themselves subject to the impaction of other bodies.[28] It is a matter of body-to-body interaction, mode to mode, thing to thing, and event to event. Emotions take us "to the things themselves." Husserl's celebrated shibboleth might well apply to Spinoza at this level of his analysis in the *Ethics*. Around us at all times is a world of real things that are decidedly outside us—*en dehors, äusserlich.*[29] It is to this outer realm of real things that emotions, borne by bodies as their indispensable carriers, and accompanied by more or less adequate ideas and trailing images, take us. Wallace Stevens alludes to this realm in his poem "Not Ideas about the Thing but the Thing Itself" when he writes of "a new knowledge of reality" that is "coming from outside."[30]

Spinoza is telling us that emotions give us a uniquely configured "new knowledge of reality." Not only because they have cognitive or conceptual dimensions—which they do—but mainly because in their expressiveness they take us outside ourselves and beyond ourselves: beyond the domain of subjective feeling into the light of what Stevens calls the "colossal sun" in which we are other to ourselves in the presence of other animate beings and, more generally, the environing world. Emotions are uniquely effective means by which we come to know the real actively: know it in ways that do not depend on elaborate theoretical schemata of the sort we find in Kant's *Critique of Pure Reason* or in the formulas of modern natural science. Spinoza allows us to affirm a genuine *emotional knowledge* that we are always already generating from within the affective presence of the life-worlds we actively inhabit.

Bodies as the concrete carriers of modal inter-influence register "affections" (*affectio*) in the form of transitory images and by way of passing ideas—all of which are confluent in the durational immanence of feeling. At the same time but at another level, the human body is the source of affects (*affectus*) that have everything to do with the bodily subject's power to act, a power that is fully activated by way of adequate ideas, and thus to realize its own force of existing amid the challenges and solicitations of the world. The incoming of affections as they form a stream of immanent feeling exists in equipoise with the expressive outgoing of emotions as affects. Our affective life consists of the continual negotiation of this two-way stream.

IV

Spinoza's model lends itself readily to grasping affirmative emotions such as joy, interpreted as an "increase in the power of acting," and love, when "the affect comes back upon the idea from which it follows."[31] Both joy and love are, not surprisingly, highly valorized as contributing to the state of "blessedness." But certain emotions are destructive and even violent: how does Spinoza accommodate emotions such as anger and hatred, given that his ambition is to account for any and every emotion? How does he understand emotions that are outright disruptive insofar as they diminish the "force of existing" in that with which they interact? Let us focus on hatred as a case in point. Spinoza's most economic definition of hatred (*odium*) is: "Hatred is simply pain, with the accompaniment of the idea of an external cause."[32] This straightforward formulation has more nuance than meets the eye at first. He is not asserting that the external factor itself forces us to feel hatred; for we are dealing with the *idea* of an external cause—that is, something *in us*, and more precisely in our response to being affected by something that exists outside. This response as such is neither coerced nor predetermined. For it can come about merely by imagining certain things about the external cause, as Spinoza makes clear soon after the just-cited definition: "From the mere fact that we imagine a thing to have something that is similar to an object which is accustomed to affect our mind with pleasure or pain, we shall love or hate that thing, even though that in respect of which it is similar to the object is not the [actual, literal] efficient cause of those emotions."[33]

    This last point has direct application to premeditated acts of hatred such as, for example, the arena bombing in Manchester, England, in May 2017. Twenty-three people died, including the suicide bomber himself, and more than half of the 139 injured were children. This was surely a "hate crime," as we glibly call it—without thinking about just how hate was involved. Motivated by the deep anger of the bomber, Salman Abedie, it was an act of indiscriminate killing and maiming. That the bombing was timed at a moment of expansive joy—at the end of a concert by Ariana Grande just as the crowd was flowing out of the auditorium, ebullient and inspired—adds to anger and hatred a factor of gratuitous cruelty. No formula can fully capture the complex perversity of the bombing, which was a combination of anger + hatred + cruelty + ideological justification (presumably to further the cause of ISIS). A very dense emotional embroilment was in play. Can Spinoza's model of emotion help us to understand it better?

It would be misleading to claim that the ways in which the people of Manchester have treated Muslims abusively—whether directly or indirectly—simply *caused* the bomber to lay his plot and carry it out. These modes of real and documentable abuse were clearly a factor in Abedie's planning, perhaps even its literal instigation; but what mattered still more was the way he *thought* about this treatment, imagined where it was coming from, and more generally contemplated its origins and effects. In Spinoza's own words: "From the mere fact that we have contemplated some thing with the emotion of pleasure or pain, of which it is not the efficient cause, we are able to love it or hate it."[34] In other words, what matters more than a demonstrable chain of efficient causation is how Salman Abedie *contended with* a discriminatory and hurtful situation: what he made of it after—and as a result of—thinking about it and brooding on it. In doing this, he was operating at the level of "affection" (*affectio*), that is, the taking up of his image or bare idea of this situation in the durational flow of his feeling. This uptake is not forced but nuanced insofar as the image or idea at stake can be acted upon in various ways, or not acted upon at all. The tragic truth is that Abedie might not have been led to the action he undertook had he thought about it differently, and as a result acted differently.[35]

We can detect a comparably nuanced insight on Spinoza's part when it comes to his insistence that hatred is *pain*. By this he means at least two things: first, to feel hatred is itself painful; and second, hatred consists of projecting a situation in which the hated person or thing is made to feel pain as well. Thinking this way dispels any suggestion that hatred is just a creature of a person's mind, a matter of sheer fantasy—that we hate in a vacuum. Instead, we come to hatred from pain which we, and others with whom we are close, have experienced. (In Abedie's case, these would almost certainly have included fellow Muslims in Britain and elsewhere.) In hating those who perpetrated this pain, one wishes to put anyone associated with these perpetrators in pain by way of a forceful counteraction that involves an element of revenge—which Spinoza defines as "the endeavor to repay harm that has been inflicted on us."[36] The implicit logic is: "They have made me and my kind suffer, so I shall make them and their kind suffer in turn."[37] At stake here is the empathic dimension of an emotion like hatred, which can commence with a sense of shared suffering—pain felt in common—accompanied by the wish to induce suffering in those responsible for such pain, including those allied with them by way of contiguity in space and time, and/or by racial or ethnic identity.

Abedie's deadly action may well have originated in an incident hurtful to him or other fellow Muslims—an incident occasioned by racism and exclusion, acutely felt, and which was then intensified by a labile imagination. By the time the plan for his action became consolidated in his mind, this hurt or pain was absorbed into the hatred manifest in the plan itself—a hatred that was expressed in the concrete steps of constructing the lethal weapon, concealing it, and entering the auditorium in Manchester. In his mind these malevolent actions became not only practicable but virtually irresistible. This doubtless brought with it its own perverse pleasure, very possibly heightened by an element of self-glorification as the self-chosen agent of ISIS. This would also be in keeping with Spinoza's general rule that "active" emotions, in contrast with passive ones ("passions"), are always accompanied by pleasure.[38] More directly put, "someone who imagines that what he hates is destroyed will feel pleasure."[39]

Spinoza points to one other aspect of hatred: this is that *anger* is always at stake in hatred, indirectly if not directly. He remarks: "The endeavor to inflict harm on a person whom we hate is called 'anger.'"[40] We might say that anger is an emotional *force* that fuels hatred. It supplies the precipitating condition for the eventual release of hatred. For anger emerges from displeasure or disapproval of something others have done that is felt to be harmful to oneself or those with whom one is closely affiliated: moving to hating those others is all too tempting. Spinoza himself, as a member of a persecuted minority (persecuted much more overtly in Spain and Portugal than in Holland), was aware of the collective dimension of hatred, as is evident in his statement: "If anyone has been affected with pleasure or pain by someone who belongs to a group or nation that is different from his own, and this is accompanied by the idea of that person, under the universal name of that group or nation, as its cause, then he will love or hate not only the person in question, but all the members of that group or nation."[41] The massification of hatred is a form of overgeneralization that has enormous detrimental potential—as becomes particularly evident in the case of genocide, when whole peoples are targeted for elimination on the basis of their racial or religious identity.[42]

V

It is something of a general pattern for Spinoza to employ dichotomous language only to overcome it. He does this in the case of love versus hatred, which can realize various hybrid combinations that are discussed in detail in the *Ethics*.[43] Another telling case in point, of particular interest here, concerns his use of the contrastive language of "inside" versus "outside," as in this passage: "I say that we act when something occurs either in us or outside us of which we are the adequate cause; that is . . . when there follows from our nature, either in us or outside us, something that can be understood clearly and distinctly through that nature alone."[44] But the very distinction of inside/outside is of secondary significance with regard to the fundamental point that to be the "adequate cause" of something—which entails understanding it through our own nature—is to *act* in the circumstance. Such action cuts across and suspends the inner/outer distinction, for it directly engages the larger intermodal world of which we are part. It is this world that is the true "outside"; it is sheer outsideness as it were, a domain in which everything is outside everything else. This includes *us* as singular modes, bodies in the world: we are outside ourselves thanks to our "power of acting," which situates us in interactive groupings of co-impinging modes. Even if this power "follows from our nature," our nature or essence is itself what it is only in relation with other modes. When I am actively empowered by gaining adequate ideas regarded as "the source of active [emotions],"[45] the power is expressed by emotion considered as itself an action. When we fail to be a fully effective cause—when we are only a "partial cause"—we are embroiled in "passions." The latter constitute a kind of psychic interiority, a passivity in which reaction prevails over action: "I say that we are passive when something occurs *in us*, or when something follows from our nature, of which we are only a partial cause."[46]

This passive interiority, existing in correlation with the human body as it is buffeted by the world, is not a fixed domain; since it is entirely composed of durational processes, it is in a continual state of transition and change. It is constituted by "the impressions, i.e., the traces, of objects, and consequently [by] the . . . images of things."[47] It derives from the intake of the affections that emerge from impingements with other modes. Such affective interiority is passive through and through, and as such it is akin to what Heidegger might call a "deficient mode," a moment of inadequacy, of inaction, and of passion construed in the literal sense of "suffered feeling."[48] In contrast, the active moment occurs if we can emerge from the imbroglio of this dense inwardness into the outwardness realized by the action of an emotion that is accompanied by an adequate idea of the purport of that emotion. In the case of joy—an emotion consistently valorized by Spinoza—we move from a passive sense of rising happiness, of incipient joy, as we discover that our experience has consonance with other modes, and in embracing this consonance we affirm it in forming an adequate idea of it—at which point merely passive

joy becomes fully active and we experience "the bliss of action."[49] Such
action amounts to empowerment in the realm of Nature or God, and thus
of infinite Substance.

We may take this empowerment to be the direct result of emotion
as activating. For emotion as an *action* represents the becoming-active of
that which is held in immanence within as feeling and as passion, as sheer
affection (*affectio*). Emotion itself (*affectus*) is always already on its way out,
for immanent affection holds the potential for the gaining of an adequate
idea of its own content. Activation is attained when we convert passive
reception or anticipation into forthright action by means of adequate
ideation. Emotions such as joy and love maximize our power of acting
when they are not just experienced, but are also fully comprehended,
thereby enabling us to become the fully effective owners of these emotions instead of turning away from them in the evasive maneuver that
Collingwood calls "corruption of consciousness."[50] As Spinoza can be
taken to say: if "we can be the adequate cause of [our own affections],
then I understand by the emotion an action; otherwise, I understand it
to be a passion."[51] In other words, we can transform our take on a given
affection by gaining an adequate idea of it and thereby engage in knowing action rather than passive reaction. From being held in reserve as
"knowledge in potency," the affection transmutes into an active emotion
that has real effects in our surrounding world.[52]

This transformative process can be modeled thus:

passivity of feelings as affections // formation of adequate ideas of these
affections // emergence of emotions as active affects

Crucial here is the transmutation of a feeling by the addition of an adequate idea of its content. "Such a feeling," affirms Deleuze, "is no longer
a passion, because it follows from an adequate idea in us; it is itself an
adequate idea."[53] Through this process, what we hold within in the immanence of affection or feeling comes *out* into the dynamic realm of
intermodal interaction—which is to say, out into the realm of effective
activity whereby a given emotion not only makes a difference but creates
difference itself.

VI

A fully developed account of Spinoza's model of emotion would show
two contrary motions at play in relation to the human subject. (1) On

the one hand, the world impinges on the human body via affections: the embodied subject is constituted by the history of such incomings from the surrounding world. There is no preexisting inner subject, nothing that precedes the instreaming influences from around the body—nothing like a realm of pure consciousness as in Descartes or Sartre, much less a sheer unconscious as in Freud or Jung.[54] Nor is there a tabula rasa ("blank slate") such as Locke posited. Whatever we might be tempted to consider "inside" is nothing but the registration of bodily incursions from without in the form of fleeting traces, deposited images, and inadequate ideas. The inside is thus what it is only insofar as it is generated from the outside, exogenously.[55] As a result, there is nothing inside the subject to *turn inside out*—to deflect or redirect outward. In this account, what is there in the subject is a momentary and ever-changing catchment area filled with passing affections, which are themselves the traces of impactions of surrounding modes upon the body.

(2) On the other hand, there is an opposite directionality: from the subject *on out*. Affections, when and if adequately understood, become active presences that animate the immanent durational experience of the person affected. Insofar as they remain merely received, these affections have the status of "feelings" and "passions"; but when the subject gains an adequate understanding of them, they are catalyzed into active affects, that is to say, full-fledged *emotions*. These latter are genuinely periphanous, showing themselves in their transitivity, their outgoingness. But to attain the status of an active emotion is not to be liberated from captivity within the subject, for there are no inward emotions to begin with. Within us there are only transitory affections in the form of feelings and passions which as "powers" have the positive potential of *becoming* active forces in the intermodal complex to which a given subject belongs. This happens only when they are thought adequately in their essential nature—understanding what they *are*—thereby becoming emotions or affects that actively engage with other modes. To become actively emotional is to extend beyond one's own bodily inherence; it is to go beyond the inertness of one's own inactive, merely felt passions in the durational domain, thereby exceeding one's im-passioned passivity. It is to *ex*-ist, to "stand out," and to do so in and as the activity that accomplishes existing-beyond-feeling.

If Husserl insists on the intentionality of pure consciousness and Heidegger emphasizes the *ecstasis* of *Existenz*—with Merleau-Ponty underlining the operative intentionality of the lived body—then by taking Spinoza's lead we can discern a fourth member of this auspicious series: that of a properly *emotional intentionality*, whereby the subject emerges out of itself, and is able to do so thanks to achieving an adequate grasp of its own affections, thereby converting feelings into active emotions.[56]

* * *

Spinoza's contribution to our understanding of emotions is nothing short of remarkable. His genius was to locate emotions as adequately understood feelings in a domain outside the subject, where activity triumphs over passivity. Given that he provided a powerful case for the *Aussersichsein* (being-outside-itself) of emotion, one might hope that he would go on to discuss just *where* emotions present themselves, but no such discussion is to be found in the *Ethics*, an otherwise admirably comprehensive and systematic treatise. By this I mean he did not provide *specific places* for emotions, even if it can be argued that he did pursue a model of a general *environment* for emotions. Indeed, what is outside the subject *is* this very environment.[57] Even so, he did not describe particular places-of-presentation for emotions, and thus did not specify where emotions find their own expressive location, their distinctive showplace or *Schauplatz*—the word that Freud employed to designate the "dream scene." Despite Spinoza's radical deconstruction of Descartes, in neither thinker is there a proper place for emotion to show itself. One must wait for Kant's *Critique of Judgment* to find the suggestion of a concrete model of a place-of-presentation for a particular emotion such as the sublime. But Kant only hints at this model and does not thematize it. Absent in Descartes, Spinoza, and Kant alike is an adequate conception of the placiality of emotion as expressive.

Lacking from all these philosophers is what we might call an *emotional commons*: a common space for the periphaneity of emotion.[58] The need for recognizing such a common space is pithily stated by Eugene Gendlin: "People . . . are not inside their skins, but *are* their living-in the world and their living-with others."[59] He adds that "we *are* interactions with the environment—other people, the world, the universe—and we can sense ourselves to be just such an interaction."[60] To this I would add that these interactions are often explicitly emotional. Thinkers from Descartes through Spinoza, as we have seen, and Kant, as we shall see next, lack a viable schema of emotional placement as a concrete *somewhere* that is at once periphanous and intersubjectively shareable. We shall continue our search for such placement, and for a convincing characterization of how emotions must be understood in terms of their essential outsideness, by now exploring Kant's highly suggestive treatment of the sublime.

4

Kant and the Place of the Sublime

This chapter does not ask *what* the sublime is: its essence. Others have attempted to spell out this essence: "The sublime is an aesthetic experience of awe, wonder, exhilaration, and even terror that is felt in the presence of typically vast, formless, threatening, overwhelming natural environments or phenomena."[1] The search for the elusive essence of sublimity would lead us to compare different theories of the sublime; those of Longinus with Kant, for example. Instead, we consider here the *locus* of the sublime—in terms borrowed mainly from Kant—in order to ascertain an answer to the question: *Where* is the sublime? How are we to locate something as amorphous and ethereal as the sublime, whose very name suggests vaporization, being "under the threshold" (*sub-limen*) of the determinate? What does it mean to find a place, a proper place, for the sublime? And how does this place affect its status as a powerful and intriguing but little-understood source of emotions such as wonder and awe? My aim in this chapter is to think through the location of the sublime on its own terms and in its own direction, with the aid of Kant's challenging and often aporetic pronouncements, and occasional borrowings from Edmund Burke. We will concern ourselves with this location by considering how the sublime comes to us from a certain *without,* an outside that challenges the primacy of the interiorized emotional subject who is the pivot of early modernism.

The question "Where is the sublime?" will lead us to the close imbrication of place and emotion, seeing how the one cannot be thought without the other. It will also lead us to the brink of decidedly postmodern notions of affective life. For this decisive move away from inwardizing conceptions of emotion—conceptions that he himself all too often espoused—Kant proves to be a crucial transitional figure, one who is decidedly Janusian. On the one hand, he envisages emotions as literally self-contained; to this extent he looks back to Descartes. On the other hand, his notion of sublimity manifests a force that draws us out of our enclosed subjectivity and takes us into the broader domain of the place-world; here, like Spinoza, he looks forward to models of emotion as situated outside of our self-enclosing and self-enclosed subjectivity.

|

Kant's *Critique of Judgment* (1790) presents us with a paradox of implacement. On the one hand, according to Kant, what is experienced as sublime is indissociably linked with natural things ("objects"). Even if they do not house the sublime in any straightforward way, these things are indispensable for eliciting the sublime, "arousing" it and "prompting" it, as Kant puts it in explicitly exogenous terms. They may not *hold* the sublime, but they do *intimate* it. They certainly *occasion it*. On the other hand, the generation of the experience of the sublime occurs within, in our psychical and intellectual interiority. It is to this extent endogenous, for the place of this generation is within us. As Kant writes expressly, "true sublimity must be sought only in the mind [*im Gemüt*] of the judging person, not in the natural object the judging of which prompts this mental attunement."[2]

From this viewpoint the sublime is a mental event, not a natural phenomenon. It is what happens *to us* and *in us* once we are sufficiently solicited by a natural spectacle. Requisite as the spectacle is, it does not possess the sublime as a property or power of its own. Kant adds: "All we are entitled to say is that the [natural] object is suitable for exhibiting a sublimity that can be found [*angetroffen*, "encountered"] in the mind. For what is sublime, in the proper meaning of the term, cannot be contained in any sensible form."[3] This is why Kant denies that even the most tumultuous ocean can be called sublime: it is properly termed "horrible" (*grässlich*). "The sight of it," Kant avers, "is horrible; and one must already have filled one's mind with all sorts of [preexisting] ideas if such an intuition is to attune it to a feeling that is itself sublime."[4] In short, sublimity is not found in the natural scene or spectacle that elicits it, but in something that happens within ourselves.

Kant appears to force upon us a strict choice from the start: either the sublime is something in nature (exogenous) *or* it is something in us (endogenous). In nature, it would be a property of perceived objects; in us, it is a psychical process. This difference reflects the basic difference between physical and mental being. Although Kant is determined to locate the sublime in us, he acknowledges the strong temptation to assume that it is located *out there* in nature. In fact, he succumbs to this temptation himself, given that his own prototypes of the sublime are almost invariably drawn from the natural world: "bold, overhanging and, as it were, threatening rocks, thunderclouds piling up in the sky and moving about accompanied by lightning and thunderclaps, volcanoes with all their destructive power, hurricanes with all the devastation they leave behind, the boundless ocean heaved up, the high waterfall of a mighty river, and so on."[5] These are all examples of the dynamically sublime, of nature in its sheer might (*Macht*). Yet the mathematically sublime, the absolutely large in magnitude (*Grösse*), is also most effectively presented in natural terms; that is, in terms of what appears to us in perception: "nature is sublime in those of its appearances whose intuition carries with it the idea of their infinity."[6]

Ultimately, both modes of sublimity belong to the natural world—Kant remains a naturalist despite his transcendentalist proclivities—but they do so in extraordinary ways: "In what we usually call sublime in nature there is such an utter lack of anything leading to particular objective principles and to forms of nature conforming to them, that it is rather in its chaos that nature most arouses our ideas of the sublime, or in its wildest and most ruleless disarray and devastation, provided it displays magnitude and might."[7] Such wildness serves to remind us that nature does not house either kind of sublimity (that of magnitude or of might) comfortably; indeed, when we are before an ocean that we experience as tempestuous, we may find ourselves overwhelmed and threatened by the spectacle. Yet all this may unexpectedly turn to savoring its sublimity, for something we currently experience as sublime "is now attractive to the same degree to which [formerly] it was repulsive to mere sensibility."[8] The attraction or "liking" proper to the sublime, Kant affirms, "is a pleasure that arises only indirectly: it is produced by the feeling of a momentary inhibition of the vital forces following immediately by an outpouring of them that is all the stronger."[9] It is as if drawing in our breath before the daunting spectacle were succeeded by an exhalation that brings with it an emotional appreciation of the very same spectacle.

As tempting as it is to posit sublimity in the object per se, such as a tumultuous ocean, for Kant this constitutes a false localization. Appearances notwithstanding, the true locus of the sublime lies within the subject, and it is only by a mistaken maneuver that we come to believe that sublimity belongs properly to natural things themselves. This is to fall into the error of "misplaced concreteness," in Whitehead's apt term. We attribute to nature the sublimity that arises from within us, thanks to the "vocation" (*Bestimmung*) of our cognitive powers to rise to heights that nature alone can never attain: "Hence the feeling of the sublime in nature is [ultimately] respect for our own vocation. But by a certain subreption (in which respect for the object is substituted for respect for the idea of humanity within our[selves, as] subject[s]), this respect is accorded [to] an object of nature that, as it were, makes intuitable for us the superiority of the rational vocation of our [own] cognitive powers over the greatest power of sensibility."[10] What a later era in the wake of Feuerbach, Marx, and Freud will call "projection" Kant designates as "subreption," a maneuver whereby we take to belong to the object, as something "intuitable for us," what really belongs to ourselves as subjects whose considerable cognitive powers are engaged and excited by the prospect of enormous might or magnitude.

Upon encountering a sublime spectacle outside us, our imagination is challenged to present to itself, in a single comprehensive whole, what exceeds its own limited power of epistemic representation. But this very inadequacy only serves to remind the witnessing subject of the much greater scope of its own ideas of reason, which demand an "absolute whole" that exceeds not just what imagination can encompass but what the natural world can deliver. That this absolute whole is "impossible"— impossible because no progression of images or sensible intuitions, no matter how numerous or richly laden, will ever be equal to it—is beside the point in Kant's view.[11] What is to the point is the striving to attain the equivalent of such an absolute whole from within in the very face of the absence of being able to find and thus represent that whole in the natural world without, thus gaining a "pleasure that is possible only by means of [the] displeasure [of a failed representation]."[12] The frustration incurred by a failure to account adequately for an overwhelming spectacle given in the sensible world gives way to the special pleasure of expanding our own mental powers beyond their usual modest limits.

No wonder that we are "agitated" (*bewegt*) in the presence of the mathematical or dynamical sublime, when we are brought before the "abyss" (*Abgrund*) to which it leads us.[13] In the wake of failing to be equal to the initial spectacle of the sublime, we engender a sublimity within ourselves as rational beings who seek absolute wholes wherever they are thinkable. If such wholes cannot be found in ongoing perceptual experience, they can be engendered from within. Only in the case of beauty do we have recourse to something that is adequately presented in what lies before us—namely, in the formal purposiveness of nature or in a work of art that conveys such purposiveness.[14] In the case of the sublime, by contrast, we turn *within ourselves*—to our own resources. It is precisely because we cannot find a sensible intuition or a formal concept that fits our experience of the sublime spectacle without that we turn to a different resource, that of the inherent powers of reason. No matter how striking appearances may be—even if "shapeless mountain masses [are] piled on one another in wild disarray, with their pyramids of ice"[15]—the dynamics of physical forces thereby become a psycho-dynamics as we enter into a struggle between what reason calls for and what neither sensibility nor imagination can deliver. Yet, far from being simply discouraged or set back by this struggle, we are elevated by it to a new level of experience, that of a specifically sublime emotionality.

In short: as a result of the very impasse in which an overwhelming natural spectacle places us—our never being able to encompass it by means of images or concepts—we gain satisfaction from the very recourse we can then make to our own powers of reason: a recourse that brings its own "emotional liking" (*rührendes Wohlgefallen*). Since we cannot make ourselves equal to the sublime as presented to us in perception or extended in imagination, we move within and fashion our own compensatory countersublime. Failure at one level gives rise to satisfaction at another.[16]

At this point we are led to ask two critical questions. First, why should the spectacle of the sublime, mathematical or dynamic, lead us to retreat into ourselves, that is, move away from its challenging prospect into our emotional selves? Rather than being drawn out by the spectacle, Kant argues that we are drawn back into our own emotional subjectivity. Just insofar as our subjectivity is challenged by the might and magnitude of something outside us, he beats a retreat to an internal drama that brings a self-generated emotional surge inside us. Here we see explicitly at work the early modern impulse to bury emotion in the human subject, and at the very moment when there would seem to be a rare opportunity to move beyond this subject. Second, what is the status of the daunting spectacle that occasions the generation of the sublime? Is it something purely "phenomenal," in the language of the *Critique of Pure Reason*? Or is it something more than "mere appearance" (*blosse Erscheinung*), a source that is a genuine resource, something under or beyond its mere appearance? When Kant writes in the sentence cited earlier that "nature is sublime in those of its appearances whose intuition carries with it the idea of their infinity," he only underscores the ambiguity: sublime *in its appearances* refers us to the realm of sensibility and imagination, while the *idea of infinity* invokes the realm of reason—whose proper province is the noumenal realm, that is, an overtly "supersensible substrate."[17]

The power of the sublime derives in large part from its uneasy stationing on the cusp between phenomenal and noumenal, an edge on which the sublime shimmers seductively, helping to account for its combined effect of attracting us while also frustrating us. But this precarious positioning also makes us wonder whether the options offered by Kant are the only relevant ones. Perhaps we should not assume that the sublime is to be found *either* in matter *or* in mind any more than we should we assume that it is located *either* in phenomena *or* in noumena. The exclusiveness of such binary choices cannot be taken for granted. Is there another way of conceiving the locus of the sublime that is less dichotomous and divisive?

II

Early in his essay "The Origin of the Work of Art," Heidegger poses the question: Where is the artwork? (*Wo aber ist das Kunstwerk?*).[18] This chapter began similarly by inquiring, Where is the sublime? The implacement of the sublime for Kant is complex, as we have just seen. The natural locus of the sublime certainly *seems* to be in the sensible world: in the raging ocean or the towering mountain. But here, as elsewhere in the domain of transcendental topics, appearances are as misleading as they are necessary. According to Kant, the ultimate seat of the sublime is within the human subject rather than in the external spectacle that commands our attention at first. But this seat is far from being a secure foundation. By Kant's own admission, it is a place of continual and irresolvable conflict (*Streitraum* in Heidegger's term), and is finally an "abyss" (*Abgrund*) in Kant's own preferred word.[19] The seat of the sublime is insecure; it is an unsettled and unsettling seat that will not support what we try to put into it in the effort to rise to the challenge of the natural spectacle. The incommensurability, if not outright incompatibility, of imagination and reason—the one chasing after the other—means that the very vocation of aesthetic sublimity is ill-fated. Even if it is true that in pursuing this vocation "the mind can come to feel its own sublimity,"[20] this sublimity is largely self-generated—largely but not entirely, since the sublime is at least *provoked* by an actual scene. How can it be, then, that this subjective basis for the experience of the sublime—a base that reflects its own "actual present impotence"—is something that, as Kant announces triumphantly, "elevates it even above nature"?[21]

Here we must ask: Can the role of nature in the generation of the sublime be confined to that of a mere *provocateur* of subjective psychodramas? Kant's own unabashed recourse to examples taken straight from experiences of wilderness (albeit often as reported by naturalists such as Saussure), and above all his own insistence that nature arouses and agitates us only when it "displays magnitude and might," point in quite another direction: that of acknowledging the natural world in its own force and inherent power. So too does Edmund Burke's emphasis on *terror*: an emotion that is very likely to come from some event or trait belonging to the natural world, something literally terri-*fying*, that generates terror itself. But in what do this magnitude and might, and the associated terror, consist? How do they *show themselves* in the world? What is the true *place* of the sublime, and with it the proper locus of the emotions it arouses? The sublime needs to be located if it is not to be simply free-floating. Or rather, it needs to be *re*located.

A double deconstruction is called for here. First, it will not do to situate the sublime in the human subject alone. Even if we can agree that this subject has a lot to do with the generation of the full experience of the sublime, this does not mean that the sublime per se is located in that subject exclusively, for then it would be difficult—even impossible—to distinguish from a fantasy or memory held by the same subject. Even if Kant everywhere affirms the exceptional resources and powers of the subject, it is not plausible that these resources alone are responsible for this experience, which characteristically makes some reference, however indirect, to a natural world that is outside and beyond us. But secondly, it would be equally mistaken to put the sublime entirely and only in the natural world, for then its resonance among humans would be difficult to explain. The great poets and painters of sublimity, from Wordsworth to Turner, start from a deeply immersive *experience* in nature, not from the sublime as if it were an objective feature of the natural world: a "thing" rather than an "event." The sublime that they portray is not to be found as an isolated item or event in the natural world, nakedly presented as such. Such exclusive placement would not only proceed by an illusory sub-reption whereby we project the psychical onto the physical; more importantly, to so identify the sublime with a given natural thing or event would fail to do justice to its expansiveness, its characteristic way of spreading itself across an entire domain: to be *all over the place*: as when a sunset illuminates an entire scene.

To demand that the sublime be an objective feature of nature, whether as a property or in some other way, is to presume naively that it can be literally located there: that it is *just there*, in that pinpointed locus, and nowhere else. Whitehead regards the obsession with *simple location* as "the very foundation of the seventeenth-century scheme of nature."[22] According to the doctrine of simple location, any particular thing is just where it is and not anywhere else: "it is just in this place and in no other."[23] This overriding scheme continued into the eighteenth century—with the notable exceptions of Berkeley and Leibniz—and was still formative for Kant as late as his 1786 treatise, *First Metaphysical Principles of the Science of Nature*, in which he maintains that "the place of every body is a point."[24] Such a pinpointed place is designated without reference, not even implicit reference, to any other place or places. To affirm that the sublime is to be found in a given natural thing located at a determinate place—there and nowhere else—is to restrict the basis of its ampliative powers, its capacity to inspire poets and painters as well as laypeople who marvel in its presence.

The sublime cannot be simply located in nature, then. By locating it inside the mind, Kant hints at its non-simple location there. For mind, *das*

Gemüt, is non-simple for Kant thanks to its inherent complexity, as the collective prefix *Ge-* indicates. *Gemüt* includes emotion as well as cognition, heart as well as intellect, imagination as well as memory, and via the *sensus communis,* others as well as oneself. Given this multivalence of mind, if the sublime belongs there rather than in nature, it is as the product of a complex internal process that cannot be reduced to isolated emotional states such as pleasure or displeasure, horror or terror. The location of the sublime as an "absolute whole" in the mind is all the less simple since it bears on the infinity of reason's domain, the supersensible, which is a decidedly non-simple location—and all the less simple given that the supersensible is an abyss for an imagination anchored in sensibility: reason "look[s] outward toward the infinite, which for sensibility is an abyss."[25]

Closely related to his bias in favor of the simple location of natural things is an unexamined presupposition on Kant's part that the sublime is located either in the judging subject or in the natural thing: either in Mind or in Nature. Such an exclusive choice is for Kant an "absolute presupposition"—to borrow Collingwood's term for something that is at once basic yet never questioned.[26] By insisting on this binaristic choice, Kant disallows the possibility of an *indeterminate* locus for the sublime. To understand such a locus as it is experienced by humans calls for a sense of place that cannot be reduced to bare position, and thus cannot be reduced to "site," as I call the sheer positioning of objects in homogeneous space.[27] The sublime contests any such delimited specificity of location; it calls for a locus that is more diffuse than determinate. Putting this point more positively, if the sublime is trans-subjective—phenomenologically extending beyond a discrete emotional response—it is also trans-objective as unconfinable to a given object or thing. If it is at least plausible to delimit beauty in these two ways, this will not work for the sublime.[28]

Might the alternative be to propose, then, that the sublime is *bi-*located (in Levy-Bruhl's term)? I think not. Bi-location—simultaneous location at two places—is not adequate to characterize the radicality of the implacement of the sublime. For bilocation is all too easily reducible to mere co-positioning in the same space, as in Leibniz's idea of space as the "order of co-existence." But neither will it do to talk of *omni*-location. Just as it would be exaggerated to claim that the sublime is *always* occurring, to say that the sublime is *everywhere* is to miss what is specific about its implacement. To be everywhere is finally to be no place in particular, much as taking place at every time is to occur at no specific time.[29] To be everywhere comes very close to being the mere converse of being nowhere.

It becomes clear that if we are to find for the sublime its own mode of implacement, we shall need to satisfy two criteria: first, a sense of place that exceeds location as position or sheer site. And second, a model of implacement as something other than single or exclusive (*univocal* in character) yet not indifferently anywhere or everywhere (*equivocal*). With this double demand, our initial question returns with renewed force: *Where is the sublime?*

III

On an early evening in mid-May, a sunset I could only consider sublime suddenly appeared to the west of the café in which I was writing: reddish-purple clouds collected above a zone of golden light lingering after the sun had sunk beneath the horizon. This was a scene of penumbral presence emerging at the perimeter of the local landscape composed of hills and woods as well as roads: a luminous landscape that led to its own vanishing at the edges of these clustered places. This extraordinary scene elicited my emotion: I was drawn out of my sheltered subjectivity into enthusiastic reception of a place-world that was charged with sublimity. I was deeply moved—emerging from my just-prior placidity into an unexpected emotionality in response to the scene unfolding. This emotionality combined awe and wonder with an infusion of joy. Others around me were likewise captured, leaving their tables to view it outside.

In this experience I and others were transported into a special state of psychic receptivity and appreciation: we were spellbound by the effervescent allure of the sunset. This allure was not a discrete stimulus; it characterized the entire scene and was transmitted simultaneously to each of us who beheld it. The sunset conveyed an emotional tenor that suffused the whole spectacle, not just our private selves. If I and others were involved with what we witnessed together, it was not as separate selves but as integral parts of the same scene. Whatever happened in me endogenously ("the *feeling* of sublimity") could not be adequately understood by invoking an exogenous model of ocular stimulation by the colors as such, the diminishing light or the cloud formations per se. Instead, I and others were presented with an entire layout of the sublime—in a full and singular manifestation of what presented itself. We were perceiving a coherent visuosphere that we shared in common before any considered individual or collective judgment might arise. Ours was a silent and awestruck co-witnessing; only later was there conversation among those who had just witnessed the spectacle; the moment of *sensus communis* ("common judgment") emphasized by Kant was yet to come.

An endogenous model of an isolated observer taking in a set of private and separate sensations cannot capture the full sensuous actuality of such a shared experience of the sublime. If we ask where the sublime was in this experience, we would have to say that it belonged to the visual world, and was intrinsic to its periphanous self-presentation. The sublimity, situated outside us, was visible in several converging features of the same sweeping sky; it was a scene spread out in depth as well as in height, laid out horizontally with a breadth and width of its own, all this in the midst of a scene of shifting cloud formations. These various dimensions and configurations rendered accessible the placescape constituted by the sublime scene, inviting me and others to be its active witnesses, participating in it. The participation very much included the emotionality that I and others felt in being present at the unfolding drama, taking it in so that it was not only outside us but at the same time between us. The sublime in such a circumstance was located in the visual spectacle, but it also resided in the shared experience of ourselves as its onlookers. The emotion we felt in common we can only name awkwardly and inadequately with such words as "surprise," "wonder," "astonishment," "bliss," and similar affectively intense terms. In the thrall of such a multifaceted emotionality we were *beside ourselves*, drawn *out* of ourselves—caught up in a simultaneous reaching out toward and being drawn in by the spectacle itself. The ordinary became a scene of the extraordinary, all in a brief stretch of time that was soon over as the sunset vanished into the darkening oncoming evening.

In moving from an initial exposition and critique of the dynamic and mathematical sublime in the *Critique of Judgment*, we have opened an alternative way of understanding sublimity here. In the Kantian treatment, the sublime was caught up in binary oppositions of subject and object, mind and nature, mathematical and dynamic, phenomenal and noumenal, as well as empirical and transcendental, a priori and a posteriori—the list of dyads could continue. These pairings purport to be exclusive as well as exhaustive in their conceptual reach. Yet the sublime as manifested in the sunset experience just described eludes such exclusion and exhaustion, dissolving the Kantian dyads in favor of an alternative model in which a deeper coherence triumphs over crisp bifurcations. Indeed, Kant's own model of the dynamic sublime sometimes undercuts its own oppositional binaries by employing such expansive notions as *Gemüt* and *sensus communis*, as well as by the coupling of apprehension with comprehension, imagination with reason: such pairings exhibit a dense dialectical interdependence that cannot be reduced to sheer dyadic difference. It is telling that Kant, while adhering to an early modernist model of emotion as taking place altogether inside the subject, whether at the level of sensibility, imagination, or reason—and conceiving that same subject as existing independently of its surrounding—offers these alternative notions without owning up to their full deconstructive force.

The sunset experience taking place in the sky that day undermines binarism at its own game. Descriptive terms such as "scene," "spectacle," and "visuosphere" resist binary reductions by inviting and extending special opportunities for participation, acting to situate what is located in a given place and drawing us into its embrace. Rather than being a matter of extended substance (*res extensa*) wholly apart from myself as the cognizing subject (*res cogitans*), a place belongs to me and I to it. Thanks to my lived body as the crucial intermediary, a place participates in my ongoing life and I in its—I and it participating together in this same life, given its basic accessibility. As participative in these various ways, place straddles the threshold of the sublime, complicating any effort to locate sublimity on one side or the other of a model that separates the subject from the phenomenon, separating the emotion of sublimity as felt within from a presumed external cause of this same emotion.[30] Place undoes any such dualism by being a dynamic syncretic force in the life of the subject.

Place also undoes binarities by its irrepressible plurality. For there is no such thing as *one* place only, or just *two* places, or only *thirteen*—that is, places as so many discrete, denumerable things. Places proliferate on either side of any given threshold, including that of the sublime. The threshold itself does not simply divide one place from another, any more than a horizon does. A threshold, like a horizon, is a unitive force that brings several places into proximity with one another. In other words, place is inherently *multilocular*—as was the case with the sunset I witnessed, a spectacle that occupied almost all the various regions of the open sky. Such outreaching mulilocularity is an integral aspect of the power of place: a power not just to excite and move us in singular and separable ways, but to engender a plurality of related and diverse emotions, each appropriate to a given phase or aspect of the places in which we find ourselves.

IV

To recognize the placialized presence of the sublime is to understand its power differently from the way Burke and Kant posited, and to convert its overpoweringness as outsized might and magnitude, occasioning terror or horror, into a subtle power that operates from below—*von unten*, in Karl Jaspers's suggestive phrase. The sublime sunset was above me directionally, but its force worked on me down here below: down on the ground from where I witnessed it. Its sublimity did not overwhelm me but drew me and others into its nexus. It had no simple location but was arrayed across the sky, from where it descended into our admiring bodies. It was first of all *out there*, and only from there did it reverberate in our casually assembled receptive bodies. To try to locate the sublime in just one place goes contrary to the multiple modes of its ingression into our lives. One of Wallace Stevens's poems reads: "The sky [is] acutest at its vanishing," and something comparable is true of sublimity as I am conceiving it here.[31] Much of the captivation of the sublime is found in its very vanishing as something sheerly colossal—as something awesomely *up there*, occasioning a "respect" (*Achtung*) that is akin to religious humility before God (Kant analogizes sublime might [*Macht*] to God more than once).[32] But a noncolossal, nonterrifying sublimity is found in a layout of places where it is multiply situated. Such sublimity dis-appears even as it appears.[33] Neither phenomenal nor noumenal, it oscillates on the threshold connecting subject to thing, mind to nature, self to other. It re-situates these oppositional terms in ways that underscore their coexistence and allow their differences to converge as configurative rather than as divisive.

Such a revised notion shows sublimity to evanesce in its very coalescence in places. These places exhibit the sublime without containing it, much less simply locating it. A truly dynamic sublimity exceeds any one given place and is immanent in the congeries of places that make up the landscape or cityscape from which it emerges. Such sublimity does not stand *over* places, commanding them from on high; the word "sublime" means what it says: the *limen* or threshold is approached *from below*, from the lower depths that make up the rhizomatic receptacle of appearances (in contrast with an "epi-phany," which is located *upon* appearances). Even as it may appear in the sky above, such sublimity is not transcendent, much less wholly other; it spreads throughout a skyscape that belongs to a local landscape, permeating all its assembled dimensions and the places immanent in it. The sublime to which I am pointing here is not so much *extended in space* as *distended in place*, where it acts to conjoin the *disjecta membra* of binary oppositions such as nature and mind, subject and object, self and other, above and below.

In a sublime scene such as I here describe, "all goes onward and outward . . . and nothing collapses."[34] The sublime is "a way out"—as Freud said of sublimation—in that it takes us out of the fixities and definites of a metaphysics of presence.[35] In other words, sublimity occurs by *expansion*—a term used by Kant to designate the challenge that reason offers to sensibility, thanks to "a dominance that reason exerts over sensibility only for the sake of expanding [*erweitern*] it commensurately with reason's own [infinite] domain."[36] For Kant, the scope of Ideas exceeds not only sensibility and imagination but nature itself.[37] Here one must wonder, however, if just the reverse is not the case: is it not nature that exceeds reason in its dialectical employment, thereby inducing not only a conceptual understanding but an emotional engagement? This engagement cannot be contained within the human subject. It qualifies the natural landscape that precipitates this experience. In short, *the emotionality of the sublime turns itself inside out in the experiences of the places in which it is presented to the subject.* "Everything spatial expands," wrote Theodor Lipps, and this is surely true of the natural world in its sublimity: when experienced as sublime, this world expands indefinitely in and through its horizons and thresholds.[38] But it also expands in the emotionality to which it gives rise.

In the end it is not a matter of insisting on nature, including wild nature, as the privileged, much less the exclusive, place of the sublime. True, the move to nature, and especially wild nature, on the part of the *Naturphilosophen* who were the immediate legatees of the *Critique of Judgment* was helpful in disburdening the human subject of intensely impacted transcendental machinery, as well as the oppressiveness of a triumphalist modernism. But behind all this there lies a scenography of situations, a loosely knit community of places from which the sublime emerges and is felt emotionally.[39] Kant insisted that the sublime "consists merely in a *relation,*" and for him this relation lies not only between the sensible and the supersensible, but also between imagination and reason, subject and object, immanent and transcendent: these are the bookends of Kant's discussion in the *Critique of Judgment.*[40] I have been arguing, by contrast, that the relation that matters most in the experience of the sublime—and which engenders its inherent emotionality—is that between the places that manifest the sublime—places on which human beings rely as they traverse and inhabit them in their time on earth.

This is to argue that the place of the sublime is, for human beings, a being-in-place among and between places that are felt intensely in the alchemy of a subliminal emotionality. These places include the place of the subject as well as the place of natural and artificial things, the places of social and political subjects in community, urban places as well as wild ones, built and unbuilt places, and the list goes on. In all such situations the sublime *appears*—yet without being reducible to what Kant labels as a "mere appearance" (*blosse Erscheinung*). Let us say that the sublime exists *through* these various places by qualifying them as a suffusive presence that is located in them and from there elicits our emotional response to them. The full phenomenon of the sublime is not found on any sheer surface, much less in any noumenal thing-in-itself (*Ding an sich*); it saturates the places in which it appears, from below, sideways, and every other way. Considered thus, the sublime becomes an aura of the place-world as it is encountered in its "mere being," in Wallace Stevens's phrase, a phrase that has to be heard in contrast with Kant's "mere appearance." It is elevated beyond the abyss of reason and the incomprehension of imagination without calling to be conceived as an august Verticality or a crushing Colossus. Not being "superelevated" (in Derrida's term),[41] it is distended laterally, spreading through the multiple implacements of the near and far spheres of experience. No longer merely mental, and certainly not strictly physical, it is inherently placial and thus a matter of becoming rather than a form of fixed being.

Let the poet have the last word here: the sublime is finally a "palm at the end of the mind, beyond the last thought, rising in the bronze décor. . . . [It] stands on the edge of space."[42] The sublime is indeed an edge phenomenon; it is a palmary instance of the periphanous in human experience, including the outlying emotions that are the special focus of this book. For emotions take us to the very edge of our affective lives; emerging on the perimeter of conscious perceiving and imagining, they lead us *elsewhere* than the centrated subject, out onto the fringes of that subject's scope of awareness. This dis-placement is far from diversionary or superficial, for it is capable of revealing to us new directions and unexpected parameters of our ongoing lives. That these directions and parameters are situated "on the edge of space" makes them all the more invaluable, for it is *out there, outside the subject* in these extrinsic spaces and multiple places, that we come to know the outer limits of what we are capable in the realm of emotion. This is a matter of moving from the tempting and all too customary models of exogeny and endogeny to a different paradigm: that of *exophany*, according to which things come to be shown and known in their appearing elsewhere and otherwise. This paradigm is concretized and exemplified in the actual experience of the sublime and its attendant emotionality. Kant's treatment of the sublime, despite its contortions, offers a crucial transition from the rigid subjectivism of early modernity to construals of emotion that expand its compass in directions that we must now pursue further.

* * *

The central concern of the periphenomenological study undertaken in this book is the *showing* of emotions—especially the *location* of this showing in its characteristic places-of-presentation. "Place" as a configurated and diversely oriented scene is contrasted with "space" conceived as an indifferent and empty tableau. In contrast with a *re*presentation, a secondary action of forming an image or giving a verbal description, a "presentation" signifies a direct donation or giving, whether of a landscape vista or the concerted emotion emerging in a face-to-face confrontation or in a crowd of protesters.

The early Greek philosophers, we have seen, valorized emotion in the public arena, thrusting us in medias res out there with others in the popular theater, the agora, and the Assembly. Plato concerned himself with how emotion plays itself out in relation to the polis, the city-state, in dialogue, political debate, and sometimes even (as in the *Phaedrus*) outside the city walls, a literally extramural location. Aristotle stressed the interpersonal context in which the middle range of any given emotion must be calibrated in relation to how it affects others if we are to act ethically. In his considered view, emotions are socially valuable when experienced in-between the extremes of excess and deficiency, as well as being essential to political rhetoric in the form of oratory. Aristotle also underlined the need for an orator to gauge the emotional tenor of an audience, as well as his own emotional "display." All this stands in contrast with his own effort to locate emotion "in the soul" (*en psyche*) via its embodiment. Plato and Aristotle alike acknowledge the role of the psyche as the seat of emotion (Aristotle also emphasizing the importance of the body), but for them both this role is preliminary to the extraversion of emotion in public space, where it assumes crucial instrumental roles in social and political life. Both were especially concerned with how emotion figures in the realm of open discourse and debate, in a context of interaction with others, where looks are exchanged and words passed back and forth. In all such cases, the place-of-presentation lies squarely *between us*. Emotions take us out of our closed-in selves and into the company of others in an action of *coming-out* into an affectively shared compresence.

Seneca's lucubrations on anger inserted a phase of deliberation into the epigenesis of an emotion such as anger. To this extent he anticipates the modernist emphasis on the self-determining subject. Descartes, the exemplary early modernist, was preoccupied with the endogeny of emotion: its generation within mind and body, aided by animal spirits as their critical go-between. Sensations in the body transmit various stimuli, which come from outside in a brief moment of exogeny; but in the Cartesian model these stimuli are *in-coming*, taken in by the subject as the first step in the generation of a given emotion. All that really matters takes place inside the subject.

With Spinoza, by contrast, affect is conceived in terms of its configuration at the outer surfaces of subjects. Suddenly the doors are flung open and instead of everything conspiring toward containment within the subject, all goes on and out into a space of radical *ex-posure*, a decidedly open scene. Emotion is intrinsic to this scene; it is not only occasioned in that scene; as adequately grasped, it provides its animating force, its propulsive power. The result is an interactive space that is altogether manifest, and which notably does not favor human over other kinds of interaction, such as those between different species and even between inanimate substances. Modalized substances are not only out in the open as subject to being affected by other such substances; they are themselves forms of openness.

In Kant's philosophy, other emotionalities emerge that take us out of ourselves into a more capacious, greater-than-human setting. Here anger—an intensely felt emotion of decisive concern from Plato through Seneca to Spinoza—is no longer a dominant focus, and we are invited to consider emotions like wonder or awe that have a broader base. Kant proposes that the experience of sublimity is generated from within the realm of reason insofar as we bring forth from within ourselves Ideas whose bounds exceed sensibility. Acknowledging this autogenous power is taken as compensating for the frustration of not being able to cognize sublime spectacles at the levels of perception or imagination. At the same time, Kant is the first major Western thinker after Longinus to alert us to the significance of scenes of sheer might and magnitude, scenes that lie outside and around us. Such scenes are not just *in* our circumambience; they *are* our circumambience. They *surround* us, being literally periphanous, "shown around." A sublime spectacle is a scenic showplace: a place in which an encompassing land- or sky- or seascape manifests itself, sometimes frighteningly, and in which we find ourselves re-situated from our all-too-human social world, thereby relocated into another space in which a different range of emotions is at stake. Although Kant cannot abide emotion in the context of the appreciation of beauty, where he considers it to be a distraction, he regards it as essential to the experience of the sublime thanks to its antithetical dynamic: a pleasure that derives from coping with the displeasure occasioned by certain turbulent emotions such as fright and terror.

In all, a distinctive trajectory has been traced in this first part of the book: from Plato's defiant skepticism of unrestrained emotion to Spinoza's open embrace of affect in which emotion is integral to the being and well-being of any sensitive substance. Spinoza and Kant together make way for the conception of an open field of emotionality that is not only interpersonal but radically trans-individual. They furnish a "first draft" for what is currently beginning to be spelled out centuries later, in our own time. In the wake of these emblematic earlier figures and taking clues from more recent thinkers, I shall demonstrate how emotion is turned inside out by moving from the enclosure of emotion in the human body, soul, or brain to its explicit *dis-closure* in a literally im-personal space. The very complications and limitations of predecessors make it possible to explore a radically different construal of emotion that will allow us to avoid the pitfalls of subjectivism by urging us to follow emotion out into an expanded emotional landscape whose topography we shall now trace in parts 2 and 3.

Part 2

Emotional Placescapes
The Interpersonal Dynamics of Emotion

5

The Interpersonal Domain: Merleau-Ponty and Scheler

> Show that philosophy as interrogation . . . can consist only in . . . installing itself on the edge of being.
> —Merleau-Ponty, *The Visible and the Invisible*, 260 (working note of May 1960)

In a few passing remarks, Maurice Merleau-Ponty staked out a controversial but highly promising model of emotion as decisively interpersonal: he locates emotion at the periphery of the subject in a space shared with other human beings. His brief and bold assertion, made in a minor essay of 1945 and again in a radio talk of 1948, calls for a case to be made on its behalf—a case that Merleau-Ponty himself did not take the trouble to make. Here I aim to flesh out in my own terms what he suggests schematically, seeking to show just how and why his characterization of the nature of emotion as happening *between* human subjects is compelling, in contrast with misguided conceptions of emotional life that locate emotion exclusively inside the subject. This opens a prospect that we shall further explore with the help of Max Scheler in the subsequent half of this chapter.

I

A first adumbration of Merleau-Ponty's take on the interpersonal nature of emotion is this: "We must reject that prejudice which makes 'inner realities' of love, hate, or anger, leaving them accessible to one single witness: the person who feels them. . . . Emotion is not a psychic, internal fact but rather a variation in our relations with others and the world which is expressed in our bodily attitude."[1]

This is to assert that emotion is not exclusively a first-person experience—something that belongs just to me, as if it were my own privileged possession. Rather, it occurs in an intersubjective rather than a private space. In short, it exists *between us* rather than *in me*. Merleau-Ponty confirms this in another early passage:

> Imagine that I am in the presence of someone who, for one reason or another, is extremely annoyed with me. My interlocutor gets angry and I notice that he is expressing his anger by speaking aggressively, by gesticulating and shouting. But where is this anger? People will say that it is in the mind of my interlocutor. What this means is not entirely clear. For I could not imagine the malice and cruelty which I discern in my opponent's looks separated from his gestures, speech and body. . . . It really is here, in this room and in this part of the room, that the anger breaks forth. It is in the space between him and me that it unfolds . . . anger inhabits him and it blossoms on the surface of his pale or purple cheeks, his blood-shot eyes and wheezing voice. . . . [It] is in the space we both share—in which we exchange arguments instead of blows—and not in me.[2]

This statement is all the more remarkable in that it was originally uttered as part of a radio broadcast—thus reflecting what Merleau-Ponty informally thought about emotion rather than following from a formal argument. His idea is that anger is never *my anger only*; it is what I feel *in relation* to another person who figures not just as an efficient cause of the anger but as the *occasion* for my anger, or better yet as part of a nexus of factors that have induced the anger I now register: as a place of resonance (rather than as an absorptive and possessive ego).

In the same radio broadcast Merleau-Ponty adds the following line of thought:

> When I recall being angry at Paul, it does not strike me that this anger was in my mind or among my thoughts but rather, that it lay entirely between me who was doing the shouting and that odious Paul who just sat there calmly and listened with an ironic air. My anger [was] nothing less than an attempt to destroy Paul, [an anger] which will remain verbal if I am a pacifist and even courteous, if I am polite.[3]

Merleau-Ponty here suggests not only that others show their emotion to me, but *I show my emotion to myself.* For he is insisting that anger accrues not just to what I perceive in others, but also to what I notice about myself. When I am angry, I am in effect *exterior to myself*—beyond myself as sheer subject, outside my bare consciousness: in bodily behavior that is manifest to myself as well as to others.

Although he does not explicitly address self-showing in his 1945 essay "The Film and the New Psychology," Merleau-Ponty articulates there a principle that covers both such showing and the manifestation of emotion by others: "Emotions [such as love, hate, or anger] are types of behavior or styles of conduct which are visible from the outside. They exist *on* this face or *in* those gestures, not hidden behind them."[4] Emotions cling to the surfaces of bodily activity rather than inhering in the depths of conscious subjectivity. They appear on bodily surfaces (including my own), which effect and convey "styles of conduct"—where "style" signifies something that is at once recognizable as distinctive about a person and is accessible in a portion or phase of lived space.

Of crucial importance in the statement just cited is the phrase "visible from the outside." Leaving aside the striking anticipation of what would become thematic two decades later in Blanchot and Deleuze under the heading of *le Dehors* (the Outside), we should attend to the radicality of what is here being said: that what matters most in emotional life is not what happens in psychical or physiological interiority but rather in the perceived exteriority of actions, both our own and those of others. "Others are directly manifest to us as [their] behavior," reads another assertion from "The Film and the New Psychology."[5] To this we must add: I myself am likewise directly manifest to myself in and as my own conduct.[6]

II

There is a strong temptation in the West—evident from Saint Augustine to Michel Henry—to think of emotions as coming from *deep within us*, from the hidden profundity of our being. There, in the psychical and/or physiological interior, they are presumed to be generated; there too, they are *our own*, exclusively so; others may have elicited or exacerbated them, but once they emerge in our innards they belong to us, they are constitutively part of us. As singular occurrences, they are experienced as "ours to be in one way or another," in Heidegger's telling phrase.[7] This way of regarding emotion characterizes what we have seen Descartes designate as "passions," the result of an elaborate internal apparatus that includes the senses, animal spirits, the heart, and the brain. Other modern thinkers, however different in overall orientation, have followed suit—including Kierkegaard, who sees emotions as revelatory of who we are psychically at various stages on life's way, with anxiety a key emotion throughout insofar as, felt from within subjectivity, it signifies what is sheerly possible for us at each stage. Similarly, the Romantic preoccupation with melancholy (starting a tradition of reflection that eventually leads to Freud) presents us with a model of emotion that we hold within us. In Kant's apt phrase, it exists "only in our mind."[8] For all these thinkers, emotion stems from somewhere within, however this "within" is to be interpreted, psychically or somatically; consequently, we must think of it and deal with it in its unique and literal intimacy (*intimus*, "inmost").

But all such emphasis on emotion as a matter of personal depth, tempting as it may be, overlooks another entire dimension of our emotional lives. This is its *peripherality*. In using this term, I refer to the way in which many emotions emerge at the edges of our experience and often remain there as well. Such emotions are not undergone as situated within us in some psychical *bathos* or physiological or neurological substrate; they appear at, and often as, the perimeters of our ongoing experience. As Merleau-Ponty asserts, their felt locus is extra-subjective, *out there* rather than *in here*; they are literally super-vening rather than in-hering. We certainly feel them, but we experience them as impinging upon us rather than as upwelling within us; as coming *to us* rather than stemming from *inside us*.

We need to distinguish specifically "peripheral emotions" from the peripheral dimension of all emotions. Peripheral emotions are those that are most explicitly and fully presented at the peripheries of our ongoing lives in periphanous appearings, including those emotions that come from being in the company of others among whom their transmission is favored, but also those that come when I am by myself and feeling emotions that seem to arrive from I know not where. The peripheral dimension of emotions, on the other hand, reflects the fact that all emotions present distinctive edges in the space and time in which we experience them: that is, in their distinctive places-of-presentation. As such, they call for a close periphenomenological description that pays special attention to the sundry ways in which they realize their edgewise being, forming, being at, and (on occasion) exceeding their own edges. In living experience, however, the two modes of emotional peripherality often join forces. A case from my own experience will demonstrate this collaboration.

A friend in Santa Barbara telephoned in January 2018 to tell me of the sudden onslaught of mudslides in that city. In the immediate wake of major fires that had denuded the surrounding hills, uncontrollable debris-flows were triggered by torrential rains. They had devastated more than a hundred houses—crushed outright by boulders brought down by the slides, or inundated by swiftly moving mud masses that measured up to twenty feet high; more than fifteen people had been killed in a matter of hours, and others were missing. My friend's voice was tremulous, charged with apprehension and fear—not for herself (she was near the danger zone but not in it) but for friends who were directly in harm's way. Listening to her, I did not merely infer her distress, I *felt it directly*. The effective edges of her emotional state got through to me right away— not only by way of her choice of words ("terrible," "catastrophic"), but in her tone of voice and tense pauses between words. Beyond taking in her literal words, I *took over* the emotion transmitted by her voice—a complex amalgam composed of dismay, fear, and anxiety. These were emotions *at the edge*, and each of them had its own edges. And the jagged edges of her distraught emotional state entered directly into the edges of my listening self in a dense integumentation.

For an emotion to have an edge, the emotion itself need not have a simple structure, an obvious "handle"—it can be and often is a complex composite—but if it is passed on to others or received from them (and thereby felt by myself), it must have an *effective* edge. By this I mean that the edge needs to have enough of a shape to be experienced as such even if it is difficult to specify precisely how this happens. It is this felt shape, amorphous as it may be by any objective standard of measurement, that constitutes it as an edge and that situates it at the periphery of my experience. Thanks to its edge, an emotion possesses what William James calls "the sting of reality." By means of this same edge, the emotion can be transmitted to someone who is far away, as happened in the phone call just recounted. Listening to my friend, I knew not only what she was talking about but pretty much how she felt at the time of the telling: *I felt* the very edge of what *she felt*.

Such emotional transmission is not confined to one-on-one conversations, of course. Often we "pick up" an emotion from a group of people we have just joined—say, their collective sadness, resentment, or good humor. We may not know from where this emotion stems or how it initially came about; all we know is that it reaches us now and affects us just as if it were extended to us. At first it enters at the periphery of our consciousness: outside myself but also outside other members of the group from whom I pick up the emotion. Such picking up by the edge, at the edge, occurs saliently in the midst of crowds whose "collective effervescence" (Durkheim) fosters such effects, sometimes in virtually irresistible ways—as in certain enthusiastic political rallies. But even in solitary states, readers of novels are accustomed to situations where they experience the emotions of certain characters quite directly: say, Swann's jealousy in *Remembrance of Things Past*. They are not just reading *about* the jealousy, but the jealousy enters right into them. Its edge—its peculiar poignancy—engages the outer edges of their attentive states.

Whether in a tense phone conversation, in direct pick-up from a group one has joined, or from fictional characters, we witness situations—both ordinary and extraordinary—in which we experience emotions that are not our own.[9] They do not belong originally, much less exclusively, to the subject who undergoes them. It is true that the way I process them—taking them in and up—is something that does lie in the realm of my own agency. But this becomes a matter of the endogeny of emotions and is to be distinguished from their periphaneity, their overt manifestation. Such periphaneity concerns the broad setting of a given emotion—the place where it appears—and cannot be reduced to the endogenous process of dealing with it on my own subjective terms. It may well precipitate other events, including other emotional events, but in and by itself as first experienced it is a sheer showing, an emotional display that is out there before me or around me, rather than in me. To this we must add, in keeping with Merleau-Ponty's prescient thought, that even in cases in which I experience an emotion as coming from myself ("my anger"), it is the edge of that emotion that I experience: its profile, as it were. It appears in a space that is intersubjective and shareable in principle, even if the exact target of this anger, if any, is not yet evident to me. Its coming forth is a periphanous phenomenon.

III

For the most part, the edges of my emotional life are those that intersect with the edges of the emotional lives of others, real or fictive. It is a matter of edge-to-edge situations which have analogues in other edge-fraught circumstances—for instance, the experience of being "up against the wall," as when migrants find themselves confronted with a massive structure that abruptly forecloses any movement forward. In a case such as this—experienced by all too many immigrants at the southern US border—we have to do with the hard edges of a physical structure that is more or less forcibly unrelenting. This can be set in contrast with the way, say, the outer edges of my body fit comfortably with the inner edges of the clothes I am wearing. In both these cases, as different as they are, the material structure of one set of edges is literally contiguous with that of another set.

With emotional edge-to-edge situations, by contrast, we are dealing with something essentially *labile*; something that is more likely to involve insinuation than confrontation or direct contact. Edges in these circumstances may have a certain identifiable character broadly construed—

fear, joy, anger—but they are widely variant in how they display that character. Moreover, they are *yielding*: not merely giving way to insistently applied pressure, or disappearing from sheer distraction, but reflecting the changing circumstances in which I and others are mutually embroiled. This is a matter of touching each other's emotional edges in ways that are not mere registrations of an encounter, but which actively transmogrify the encounter in ways that are variously synchronized. An example of this is my experience of the Women's March in New York City in January 2017, when I found myself part of an enormous mass of people who were experiencing, *together,* a common revulsion at the inauguration of Donald Trump. It was not that everyone in this mass of marchers was experiencing exactly the same emotion; instead, it was a situation in which an emotion roughly characterizable as "chagrin" was being *shared out,* however diversely it was experienced by individual marchers. Such sharing-out occurred at the edges and through the edges of the marchers, not just because they were walking shoulder-to-shoulder en masse (this was a material and social dimension of the experience), but because their emotional experiences became deeply confluent, despite the nuances of difference felt among individuals.

This confluence was especially evident in the phenomenon of the upswelling, inarticulate outcries generated spontaneously by the marchers: coming from far back, moving through the segment where I and those around me were situated, and then passing on to those ahead. At each stage these outcries, like collective howls, were transmitted by the edges of acoustic masses that moved through the entire crowd with a cadence and rhythm of their own. The result was that a complex but coherent collective emotion emerged from a conflux of intersecting emotional intensities that were intercommunicating at their edges, carried forward in massive waves of sound. All this manifested an interplay of near and far spaces for which no precise spatial metric could be given. The marchers felt themselves immersed in a densely qualitative matrix of emotional intersectionalities that put on dramatic display what Teresa Brennan has analyzed under the heading of "transmission of affect," to which we shall return in chapter 10.[10]

IV

If Saint Augustine could write in his *Confessions* of the "innumerable dens and caverns of memory," we can say of emotions in their peripherality something like the reverse: these emotions are found in the openings and at the surfaces of felt meaning. They come to a mode of manifestation set forth by the edges we hear, the edges we see, the edges we infer or imagine. Far from being "messy," as we are so often tempted to say, most emotions come to us with a precision all their own. I maintain that this precision—implicit as it often is—is due largely to their edge-structure, to their liminality. For it is in their edges that emotions come to appearance and attain their fullest expressive being, a theme that will be further pursued in chapter 9 and the epilogue.

Merleau-Ponty was on the right track, then, in his bold claim that emotions are "visible from the outside" and show up "*on* this face or *in* those gestures" rather than being "psychic internal fact[s]" that are confined deep within our subjectivity. To make the case for this claim, I am suggesting that we think of emotions in terms of their peripheral prowess, their capacity to take us out of any supposed interiority into a situation of disclosure—thereby attaining an accessible periphanous standing in our experience. We can regard Merleau-Ponty as making a convincing if elliptical case not only for emotional peripherality, but for how this plays itself out in intensely interpersonal situations, where my anger is not mine or yours but *ours*, shared out between us in a commonly felt edge. This is to open a placescape for the interpersonal nexus of much of human emotional experience. We shall next take up a thinker who spelled out this nexus in considerably more detail than did Merleau-Ponty: Max Scheler.[11]

V

Scheler is the Western philosopher who has given the most concerted attention to the interpersonal enactment of emotion, especially in his book *The Nature of Sympathy* (1923), in which he distinguishes between four levels of interpersonally experienced emotion: community of feeling, fellow feeling, emotional infection, and emotional identification.[12] We shall consider each of these levels as specifying an essential way that emotion is shared; each displays a modality of emotion considered as emerging between human beings rather than something happening inside them.

1. *Community of feeling.* When parents grieve over the death of their child, they feel the grief *together.* They share it, and so intimately that they can even be said to experience *the same* grief: "Two parents stand beside the dead body of a beloved child. They feel in common the 'same' sorrow, the 'same' anguish. It is not that A feels this sorrow and B feels it also. . . . No, it is a *feeling-in-common* . . . they feel it together."[13] In contrast with physical pain—which cannot be as fully shared—here we have both

parties experiencing something so similar that it can be considered the same emotion. Such a situation amounts to a *convergent participation* by the two grieving parents. This participation is felt in the first person by each parent, yet they merge emotionally with each other to the point of feeling a grief *in common*.

This differs decisively from what a friend who comes to offer condolences experiences: in commiserating with the parents, the friend engages in active sympathy and enters into a deeply empathic experience, fully appreciative of what the grieving couple are going through. Yet her commiseration—no matter how appropriate and authentic—cannot be said to co-engage in *their* grief; she remains at the fringe of the communal bond felt by the two parents, however genuine and welcome her presence may be. Her experience remains *vicarious* in a sense that might be formulated as "I can only imagine how much my friends are suffering now." She suffers *with* them—hence the *com-* of "commiseration"—but she does not suffer *as they do*. Indeed, she cannot do so, and to pretend that she could would be in bad faith. All she can do is to *offer her sympathy* without claiming to share the emotional bonding of the parents themselves: their emotion is "external" to what she feels.[14] No matter how sincere her feeling of compassion may be, it remains vicarious and "third-person."

2. *Fellow feeling.* Fellow feeling is an expansive category that signifies all the ways in which my own emotion reaches out and actively connects with another's situation, which has its own feeling component. I do not merely attend to this situation by, say, visualizing it; rather, I reach out emotionally to the other's circumstance, and to this extent I *participate in it*—in what the other person is experiencing. Yet I do not identify with it, as in the case of the two grieving parents whose feelings actually merge; rather, I *take in* the other's feeling state as I grasp it, and to this extent I react to it: "Fellow feeling proper, actual 'participation,' presents itself in the very phenomenon as a *re-action* to the state and value of the other's feelings."[15] This happens in the commiseration of the friend who visits the grieving parents, just mentioned, but it also occurs more broadly whenever I take the other's emotional state to be *real*, and this ontological ascription is what draws me out and draws me into their emotional drama: "It is through fellow feeling, in both its mutual and its unreciprocated forms, that 'other minds in general' . . . are brought home to us, in individual cases, as having a *reality equal to our own*."[16]

In fellow feeling, I see the other's suffering immediately and understand it for what it is—sheer suffering—without having to pass an explicit judgment to the effect that "this person is suffering." I can also actively *imagine* this suffering if I have been told about the other's misfortune, and this active imagining counts as genuine fellow feeling. In experiencing such fellow feeling, I am empathizing with another's difficult emotional state. Whether or not I know its full genesis and raison d'être, I can be said to understand it, to appreciate what that state must be like. Fellow feeling thus takes us into an extraordinary middle state situated between outright merging with another's emotion and an objective knowledge of it. Occupying an ampliative mid-region, fellow feeling exhibits an extraordinary range. We can have such feeling for a child who is crying miserably even if we don't know the child or his exact situation, and we can have such feeling for refugees huddled at the US–Mexico border wall in Tijuana, compelled to line up at the wall every day on the Mexican side in the (often vain) effort to be granted a preliminary interview with the US Border Patrol. Indeed, every day we are presented with circumstances that call for the kind of empathic bonding that is at stake in fellow feeling. Some of these circumstances are trivial and passing—as when we observe someone soaked with rain in an unsheltered area while waiting for a bus—while others are more markedly tragic, as when we hear of the many Uyghur Muslims being held in forced captivity in northwest China.

VI

Let me give an example of fellow feeling from my own recent experience. Chris Ebele, when I first met him at the Elizabeth, New Jersey, detention center several years ago, was in his mid-fifties. He was waiting for the court hearing that would determine whether he would be granted asylum in the United States, having fled from Nigeria because of intolerable conditions there. When he was successful in this hearing, I experienced vivid joy at the news: I felt exultant knowing that he was happy. Although we were not in the same physical space at the time (he was still in detention in New Jersey, I was in California), I actively imagined his relief and joy at this news, since now he would be released from the detention center—the grim equivalent of a federal prison—after almost a year of being held there in limbo.

A little more than two years after being released from detention, Chris received the news of a suddenly imposed travel ban on anyone coming to the United States to reside—including family members of those who had been granted asylum. Before this, Chris had been expecting his family to arrive sometime in 2020. Now their immigration was completely forestalled, at least as long as the Trump administration remained in office. When I spoke with Chris on the telephone about this bad news, his mood was dejected and despondent. It might well be many years before his wife and three children could come to the United States, especially if Trump were reelected. I felt a deep sadness descend on me. Singular though it was—I felt it as *my* sadness, after all—it was rooted in what could only be described as a family tragedy. I was feeling the likelihood of this emerging tragedy, and empathized with the despair it must have engendered in Chris. I was not *identifying* with him in that despair, but it was nevertheless present to me, even if I was far from Chris in geographical terms. I was feeling *with him* thanks to a fellow feeling that was activated by the newly impending situation that threatened to undermine the principal motive of his coming to the United States.

This experience illustrates an essential feature of fellow feeling: its being directed toward others and taking oneself out of self-preoccupation. To this extent, it is literally *altruistic.* But not all fellow feeling is concerned with the welfare of others. Scheler points out that torturers understand quite well the kind and degree of pain they are inflicting through their sadistic actions. But instead of feeling compassion for the tortured other, they take an active pleasure precisely in causing and increasing the pain. We have to do here with a perverse and intense alliance of the torturer with his victim. As Scheler writes: "The cruel man owes his awareness of the pain or sorrow he causes entirely to a capacity for visualizing feeling [of the tortured person]! His joy lies in 'torturing' and in the agony of his victim. As he feels, vicariously, the increasing pain or suffering of his victim, so his own primary pleasure and enjoyment at the other's pain also increases."[17] Here we can say that empathy and understanding have been *perverted* in a literal sense—"turned through"—so that fellow feeling has been turned back upon oneself, a self who takes pleasure in others' intense pain, especially as engendered by one's own actions. Instead of having the other's welfare in view, here the other's *malfare* is the primary objective and source of pleasure. Fellow feeling can be turned either way, fueling a concern for the other's well-being or providing the basis of a sadistic pleasure.

VII

We move now to the third of Scheler's four levels of interpersonally experienced emotion.

3. *Emotional infection.* Also termed "contagion" by Scheler, this refers to situations in which emotion is *passed along* while being lived through. Even if originating with others, the subject feels the emotion as *her own.* She takes it over from others; but her concern is not with how *they* feel (as in empathic outreach) but only with what she is now feeling. No wonder, then, that Scheler insists that we are not dealing with fellow feeling here.[18]

For, as we have just seen, fellow feeling requires a certain participation in others' emotional experiences, or at the very least an "intentional reference" to these experiences.[19] In emotional infection we have to do with being *caught up* in an emotion, no matter what its source: so caught up that we take it to be our own even though it is generated in the company of others and would not have happened without them.

Precisely because of taking up an infectious emotion as if it were one's own, we can say that we have to do here with a form of attenuated and generalized narcissism, to employ terms more familiar to Freud than to Scheler. Each person in an emotionally contagious circumstance of common fury can say in good faith, "*I* am angry." I experienced this myself when I participated in the Women's March of January 2017. I took over for myself what must nevertheless have been very similar emotions felt by my fellow protesters. But I was not focusing on their emotional experience as such. What moved me—literally moved me through many city blocks in Manhattan that chilly Saturday—was what *I* was experiencing in the presence of others: others who were "sharing common ground" with me in an intensely convergent political critique.[20] A corollary of this is that many of those who deliberately incite emotional contagion in crowds are themselves narcissists who revel not only in the audience's attention to them, but in their own being carried away by their own words and gestures; witness Donald Trump's evident pleasure in making speeches to his base.

In Scheler's emphasis on how individuals in crowd situations are emotional on their own he downplays the sense in emotional infection that one is feeling a contagious emotion *with others*. Even in the context of what he terms "mass-excitement," he omits mention of how each member of such a mass has *some sense*, some *felt sense*, of how others are feeling—however marginal and inconstant this sense may be. At the Women's March, I certainly felt my own emotions, but I was aware that others around me were having comparable feelings. This omission is all the more surprising insofar as Scheler himself says that "the feelings concerned *gather* momentum like an avalanche."[21] If so, surely individuals in a crowd on such an occasion are aware, however indirectly, of what others are experiencing in the shared space that surrounds them. This is all the more so if it is the case that, as Scheler adds, in mass-excitement there is a "*reciprocal effect* of a self-generating mechanism which leads to the uprush of a common surge of emotion."[22] Scheler himself asserts that in such a situation the crowd itself is "easily carried beyond the intentions of every one of its members, and does things for which no one acknowledges either the will or the responsibility. . . . [This crowd] generates purposes beyond the designs of any single individual."[23]

Included here are circumstances where crowds turn violent and do things that no one in the crowd may have planned or even imagined when first joining up with others. A striking instance of this occurred in the uprising of white supremacists in Wilmington, North Carolina, in November 1898. No concerted action had been planned in advance, though one orator at the local opera house had proclaimed in an incendiary speech that "Cape Fear will be strewn with carcasses"—alluding to bodies of African Americans, who had been making major advances in state and local government in the 1890s. Soon after, the same orator read before a gathering of white citizens "The Wilmington Declaration of Independence," which stated that whites had the right "to end the rule by Negroes."[24] By the next morning a group of 500 armed white citizens that had gathered in town proceeded over the next few hours to shoot virtually every African American they encountered, killing at least 60 of them. It was notable that no one person or group of persons was giving orders; the crowd moved along with its own hate-propelled energy. This was not an organized protest of the sort that took place the day after Trump's inauguration, but a marauding mob that propelled itself toward hateful aims that were never discussed as such. In such a situation no leaders are needed; the contagion of hatred is motivation enough. One can only imagine how individual participants in this mob must have been caught up in the fervor of the moment, imbibing the pervasive resentment and hatred felt by virtually everyone to some degree. As Anthony Steinbock puts it, in such a situation "one has already grasped in some sense the gesture, cry, bodily movement, in its 'reproduction' such that its sense can be 'realized' even in varying movements or different facial expressions, gestures, etc."[25]

Being surrounded and egged on by the decisive gestures of one's fellow white supremacists is not only a matter of picking up clues as to what is moving them—*their* emotions—but of reinstating ("reproducing" in Steinbock's word) them in one's own active bodily movements. In such revealing cases of emotional infection, the decisive clues come from the peripheries of one's perception as one takes in the emotional purport of the environing gestures, facial expressions, and bodily movements and makes them one's own. As elsewhere in the realm of emotion, the interpersonal precedes the personal, leading the way and clearing the path—even when the result turns out to be destruction and death.

VIII

The last level of interpersonal emotionality in Scheler's model is complex but important.

4. *Emotional identification.* We have just seen that the minimal unit of interpersonal emotional sharing (the intensely intimate relationship between two people) dissolves in the open-ended confusion of emotional contagion such as happened that infamous day in Wilmington, North Carolina. But the dyadically interpersonal can dissipate in another direction by way of what Scheler calls "emotional identification." In this latter case, any sense of myself as a separate being fades as my distinctive self-ness vanishes *in the other,* or conversely the other's self-being merges *into me.*[26] The former case is that of *heteropathic* identification, the latter that of *idiopathic* identification. In heteropathic identification, I "am so over-whelmed and hypnotically bound and fettered by the other 'I' . . . that my formal status as a [separate] subject is usurped by the other's personal-ity."[27] I lose myself in the other—whether a parent, a lover, a charismatic leader, or a therapist with whom I am bonding intensely. *My* identity is determined by *their* identity. We might say that this is a form of positive transference carried to the limit—a limit reached when I am at the beck and call of a hypnotist who guides my every behavior. "The hypnotic sub-ject," writes Scheler, "is continuously 'wrapped up' in all the individual personal attitudes of the hypnotist, thinks only his thoughts, wills only with his will, esteems his values, loves with his love, and hates with his hate." Another form of heteropathic identification occurs when I identify with an ancestor. In cultures where this is valorized, a given person "is not merely like his ancestor, or guided and ruled by him, but actually *is,* in his present life, at the same time one of his ancestors."[28] In both of these paradigmatic cases of heteropathic identification, I do not simply lose my own identity, but *replace* it with the identity or being of an other. This other can range from a teacher with whom I identify, to a mesmer-izing political leader, to God in a monotheistic religion. With the radical loss of my personal self, my emotions are displaced onto the other with whom I identify—and in the most extreme cases are actually *replaced* by the emotions of this heteropathic other. This points not just to the lability of emotions, but to the real possibility of their radical *de-personalization.* Extreme as these instances are, they illustrate that emotions *do not belong to me exclusively.* They are transferable from myself to others. They are not simply "mine" as per the models of interiorization and privatization that early modernist views of emotion promote. They can become *yours,* or *his* or *hers,* or even *its* (e.g., that of a totemic god).

In idiopathic identification, by contrast, I identify others with myself and overlook how others differ from me; I assimilate them all to myself. This is particularly pronounced in what has come to be called the "nar-cissistic personality," where one's own ego absorbs others—their beliefs, their interests, their lives. As Scheler describes it, it is a matter of "the total eclipse and absorption of another self by one's own, [this other self] being thus, as it were, completely dispossessed and deprived of all rights in its conscious existence and character." We recognize this in the case of a narcissistic leader who overpowers his subjects and presumes that their interests are his interests. Examples abound in the case of tyrannical leaders such as Franco or Putin, Mussolini or Bolsonaro. Scheler calls such figures "despotic idiopaths."[29] Illusory as such extreme idiopathic identification may be—can the other really become oneself?—it can play itself out in the real world with devastating effect. Once again, it illustrates the transferability of emotions, in this case from others to oneself.

In heteropathic and idiopathic emotional identification alike we see vividly displayed the fact that emotions do not belong exclusively to me, or to you, taken as separately existing human subjects. The motility of emotions—their not being anchored in individual human subjects alone—is highlighted here. Many other situations that stop short of being instances of full identification in either of the extreme senses discussed by Scheler manifest much the same motility, if less dramatically; as, for instance, when I ascribe a jealousy to you that in fact stems from my own jealousy, unrecognized and projected onto you. Here *my* emotion, unacknowledged, is presumed to be *your* emotion.

IX

The four levels or "planes" distinguished by Scheler in his major book *The Nature of Sympathy* are discussed there not for their own sake—fascinating as each plane is on its own terms[30]—but as instances of two critical aspects of human emotionality: plasticity and shareability. Let us consider these briefly.

1. *Plasticity*. Like Proteus, emotions change shape continually, assuming one form and then another. This is one reason why they are so notoriously difficult to name and specify, to pin down with precision. In this book so far, we have seen in early Greek thinkers and Seneca, in Merleau-Ponty and Spinoza, the considerable range of experiences that can all be considered instances of "anger." In view of the sheer variety of candidates for what has been called by one name, I have avoided a single definition that fits all cases. That would be an arbitrary and vain endeavor, given the range of what counts as "anger." By the same token, the various levels of emotion distinguished by Scheler cannot escape an element of the arbitrary; nor can significant overlap be avoided—for example, between "emotional infection" and "emotional identification,"

each of which brings out different aspects of being emotional when with others. At stake here is what I call "elasticity" in chapter 10; instead of fitting into neat containers (including the human subject), emotions stretch out as if occupying an open territory that is quite the opposite of a Procrustean bed.

2. *Shareability*. Emotions are not inherently private possessions. Even if they are often thought and said to be "mine," they are this only at the level of what I call semi-technically "feeling." If emotions are indeed frequently *felt as mine*, many of them are not mine at all; they pertain not to me but to *us*. Each of Scheler's planes of feeling represents a distinctive way of sharing emotions: whether as a closely shared "community" of grief, as a "fellow feeling," as emotional "infection," or as "identification." At stake in each of these situations is the sharing-out of emotion, its democratization as it were. This need not happen as overtly as was the case in ancient Athenian popular theater, but can occur in more quiescent settings such as in mutual mourning and in idiopathic or heteropathic identification. We may regard Scheler as something of a master sleuth who detected and named major ways of experiencing emotion *entre nous*—between us—where this phrase is also taken to mean among us, around us, in our company, with others, and the like. He takes us squarely into the realm of the interpersonal—there where emotions commingle and connect outside the separate subject. In this way, he prepares the way for figures and themes to be taken up in the remainder of part 2.

6

Ahmed's Contribution: Emotion Splayed out between Signifying Surfaces

Affect, as the openness to being affected, is directly relation. It is pure sociality.
—Brian Massumi, *Politics of Affect* (205)

Sara Ahmed's book *The Cultural Politics of Emotion* was published in 2004 in the immediate wake of the US invasion of Iraq. In the conclusion to this book, Ahmed recounts the British nation's response to the suffering of Ali, who lost both of his arms in a Baghdad bombing raid in 2003. This tragic episode anchors Ahmed's discussion of emotion, situating it in the actuality of events that occurred as she was writing her text. Citing this event reflects her commitment to the thesis that emotions are "social and cultural practices."[1]

As such, they are performative, realizing a special "form of cultural politics" that is tantamount to "world-making."[2] Also in play is her emphasis on "the very public nature of emotions, and the emotive nature of publics."[3] The book as a whole tries to bear out this double emphasis, which is deeply consonant with my own stress on the outgoingness of human emotions: their periphanous placement around and beyond myself as experiential subject.

Ahmed offers her own distinctive version of how such periphaneity is at play in the emergence of emotion in the space between people, whether they are in proximity or at a distance. In the chapter entitled "The Organization of Hate," she relates a childhood incident on the A train in New York City as recounted by Audre Lorde, the black feminist poet and essayist:

[Once seated, I find myself next to] a woman staring at me. Her mouth twitches as she stares and then her gaze drops down, pulling mine with it. Her leather-gloved hand plucks at the line where my new blue snow-pants and her sleek fur coat meet. She jerks her coat closer to her. . . . I do not see whatever terrible thing she is seeing on the seat between us—probably a roach. But she has communicated her horror to me. It must be something very bad from the way she's looking, so I pull my snowsuit closer to me away from it, too. . . . And suddenly I realize there is nothing crawling up the seat between us; it is *me* she doesn't want her coat to touch. The fur [of her coat] brushes past my face as she stands with a shudder and holds on to a strap in the speeding train.[4]

This episode shows racism at work in the tenuous gap between the two women's bodies. The outer surfaces of each, as covered by their coats, are touching to begin with; but very soon there is a separation of these surfaces—in one case, an abrupt withdrawal of the white woman's fur coat, in the other Lorde draws back after looking down at her snowpants to see if anything disgusting is to be found there. Initially intermingling surfaces are thrust apart by way of looks and hand motions as the two bodies draw apart—one in visible disgust, the other in deep puzzlement.

There is a shifting scene of affects and gestures in one brief event such as this.[5] In particular, we witness a concrete instance of Ahmed's thesis that hate "works by working on the surfaces of bodies."[6] Hate is not something that is felt inwardly—no access is given to either person's interior feelings—but is found to "circulate between signifiers in relationships of difference and displacement,"[7] not unlike the circulation of capital: hence Ahmed's choice of the term "affective economies" in which a "movement between signs or objects converts into affect."[8] In a scene such as that recalled by Lorde, "hate is economic, and it does not reside positively in a [separate] sign or body."[9] Much less in a private mind!

This is to say that hatred, and racial hatred in particular, are *interstitial*. Such hatred is a relational, and most especially a contrastive, matter—as conveyed in Zora Neale Hurston's famous essay "How It Feels to Be Colored Me," in the line: "I feel most colored when I am thrown against a sharp white background."[10] Hate happens in a space of the between: not only between two people, as in the subway incident just recounted, but between members of whole groups of people who align themselves—for example, as white nationalists—against other groups such as immigrants, those of Muslim origin, mixed-marriage couples, or people of dark skin color. The hatred of a given group is often generated by a shared grievance—lack of jobs supposedly taken by immigrants, a decline in America's "greatness," and so on—that is felt as an affront to the "pure" race. In this respect, hate draws close to anger, which as Aristotle emphasized, begins with a sense of injury and seeks to defend itself from further injury; but more readily than anger, hatred tends to form alliances whose common bond is something ideologically specific such as racial supremacy or nationalist fervor. In the case of a white nationalist group such as the British "Aryan Nations," such a bond acts to "stick or bind the [ostensibly injured] subjects and the white nation together."[11]

The *where* of an emotion such as racial hatred is as critical as knowing *what* it is. If Ahmed is deliberately vague when it comes to defining such hatred—showing us rather its complexities, including its close alliance with love—she spells out with precision the place of this hatred as it occurs.[12] It happens in the interaction between human bodies: in the specific "contact" between these bodies, real or imagined. At such points of contiguity, "impressions" are generated in those thrust together.[13] Regarding impressions, Ahmed writes that "we need to remember the 'press' in an impression. It allows us to associate the experience of having an emotion with the very affect [*sic*] of one surface upon another, an affect that leaves its mark or trace. So not only do I have an impression of others, but they also leave me with an impression; they impress me, and impress upon me."[14] In this statement, she pointedly writes "affect" where we might have expected "effect"; this is a deliberate gesture toward Spinoza, whose theory of affect (as *affectus*) has everything to do with the impingement of bodies upon each other. Ahmed signals this debt when she remarks that "in Spinoza's terms, emotions shape what bodies can do, as 'the modifications of the body by which the power of action on the body is increased or diminished.'"[15] Thus, the location of emotions lies not in mentalities or physiologies but in the interaction of bodies with one another—an interaction whereby impressions in the form of affects are generated by bodies in contiguity. "Whatever we do," she observes, "is shaped by the contact we have with others."[16]

It is precisely because "emotions are relational"[17] that they can become cultural and political; or rather, they are already cultural and political, thanks to the "power" that gives to relationality its force. For emotions "show us how power shapes the very surface of bodies as well as [entire] worlds."[18] Even if Ahmed explicitly borrows the term "power" from Spinoza, Foucault's use of the same term is also relevant here—for instance, in how the white woman's haughtiness in the Lorde incident reflects a power differential at the level of institutionalized class and economic differences. This differential, in close alliance with this same woman's racialized perception, calls for an analysis of the scene in specific social-political terms.

For Ahmed, then, emotions work by shaping the surfaces of bodies, giving to them a peculiar configuration that is decisive (and all too often divisive) in the interhuman realm. This is the *specific action* of emotions.

As she says at the outset of her book: "I [will] explore how emotions work to shape the very 'surfaces' of individual and collective bodies. Bodies take the shape of the very contact they have with objects and others."[19] Closely affiliated with surface is "boundary": "emotions are not 'in' either the individual or the social, but produce the very surfaces and boundaries that allow the individual and the social to be delineated as if they are objects."[20] The addition of "boundaries" to "surfaces" is not a trivial step. For this is to bring in considerations of shape and limit, which accrue to any and every surface—which is not merely the outer layer of something, but that which relates to other surfaces by way of its extent and figure. Surface is the basis of contiguity between bodies—a contiguity that has everything to do with emotion.

To this I would only add that what establishes the boundary or limit of a surface is its *edge*—a term that, even if not invoked expressly by Ahmed, is implicated in her analysis. Just as there is no surface without an edge, so there is no edge but of some surface. A surface cannot interact with other surfaces except through the communication between the edges of each: the affective force of surfaces is conveyed by the interplay of their respective edges.[21]

Ahmed conceives emotion as a function of how the surfaces and boundaries of bodies—and thus their edges—are thrust together in emotionally charged encounters. This is to think of emotion as a pervasive medium that acts to connect widely diverse histories, psychologies, and thoughts across shared spaces and times. For this reason, Ahmed insists that what matters are not so much discrete emotions, objects, bodies, and people—each taken by itself on its own terms—but the circulation by which emotions serve to link objects, bodies, and people thanks to their quality of being adhesive or "sticky" (one of her favorite words). Emotions stick together otherwise very disparate things in the dense and diverse life of human subjects in interaction with each other. The white woman's air of disdain so evident in her separative actions altered the black girl's self-perception forever in an incident she never forgot—this disdain *stuck to* her sense of who she was—not unlike the moment when W. E. B. Du Bois first became painfully aware of his blackness when his schoolmates suddenly fixed their looks on him as *different*: these looks stuck to him for life, giving rise to his idea of "second consciousness" as endemic to racist perception.[22]

In emphasizing such stickiness, Ahmed departs from Spinoza, who allows only impact and impingement between modes.[23] Granting the importance of these forms of contact as a minimal condition of intermodal activity, Ahmed asks: What will explain such things as attraction, lasting effect (and affect), and ongoing connection—all essential to emotional experience? The stickiness of emotions helps to make the disparate parts of human experience cohere, however hurtfully or painfully. The particular form it takes in Ahmed's analysis of racial hatred is that the enactment of such hatred consists of sticking *signs* onto bodies: signs that indicate such things as being "dark," "foreign," "intrusive," and "unfairly entitled."[24] In Husserl's nomenclature, these designators would be labeled "indicative signs" (*Anzeichen*) that point to existing objects in perceived space. But for Ahmed, it is a matter not just of physical space, but of a space that is socially and culturally specified. For "the association between objects and emotions [say, blacks and hatred] is contingent (it involves contact), but . . . these associations are 'sticky.' Emotions are shaped by contact with objects. The circulation of objects is not described as freedom, but in terms of sticking, blockages and constraints."[25]

Ahmed's model of emotion picks up on what we already found so auspicious in Spinoza while also valorizing the special sensibility to the public life and fate of emotion that is evident in Plato and Aristotle alike. But her model offers a special twist by adding the dynamics of "affective economies" to the mix: that is, a way of considering the course of emotions in terms of such quasi-economic terms as "circulation" and "return." In my own preferred language, Ahmed provides a new take on the *placement* of emotion, locating it in the sticky interface between bodily surfaces as mediated by verbal signs (e.g., racial slurs) as well as visual images (as in lampoons of blackness such as the beaming face of Aunt Jemima).[26] Her arresting analysis of such emotions as racial hatred—as well as fear, disgust, shame, and love in other parts of her book—offers confirmation of the power of the periphanous dimension of emotions: their emerging and evolving in the spaces between human subjects, animating and populating these spaces, whether for good or ill.

II

One major problem with Ahmed's ingenious and insightful model is its failure to include a place for human *agency* in emotional life. She almost admits as much when she says that "attending to emotions might show us how *all actions are reactions*, in the sense that what we do is shaped by the contact we have with others."[27] This is to depart from a tradition of considering emotions as agential in certain basic respects. While Spinoza made room for agency through gaining "adequate ideas" of emotions, Seneca allowed humans to be momentary masters in their own houses in the middle ("deliberative") phase of his model of the generation of emotion. Aristotle conceded to the emotional subject the capacity to aim at a measured intermediate expression of a given emotion, and Plato found in the chest or *thumos* the seat of emotions that bear on courage on the part of citizens of the republic—where courageous behavior is itself a paradigm of voluntary action.

In Ahmed's writing I find a singular lack of any such forms of agency. It is as if emotion occurs entirely in the circulation of objects and signs and images—in the intertanglement of their surfaces and boundaries and edges. We are led to ask: Where in the midst of such circulation is the *person* who could change its course by a decisive action that is not merely reactive to the intrusion of other bodies (with their incumbent histories) into the sphere of that person's own life, and who could take an initiative in deciding to go her or his own way?[28]

Despite this lacuna in Ahmed's model, I find immensely promising for our purposes one particular aspect of this model: her emphasis on surface and boundary (and therewith edge) in the determination of given emotions. This was already in evidence in the incident reported by Audre Lorde: the disdainful look of the white woman not only implied that something was concealed in the space located *between* her fancy fur coat and Lorde's inexpensive snowpants: that is to say, in the common boundary wherein they touched by the proxy of their coats. The offended lady saw nothing, but by her glaring *created* a chasm of diverse surfaces and edges that is synecdochal for the negative dynamics of racial hatred. No words were spoken, no explicit signs were exchanged, but her haughty and contemptuous look spoke volumes and embodied racial hatred—thus generating a traumatic experience for the young Audre Lorde. Two female bodies had been thrust together on a New York subway car only to be subject to both emotional and spatial alienation (the latter enacted concretely by the white woman's precipitous standing up, still staring at the young girl): one alienation linked closely with the other. The suspicious looking down and the abrupt standing up, taken together, *performed racism*, and they did so by way of quite singular surfaces and the real or imaginary edges they possessed.

Just here is where Ahmed's work and my own preferred schema of emotion converge productively and in two major ways. First, both she and I are critical of customary ways of construing emotions that regard them as fully formed and finalized inside the subject, and only then projected outward. I have been maintaining that it is more productive to advocate the converse: namely, that many emotions are to be found primarily around and about us, rather than residing inside us as "feelings," that is, those affective states which are held back from overt expression even though they are fully experienced. The young Lorde experienced racial hatred as *coming from* the white woman, as exuded by her overt repulsion.

Nevertheless, this way of putting things carries its own problems. As Ahmed states, it might seem to imply that emotions as "out there"—as social, political, or historical entities or events—are something we experience as if they were a kind of commodity. Yet this is not to take into account the fact that emotions are continually altering, often so subtly that we cannot catch them in full flight; we can only pick up their fleeting traces, their "remnants" (*leur reste*, in Derrida's phrase). They are not fully consolidated presences around us or outside us, just as they are not determinate entities within us either. Ahmed remarks acutely: "Indeed, the 'outside in' model is problematic precisely because it assumes that emotions are something that we 'have' . . . emotions are not 'in' either the individual or the social, but produce the very surfaces and boundaries that allow the individual and the social to be delineated as if they are objects." In this view, the very distinction between *inside* and *outside* is secondary, being the outcome of the interplay of emotions themselves: "Emotions create the very effect of the surfaces and boundaries that allow us to distinguish an inside and an outside in the first place."[29]

This is a telling point—an undeniably important deconstructive move. It deconstructs the idea that emotions are somehow secondary, caught between the insides and the outside of the subject. Instead, it proposes that emotions are primary insofar as it is they which establish the very difference between inside and outside. To claim this is not just to engage in deconstruction in its first phase, that of the reversal of classical binaries in which philosophers and others have often become stuck. For it is not a matter of reversing the priority of inside and outside, but of showing how this very difference itself stems from another level or kind of being—that of emotion itself. This is to enter the second stage of deconstruction whereby a certain basic process is identified, one that is responsible for the very dyad whose order of priority was reversed in the first stage. For Derrida, this process is what he calls "dissemination" or more generally *différance*; for Ahmed, the comparable operative principle is the differential interplay of surfaces and boundaries occurring in and as emotional experience.[30] Notice that in neither case is it a matter of human agency; rather, it is a matter of the productive basis of finite differentiations of diverse kinds.

Despite the merits of this deconstruction of inside versus outside and its replacement by a dynamic principle of sheer differentiation, it remains the case that many crucially formative emotions are experienced as coming from a certain outside: not a literal outside of the human subject (outside, as the tree in my garden is outside my house), but a felt or sensed outside that I characterize as implaced somewhere around or beyond myself as an experiencing subject—somewhere out there: in your conduct, or that of others in a group I have just joined, or in the surrounding landscape. *This* sense of outside is not just the converse of the inside but is something experientially cogent: as appearing to me from a certain place-of-presentation. It is this outsideness, this exophany, which has been neglected in previous accounts of human emotion.

A second area of convergence between myself and Ahmed concerns the role of boundaries and borders in interpersonal interaction. For Ahmed, we have seen that the differentiating force of emotion is registered in the space of contact where impacts and impingements occur and in which bodies connect or pass each other by. These interconnecting bodies are receptive to the affixing of signs that name emotional states such as "hatred" or "disgust," and so on. Thus for her, emotions work themselves out in the spaces between moving bodies supplemented by the ascription of indicative signs and telling images. It is precisely in this space that the role of surfaces and boundaries is critical.

For Ahmed, "surfaces" refer to *surfaces of inscription*—exposed two-dimensional planes suitable for the affixing of signs and images, whether only in passing or more lastingly (as when racial epithets stick). "Boundaries" are where such inscriptive surfaces come to an end. As I have insisted, boundaries possess edges; to this I now add that these edges are *permeable*—in contrast with "borders," which I construe as historically established nonporous limits that delineate the extent of national or state territories, exemplified by border walls that concretize what is only a line on an official map: such as the wall at the US–Mexico border or the Israeli–Palestinian separation wall.[31] I take it as revealing that at one point in her chapter "The Organization of Hate," Ahmed substitutes "border" for "boundary":

> The organization of social and bodily space creates a border that is transformed into an object, as an effect of this intensification of feeling. The white woman's refusal to touch the black child does not simply *stand for* the expulsion of blackness from white social space, but *actually re-forms that social space through re-forming the apartness of the white body* . . . the [color of the] skin comes to be felt as a border through the violence of the impression of one surface upon another.[32]

Exactly so: at the moment of hateful perception, the black girl's body is "re-formed" *as an object*—and thus something which can be held at a distance and despised as such. No longer are we dealing with permeable boundaries between human beings sharing a common space; we are talking about an exclusionary border created by an alienated perception in which "*apart*ness" (echoed in the word *apartheid*) predominates.

From this spontaneous but momentous creation of a racial border between one person and another, it is an all too tempting step to congregate white bodies in a single hate group that constitutes an aggressive collective body set over against black bodies amalgamated into a single mass, thereby effecting an apartness and alienation at a collective level that becomes the basis for hate crimes of a more systemic character. Racism considered as "a politics of hatred" builds on this tacit but pernicious alignment of us versus them.[33] It rejects or ignores the openness of boundaries that we find in fluid friendship and in practices of open hospitality, and favors instead the (en)closure of fixed borders—borders now not only between nations but between people of different races, religious beliefs, or countries of origin.

III

In the end the distinctions between inside and outside, borders and boundaries, can be seen as closely affiliated. To recognize the full force of the distinction between borders and boundaries is to affirm a dynamic sense of space that allows both for the shifting directionality of inside versus outside and for the creative interfusion of both. Borders are paradigmatic for their role in *keeping out*—excluding unwanted immigrants and others deemed unfit for inclusion in the nation whose external limits they demarcate. The citizens of such a nation are thereby ensconced securely *inside* exclusionary borders. In the case of boundaries, we have a situation in which inside and outside are interfused in circumstances of conversation and community, hospitality and fluid creativity. A striking case in point is that of "borderlands" (*la frontera*) as conceived by Gloria Anzaldúa: a porous region that welcomes the contributions of very different cultures to the creation of a literally bi-national, bi-lingual, and bi-racial people. In a genuine borderland situation, we witness the merging of borders with boundaries, and of inside with outside: the dissolution or suspension of the most divisive differences.[34]

If I have emphasized the importance of what is outside the conscious subject in this book, it has been in order to gain a critical purchase on early modernist models of emotion that favor its endogenous insideness and thus the inherent subjectivism that this emphasis brings with it. In a more embracing view, we need to endorse a schema in which inside and outside alike play a productive role even as their distinction remains of critical importance. This is to valorize a situation in which there is mutual differentiation of inside from outside, of outside from inside—and of border from boundary, boundary from border. In such a bivalent (but not rigidly binary) perspective, each of these pairs of terms becomes a version of what Plato designates as an "indefinite dyad"—whose respective members are at once like and unlike, odd and even, same and different.

A further twist is that both dyads (border versus boundary, inside versus outside) can be productively conceived as forms of *edge*. Here I would suggest that Ahmed's basic analysis can be usefully recast in terms of edges: the very stickiness of racist epithets is due to the interaction of agglutinative edges of bodies and surfaces. The "shaping" to which Ahmed often refers in her book can be construed as an action of configuration and reconfiguration that is best discussed in terms of the edges of things, of events, and especially of the bodies of those caught up in racially divisive situations. When the Minnesota police officer Derek Chauvin put a chokehold on George Floyd's neck, the abrasive edges of his knee were brought up against the passive edges of his victim's prone body and kept there long enough to kill him.

Thinking in this direction, I would suggest that the "motion" at stake in "e-motion" can be considered as a movement in and through preexisting edges of many kinds: placial, temporal, historical; social, cultural, and political; abiding, imposed, transitory; personal, institutional, environmental. But it is also a movement that generates new edges in the course of its action: emergent, novel, anticipatory, horizonal, indeterminate, plural edges: "active edges," as they can be designated.[35]

Emotions themselves *stick to edges*, adhering to the edges of particular situations and of the bodies that actualize them—sometimes stopping at the frontiers they instate personally and interpersonally, but also bypassing them on the way to discovering or creating new edge-bearing circumstances. Edges, we might say, provide *hooks* by which emotions come to attach themselves to emotive subjects (including whole groups of such subjects), whether to communalizing or divisive effect. They are the very basis of the "stickiness" underlined by Ahmed, just as they are the affective (and effective) exoskeletal outlets, the very ex-pressions of human emotional life. They are where the periphanous power of emotions emerges with special force: luminously and sometimes resplendently, but also all too often hurtfully and with brute force. Here I am suggesting that Ahmed's innovative model of emotion can be productively modified and rethought in terms of edges. This would be to extend Ahmed's groundbreaking work by the supplemental idea that edges of all sorts—including emotional edges—serve both to delimit and to extend the surfaces regarded as the indispensable constituents of all bodies, human and otherwise. Where J. J. Gibson claimed that "surfaces are where the action is," I would say instead that *emotional edges animate and configurate the scene of affective action and interaction.*[36]

Sara Ahmed's *Cultural Politics of Emotion* concerns the social and political dimensions of emotion that characterize interactions between two or more persons. The Lorde incident exemplifies an intense, racist encounter between an innocent child and an offended adult, arising in the awkward interval between the two parties—their *Zwischenraum*, the literal between-space, where the edges of the outer garments of each female came into contact. In hate groups such as the Aryan Nations, we have to do with emotions deeply shared by members of the entire group: emotions directed at nonwhite subjects who are the targets of the group's venom. In either case, we have to do with situations in which emotions play a divisive and detrimental role by adhering to and exacerbating manifest differences between bodies construed in terms of their juxtaposed surfaces and associated edges. The bodies are regarded as objects rather than as living presences—objects to which hateful gestures and racist epithets are directed in such a way as to stick and then all too often become internalized as lasting traumas. Rather than entering into a productive dialectic of genuine *conversation*, those involved are engaged in an *antilectic* of pain and hurt.

* * *

We shall now move forward by following out the conjoint lead of Merleau-Ponty, Scheler, and Ahmed into an expanded analysis of the emotionalities that occur in group and crowd settings. In this way, we will continue to exit from the forced detention of emotions in the interiority of human subjects. In their animated restlessness and sheer variety, emotions are always moving on: moving on from their containment as virtual prisoners in the early modern subject as analyzed by Descartes, out toward an expansive circulation around and beyond this subject where others are encountered. This de-incarceration occurs by way of the operative intentionality of emotions—by their active coming-out into the public and social realm to which human subjects belong and which draws them out of the intimacy of their inner selves into the "extimate" (as opposed to intimate) existence of other people, other species, and inanimate things, out into open spaces where emotions are located not *in here* but beyond our private selves, among and with others in the surrounding world.

Affective Attunement and Emotion in the Crowd

Stern, Le Bon, and Incipient Fascism

> Affects are preeminently social . . . they are there first, before we
> are. They preexist us; they are outside as well as within us.
> —Teresa Brennan, *The Transmission of Affect* (65)

While shopping in a popular local supermarket, Lazy Acres, I sensed
something unusual going on. It was nothing overtly dramatic but rather
something concerted and pervasive. An atmosphere of *gravitas* was everywhere, both on the part of customers and store employees. Something
serious was in the air, even if no one was talking about it as such. People
were preoccupied even if they did not name the source of their preoccupation. The source itself was not difficult to track: it was the long shadow
of the coronavirus that was cast over everyone in the same open space. For
being undiscussed and unnamed, it was no less present and telling. The
coronavirus had only recently emerged as an imminent danger—it was a
Saturday in early March 2020—but it had already struck the United States
in several locations, including cities close to Santa Barbara. Its spread was
common knowledge, so much so that no one at Lazy Acres felt any need
to name it: the danger it brought spoke for itself. The crisis was hovering,
even if there was no sense of panic, only an elevated level of anxiety that
was compatible with staying focused on shopping.

Especially striking was the fact that few people were talking at all.
Normally, in this same store, there is a certain jocular spirit of making passing semi-humorous remarks, or at least greeting each other in
friendly ways. Such levity was now notably missing. This was notable in a
setting that must have numbered several hundred people. It was as if each
person was "going about their business" without needing or wanting to be

sociable. Something else was on their minds—presumably the threat of the virus, hanging over each and all, however nebulous the threat itself was. (It was nebulous enough at this early moment so that no one was yet wearing a mask, nor was there an effort at social distancing.)

There was a noticeable sense of malaise—a literal preoccupation—some significant part of which was felt by everyone. Despite the doubtlessly differential anxieties experienced by individuals, there was something that was shared: that *all felt*. This was somehow the *same* emotion—a "same" that, in keeping with the Heideggerian contrast of sameness with identity, allowed for considerable differences in what individuals experienced. Had I interviewed my fellow shoppers, these differences would doubtless have sprung forth in various verbal formulations, adding personal nuance to what was otherwise an emotion experienced in common.

|

That this emotion was not easy to specify does not make it any less real—any less distinctly felt. For we have before us a case of *affective attunement* whose exact designation in words is elusive but whose impingement was felt by virtually everyone who was present. My own struggle to put this experience into words in the preceding paragraphs exemplifies the challenge such attunement poses when it comes to its precise verbal description. But we can get a handle on such a description, fugitive as it is, by observing that it was as if all the shoppers at Lazy Acres, including myself, were attuned in two ways: first, attuned to each other's emotionality (which one might call "interaffective attunement"); and second, attuned to the event in which the attunement itself emerged ("attunement to the occasion"). Let us discuss these briefly in turn.

Interaffective attunement. This is the way in which my emotional state can be said to have been attuned with that of others. This happened all at once—almost as soon as I set foot in the supermarket—and so spontaneously that no effort was required to attune myself more fully. The grave mood of the scene was not inferred but was immediately present to me. I felt as if my emotional state was keyed, immediately, into that which I sensed coming from the others on the scene. It was not that I confused their mood with mine; but I was aware that I was somehow in direct touch with their feelings—attuned to them, as if we were not only converging in being in something like the same musical key, but in together experiencing the same melody in that key. This was not an inference but something that I experienced fully and at once: their song was my song.

That the musical analogy is not idle was demonstrated when, one week later, news clips aired of Italians singing out loud on apartment balconies as well as playing musical instruments and banging pans together in a bold and uplifting collective display of interaffective attunement. Hearing neighbors being clamorous brought many out to sing on their own balconies, thereby creating a virtual chorus that combined hope with defiance. Similar spontaneous events soon sprang up in New York and elsewhere around the world in subsequent weeks, as if by a special kind of emotional-musical contagion.

Attunement to the occasion. It is one thing to feel attuned to others in a shared intersubjective matrix, but it's something different to experience attunement to *the occasion itself* on which such attunement arises. The first is a modality of my being-with-others that involved being in consonance with them; the second is a matter of how I relate to the circumstance in which I find myself, thus of how I take in the entire situation, resonating with it. This is what I felt as soon as I entered Lazy Acres that day: the *whole scene* was somber. It was on the basis of this initial apprehension that I was able to observe more particular expressions of this somberness—whether in the person who stood next to me at the dairy counter, or in another person standing glumly in the checkout line. (In the case of the Italians who sang and played forth, we can say similarly that they formed spontaneous groups-in-fusion—in Sartre's telling term—in that their musical expressions were unrehearsed responses to the occasion of the unusually intense outbreak of the virus in several parts of Italy. These responses, unorchestrated as they were, were all the more moving to witness halfway around the earth.)

Attunement to the occasion is typically established first of all; attunement to others follows forth. But this is no simple sequence. It can seem to happen all at once, or so I experienced it that Saturday at Lazy Acres. In the end, the two sorts of attunement are co-determinants of one single ongoing event; they are distinguishable only in terms of differential emphasis, whether on the circumstance or state of affairs or on the compresence of other sentient beings who together animate the occasion by their presence. With these other beings I find myself *consonant* when I'm affectively attuned to them in conjoint and continuous ways; while with the circumstance or occasion itself, I am *resonant*: I resonate with it as it moves through me. In the one case, I "sound with" the others present on the occasion (as *con-sonare* literally signifies); I con-sonate with them. In the other case, the occasion "sounds back" to me: I *re*-sonate with it. In both of these ways, I find myself in the midst of a massive affective attunement that is all the more impressive for not being articulated in so many words (though, in the case of the singing Italians, it is articulated in distinctively expressive sounds, some of which are verbal). Such two-way attunement happens *among* those present, drawing together a group of human beings who are suffused by a shared emotionality—whether while grocery shopping on the floor of Lazy Acres in early March or when singing from balconies in Italy a week later.

II

But granting that affective attunement does occur in these two forms— often in quite unexpected ways (I did not anticipate what I would find at Lazy Acres, nor what I would see on video from Italy)—how does such attunement come about in human beings? To begin to answer this question, we must go back to early childhood and in particular to the early period of nine to fifteen months in the life of the child. It is in this period that Daniel N. Stern has located the origins of what he calls *affect attunement*—in his words, "the sharing of affective states" between a child and a responsive parent or caretaker. Stern defines such attunement as "the performance of behaviors that express the quality of a shared affective state."[1]

Notice that the emphasis here is on the *quality* of affective states rather than on their behavioral manifestation. Affect attunement must not be reduced to bare imitation, which emphasizes only "outer behavior"—bodily movements as such—rather than the emotional state of those who are attuned. It is true that the caretaker, who is the one who completes the cycle of attunement, must engage in some bodily behavior that is relevant to the child's initial affect—behavior that is correlated with this affect to some degree, enough so at least that the child recognizes it as bearing on its own experiential sense of the affect: "the infant must be able to read this corresponding parental response as having to do with the infant's own original feeling experience and not just [as] imitating the infant's behavior."[2] So the caretaker's attunement to the child's felt affect is a matter of expressive behavior that is at once spontaneous and yet closely synchronized with the infant's emotional state. Examples of this kind of situation include these as recounted by Stern:

> A nine-month-old boy bangs his hand on a soft toy, at first in some anger but gradually with pleasure, exuberance, and humor. He sets up a steady rhythm. [His] mother falls into his rhythm and says "*kaaaaa-bam, kaaaaa-bam,*" the "*bam*" falling on the stroke [i.e., the child's beating his hand against the toy after holding the hand up] and the "kaaaaa" riding with

the preparatory upswing and the suspenseful holding of his arm aloft before it falls.

[Another] nine-month-old boy is sitting facing his mother. He has a rattle in his hand and is shaking it up and down with a display of interest and mild amusement. As [his] mother watches, she begins to nod her head up and down, keeping a tight beat with her son's motions.[3]

These examples, and others given by Stern, make it clear that affect attunement happens (a) between the child and the mother, in their very interaction; (b) occurs in two stages: the child's affective experience emerges first and spontaneously, while the mother's activity is a response to this, though one that is not pre-cogitated and that occurs on the spot and in a form that closely fits and reflects the child's initial activity; and (c) the mother's behavior is immediately recognized by the child as closely correlated with its own just-previous activity: as neither a set of random movements nor a deliberate imitation of the child's own initial action but as a meaningful response to this action.[4] Affect attunement, so understood, need not announce itself as a separate activity; it is often so "embedded" in the interactions of the caretaker and child as to merge with these interactions.

The attuning action is also often cross-modal. Thus, in the first example given above we read that "features of the boy's arm movements are matched by features of the mother's voice."[5] The word "matched" is a key; it indicates a certain freedom from imitation by outright repetition, which would require that the imitating action be in the same bodily mode as the child's initial activity. But a *matching* response, though enacted across quite different sensory modalities (here, voice matching arm motion), signifies a response that has the same character or tenor—and thus exhibits the same *élan* or "spirit"—as that which is being matched. As Stern comments: "What is being matched is not the other person's [i.e., the child's] behavior *per se*, but rather some aspect of the behavior that reflects [this] person's feeling state. The ultimate reference for the match appears to be the feeling state (inferred or directly apprehended), not the external behavior event. Thus the match appears to occur between the expressions of inner state[s]."[6] What Stern calls "inner state" and "feeling" I would designate as "emotion." This is clear from his emphasis on "behavior as expression" and his claim that the child and mother, in their synchronized actions, "express the quality of feeling of a shared affect state."[7] Such feeling is the emotional tenor of the activity engaged in by the child and picked up by the mother, who reenacts this tenor in her responsive matching action(s).

Stern's groundbreaking research is important not only as giving a coherent account of the epigenesis of affect attunement—the early origins of the much more general phenomenon of "attuned space" as discussed by Elisabeth Ströker (as invoked in chapter 2)—but also as pointing to a crucible of factors that such attunement entails: a bodily proto-action, an equally corporeal response on the part of the mother (or other responsible caretaker), an emotionality that gets spontaneously shared, and a recognition on the part of the child that the caretaker's actions express an attunement with the child's own affective state. No higher-order cerebral factors need to be invoked in this body-to-body situation in which emotion is spontaneously reciprocated between child and caretaker. This allows us to appreciate how affective attunement often arises with little or no preparation on the part of those who become attuned, much less by conscious planning. Such unrehearsed attunement also holds true for settings that are populated entirely by adults, as was the case at Lazy Acres. Those who were present there found themselves attuned in terms of the ominous tacit shadow cast by the impending coronavirus. No more than a parent needs to anticipate her child's emotional-cum-bodily expressivity did I need to expect what I was going to experience in that supermarket scene in order for it to impress itself upon me as much as it did. The customers may not have made expressive gestures toward each other, but this was not necessary: *the emotion was there among us*, and it was felt— however differentially—by whoever was present, including myself.[8] (Much the same was true of the amateur musicians on their balconies in Italy, even if they were more overtly expressive.)

Something comparable holds for the child and his mother as observed by Stern. Despite Stern's wording, the child was not so much expressing an "inner state" (which implies a self-enclosed mind) as emoting in and through his bodily actions and gestures; he was making felt (but not discursive) sense with them. As Stern goes on to say, the variables that matter most in such a situation are such things as the intensity, the timing (the beat or rhythm), and the shape of his movements (such as the arc formed by his arms). These variables help to structure what Stern calls "vitality affects," which are defined as "those dynamic, kinetic qualities of feeling that distinguish animate from inanimate."[9] What is conveyed by the child are these very qualities, which become manifest in his bodily movements—so manifest that his mother immediately picks up their affective character or tenor and attunes herself to it by her own bodily gestures. For "[her] attunement is to a vitality affect" as this shows itself in the interpersonal space shared with her child.[10] She has a "feeling-connectedness" to the unrehearsed performance of the child's affective state at a given moment. For vital affects are not *in* the child, as if contained within himself. Instead, they characterize the accessible expression of a given affect as more or less intense, as more or less quickly enacted, and as tracing out a certain shape. If they are "in" anything, they are in the intersubjective space between mother and child; but this is to be outside each of these latter regarded as separate or separable agents.

It will be noticed that the situation described by Stern combines the two forms of attunement I distinguished earlier in this chapter. It is certainly a case of interaffective attunement, since it brings together the affective states of mother and child in close calibration with each other: the mother noting her child's affect and then reenacting it in her matching gestures. And it is equally a matter of attunement to the occasion—being a mutual engagement of each with the other on the same continuous (however brief) occasion: an occasion of the interpersonal exchange of emotion.[11] The result of this exchange is the formation of an "interpersonal communion" between mother and child in which the child's emotions as performed bodily are "forms of human experience that are shareable with other humans."[12] Where Kant based his idea of *sensus communis*—a community formed by those who appreciate a given work of art—on the convergence of reflective *judgments*, Stern is arguing that there is a protean, emergent community already happening between mother and child without any need for any form of judgment to intervene. The basis of this community lies not in judgment, much less in the words by which a judgment is formulated, but in the *transaction* that occurs between mother and child at the moment of affective attunement itself: an action in and through and *across* (the literal meaning of "trans") their affective interchange.

This is an interchange between two human beings whose experience is for the most part limited to the felt sense of the bodily activity of each in relationship to the other. As Stern sums it up: "attunement is a distinct form of affective transaction in its own right."[13] "In its own right" means it is taking place between two human beings who need not exchange words or thoughts, but who are engaging their respective emotionalities in spontaneous bodily movements that are in affective synchrony with each other. This happens in what Husserl calls the "near sphere," which provides the place for a mutual attunement to each other's emotion even if the earliest phase of the attunement is of the caretaker to the child— who then in turn recognizes the caretaker's response as keyed to their own initial emotional state: as matching it, albeit often in a different behavioral modality (e.g., in hand-raising rather than hammering). This is so even though "the attunement *process* itself occurs largely unawares."[14] This process continues apace in post-infantile life—in such embedded and spontaneous ways that adults rarely have an explicit awareness of it. For instance, I suspect that I was among the few who took particular note of the somber mood I found at Lazy Acres: for most of those present, it was *undergone* rather than being an explicit object of awareness.

With Stern's observations, we find ourselves present at the ontogenetic birth of interpersonal emotionality as this comes to be delineated in its adult forms by Merleau-Ponty, Scheler, Ahmed, and others. But we are also present at the birth of a more radical thesis—namely, the liberation of emotion itself from the self-contained inwardness of the human subject, its coming into its own as it were: inhabiting its own space and time and no longer bound to a particular dyad, including that of mother–child. For affective attunement can and does occur much more broadly— whether on the floors of Lazy Acres or on balconies in Naples and Rome, in a march protesting Trump's 2016 election or in a crowd hell-bent on punishing African Americans for their political victories.

III

We have just noted the close imbrication of bodily movement and emotional expressivity in the case of the mother–child dyad. Although only two human beings are engaged in this dyad, it is already an instance of bodies-in-proximity—bodies close enough to enable the biphasic attuning process to occur. Indeed, such attunement could not happen without the close juxtaposition of the bodies of the two parties—close enough in any case for affect attunement to emerge. The two bodies form a *mass of two*, and on this basis they interact intensely at an affective level.

In larger groups and especially in entire crowds, the massification is much more considerable; but the interaction remains that of body-to-body—most conspicuously when one finds one's own body chock-a-block with other bodies. But it also obtains for all the ways in which one finds oneself *in the midst* of other members of the same crowd, *with* them yet not literally *alongside* those who are not proximal to oneself. Whether the juxtaposition is up close or more distant, we are able to read particular expressivities conveyed by the bodies that surround us. We often say that we "catch their mood," yet we do not pause to consider what this phrase means. We may not be able to read the minds of the other members of the crowd of which we are a part, but we can discern their emotional tenor. This is just what happened at Lazy Acres: I had access to the darkened mood of my fellow shoppers by a glance at their concerted bodily movements, sober facial expressions, and general air of preoccupation. All of this occurred without a single word being exchanged between myself and the other shoppers, and with few words passed among themselves either.[15]

Not only could I discern their shared emotionality, but I found myself immediately attuned to it, sensing in myself—in my lived body—an affective analogue of what they were feeling.

Crowds and crowding in the familiar and numerous forms to which we have become accustomed in the last century and a half are a relatively recent phenomenon. Certainly there have always been clusters of human beings who convene or converge for quite specific purposes: as at the Assembly in Athens or in annual pilgrimages to Mecca. But increasingly common in the late modern era is the phenomenon of crowds whose intensity and numbers could not have been foreseen and who gather to make protests or to celebrate a recent event. In these instances, people join forces in order to make a particular point, whether directly, when the point is spelled out, or indirectly by implication (as in their sheer presence). Both kinds of crowd, whether organized or spontaneous in origin, exhibit two major characteristics: the amassing of bodies and the collective attunement of emotion among those assembled in a given group. These characteristics are not unrelated.

Bodily interaction—*interembodiment,* as we can call it—is indispensable to the kind of affective attunement that characterizes being a member of a given crowd, no matter how different the reasons for the assembling of human beings may be on a given occasion. Without it, affective attunement simply could not occur. Whatever proponents of panpsychism may claim, the lived body is sine qua non for the kind of attunement that occurs in crowds. The lived body is not only essential to the emergence and conveyance of the singular subject's own emotions, but also to the sharing of the emotions of whole collections of people who gather together to form crowds. But how is this so?

IV

Husserl offers a clue in his emblematic if enigmatic phrase "activity in passivity."[16] The scope of this phrase is not limited to the noetic intentionality of pure consciousness but extends to the lived body, whose apparent passivity as physical is animated by a specifically bodily intentionality—an intentionality whose full scope had to await description in Merleau-Ponty's *Phenomenology of Perception.* This intentionality is what enlivens an otherwise torpid physical body, allowing it to be designated precisely as "lived." What I have been casually calling bodily expressivity in the case of mother–child attunement reflects this particular genius of the body to activate itself through its own intentional projects, that is, by way of its fully "operative intentionality," in Eugen Fink's phrase as taken up by Merleau-Ponty.[17]

Building on the core dynamic uncovered by Husserl, Fink, and Merleau-Ponty, I want to suggest that what I am calling "affective attunement" is not only reliant on the lived body as active/passive, but possesses an *activity-in-passivity of its own*. We have seen something very much like this at work in the observations of Daniel Stern. Not only are the bodies of the mother and child active as expressive of their emotionality, but each party engenders and undergoes—often both at once—an active bodily outreach to the other: at first, the mother taking note of her child's emotional state (exuberant, defiant, sulky, or the like) and then responding with matching motions of her own, followed by the child's active recognition that her gestures amount to an acknowledgment of his own emotionality. Similarly but less dramatically, in Lazy Acres my attunement to other shoppers was at once active (as attentive to their decidedly somber state) and passive (as receptive to this state considered as a collective given). My experience was not as neatly divisible into several phases as occurs in the mother–child dyad as analyzed by Stern, but it was nevertheless an instance of bodily activity-in-passivity. As soon as I entered the store, I actively attuned myself bodily to what was going on, by my merely glancing around at what was happening around me; but what I found was also given to me as its receptive (and to this extent passive) witness. The two phases of activity/passivity were enacted together in one continuous sweep of my bodily awareness.[18]

Affective attunement is at least bi-phasic—not in literal sequence, but insofar as two phases, one active and the other passive, are discernible upon analysis. This means that such attuning is not an entirely passive process, as we might be tempted to assume if we think of attunement as happening automatically (as with a tuning fork: here a misleading paradigm). Nor is it, on the other hand, solely active, as when we consider it to be our own achievement. It is an amalgam of *both*, wedded together in a subtle but powerful commixture. As with listening to music, we don't just *undergo* attunement but *undertake* it, albeit spontaneously and often on a moment's notice. As soon as I hear jazz I know I like, I take it in, actively enjoying it even as various passive elements may well also be present (for example, the sheer memory of hearing the tune before and thus the familiarity that is now "given" with my current listening). The activity here may take the form of tapping my feet or shifting my head in rhythm with the music, but it can be more subtle than this—"internalized," as it were. Either way, I find myself attuned to what I hear, and am aware that what I hear—its activity—is integral to my own experience as something that is at once active and passive.[19]

V

Gustav Le Bon's *The Crowd: A Study of the Popular Mind*, published in 1895, broke new ground in understanding crowd behavior. His focus was on what he called the "psychological crowd." This is not just any collection of human beings, but one in which a "collective mind" emerges—a mind that is so largely determined by "unconscious considerations" that there is both a reduction of critical thinking and "a complete transformation of the sentiments."[20] This transformation is occasioned by the predominance of concerns and issues that move the crowd to actions that would not have happened in ordinary solitary life, but which seem entirely justified once one has joined the crowd. This is so even if these actions are violent: such as the mass guillotinings during the French Revolution or the numerous lynchings in the American South from Reconstruction onwards. In crowds, what the anthropologist Levy-Bruhl called *l'abaisement du niveau mentale* (the lowering of the level of mentality) predominates and acts to suspend whatever moral scruples individual crowd members may have on their own.

But in a crowd as conceived by Le Bon there is no "on their own," for the crowd acts to de-individuate and agglomerate members of the crowd who have lost their "conscious personality"[21] by throwing in their lot with others to such a degree that they have lost any critical distance from what the crowd as a whole does when acting as a single mass. As Le Bon sums up his basic take on psychological crowds: "Whatever be the individuals that compose it, however like or unlike be their mode of life, their occupations, their character, or their intelligence, the fact that they have been transformed into a crowd puts them in possession of a sort of collective mind which makes them feel, think, and act in a manner quite different from that in which each individual [one] of them would feel, think, and act were he in a state of isolation."[22] In this description, we recognize an uncanny anticipation of the crowd behavior in the Wilmington episode that was discussed in chapter 5: an episode that occurred just three years after Le Bon's book was published in 1895.

Our interest in crowd experience is focused on the role of emotion in such a circumstance even if Le Bon himself is equally, if not more concerned with issues of ideology, morality, imagination, and historical sense. In his analysis, the emotions of those caught up in crowd situations are "transformed": they are altered from emotions that are more or less under the control of rational agency to being out of control because of "transformed sentiments," a key descriptive phrase for what happens to emotions when in the midst of an impelling crowd.[23] Le Bon picks out three major traits of transformed sentiments that occur in intense crowd behavior:

Shared. Emotions are held in common when, in the midst of a crowd, human beings revert to basic emotions that are possessed by all human beings: "men the most unlike in the matter of their intelligence possess instincts, passions, and feelings that are very similar."[24]

Unconscious. When in crowds, "the heterogeneous is swamped by the homogeneous, and the unconscious qualities obtain the upper hand."[25] Le Bon is saying here that such emotions reside properly in the unconscious even if they *become conscious,* indeed often *hyper-conscious,* in the context of crowd behavior.

Excessive. Le Bon says that "given to exaggeration in its emotions, a crowd is especially impressed by excessive sentiments";[26] in short, crowds do not encourage timid expressions of emotion but favor the boisterous and the vociferous.

Thanks to being shared, unconscious, and excessive, the emotions experienced in crowds are powerful and often wayward forces. In Le Bon's analysis, such emotions operate on the basis of two dynamic processes: *suggestibility* and *contagion.* Each of these deserves a closer look.

Suggestibility. The concept of "suggestion" had a rich history in the last half of the nineteenth century. It was considered to be the main mechanism of hypnosis—whereby the hypnotist planted the idea of a particular action in the receptive subject, who then acted it out at a subsequent moment without hesitation or reflection. It was a matter of the direct influencing of receptive subjects. Le Bon extends the model of suggestion beyond the limited scene of hypnotism and applies it to entire crowd scenes:

> The most careful observations seem to prove that an individual immersed for some length of time in a crowd in action soon finds himself—either in consequence of the magnetic influence given out by the crowd, or from some other cause of which we are ignorant—in a special state, which much resembles the state of fascination in which the hypnotized individual finds himself in the hands of the hypnotiser.[27]

"Suggestibility" names the situation in which whole groups of people become in effect hypnotized—not because of the actions of a single figure predesignated as a "hypnotist," but by way of a charismatic leader or, in the absence of any such leader, by the presence of a disturbing or inspiring idea that draws out the concerted emotionality of members of the crowd. This is a version of what Scheler termed "mutual coalescence":[28] people converging around a shared aim or experience. Something akin to this happened in the case of my Lazy Acres experience. No one present in the store needed to speak of the threat of the coronavirus; this threat hung in the air and had a certain mesmerizing force that is comparable to hypnotic suggestion. By that moment in early March, we had all *become subject* to the threat, which subtly but pervasively influenced our actions as mere shoppers, as if guiding these actions from afar, from an indeterminate but ominous future. Albeit tacit and undiscussed, this threat held the power of suggestion.

Le Bon claims that suggestibility works as powerfully as it does because the *credulity* of the crowd emerges as critical, and skeptical minds recede in such a group setting. As part of the crowd, I *find myself believing what others around me are almost certainly also believing.* The power of suggestion is such that I do not need any independent evidence; I share with others an implicit *credo*. An explicit credo is a profession of something I believe and which I am willing to affirm publicly. In the case of crowd suggestibility, however, I need not profess anything explicitly; what matters are not words that commit me, but actions that I take up along with others: actions that may be accompanied by silence or by words such as "Black Lives Matter!" These actions are the bodily acting-out of the beliefs I have been led to hold in the presence of others with whose committed actions I merge in movements of "lived synchronism," in Eugène Minkowski's phrase.[29] These movements range from actions of chanting and shouting to staying quiet and taking in passively what others are saying stridently. What counts is not so much the literal sense of the words I hear—"Build that wall!"—as the sheer fact that I experience these words as powerful inducements to join with others in common actions that are as emphatic as they are unreflective. If I resist, it is because I am listening to other voices that say things quite different from what I am hearing from the dominant "oracular" voices at the time.[30]

The effect of all this on the individual is one of almost instantaneous *empowerment*. "Under the influence of a suggestion," concludes Le Bon, an individual "will undertake the accomplishment of certain acts with irresistible impetuosity . . . the suggestion being the same for all the individuals of the crowd, it gains in strength by reciprocity."[31] The reciprocity here is two-way: between the leader and the members of the crowd, but also, in the absence of such a leader, between those in the crowd who allow the reigning suggestion—as given in advance announcements or articulated on placards or from a shared mood—to guide their bodily movements. All this, enacted en masse, constitutes what Le Bon designates as "contagion."

Contagion. Contagion ensues from suggestion: it is "neither more nor less than the *effect*" of suggestion.[32] For it, like suggestibility, is "of a hypnotic order." Contagion is what happens when a given crowd gets carried away in the wake of a suggested idea, whether this takes the form of something inspirational or a threat (or the two together). In such a situation, "every sentiment and act is contagious, and contagious to such a degree that an individual readily sacrifices his personal interest to the collective interest."[33] Contagion is thus not just a matter of sharing and passing on mutually experienced emotions—a matter of interpersonal attunement—but one in which there is a bracketing-off of my own aims and my own voice in that transmission. All that matters now is the sheer spreading of the emotion as this is realized person-to-person and sub-group to subgroup. This is a quite dynamic process—so much so that individual interest, including individual assessment, is rendered secondary or superfluous. Operative here is what William James calls "the dynamogenetic effects" of "excitements" generated in such a situation.[34] Put otherwise, there is a "fascination" at work in contagion that draws individuals out of themselves and into an unwritten emotional contract with others who find themselves likewise swept up by the contagion.[35]

Le Bon's model can be summed up this way: individuals who gather in groupings that are not merely casual have a virtually irresistible proclivity to join with others to form a crowd (*une foule*) and to follow their lead, no matter how irrational or destructive their collective actions may be. Although sometimes, as Le Bon acknowledges, such a crowd can aim at something morally or politically admirable, this is exceptional in his view.[36] Those caught up in such a crowd act in accordance with whoever or whatever possesses the most persuasive suggestibility, whether or not it is articulated in so many words or not. Once something highly suggestive is taken up by the crowd in ways that are difficult to control or predict, it has become contagious; that is, it has a life of its own that is self-perpetuating as members of the crowd interact intensely with each other. Both the suggestibility and the contagion carry an intense emotional charge, which acts to dynamize the fervor of the crowd. Weak suggestions will fail to precipitate genuine contagion; they will fall to the ground rather than circulate and animate members of the crowd. The crowd itself is not a matter of sheer numbers, or of experiences shared in advance (though the latter can be contributing causes); its unifying force is supplied by a collective mind-set that holds the group together as a single gathering of human beings: a mind-set that mirrors what they share when shorn of individual histories, separate belief systems, and independent moral judgment.

In Le Bon's model of crowd behavior, both contagion and suggestibility are at once psychical and social: as psychical, they belong to the group mind; as social, they are matters of actions taken in common with others. Curiously, Le Bon says very little about the role of *bodies* in his paradigm. His concern is much more with the "collective mind," a species of what Durkheim would designate as "collective consciousness." Bodies are implied but not discussed as such by Le Bon; yet they are basic to concretely interacting with fellow members of a given crowd. Just as strikingly, little is said of the role of *emotions* as such except to designate them as "excessive sentiments"—which is only to refer to their comparative intensity. Nor is there any mention of attunement or its equivalent, even though this is surely an important ingredient in contagion and suggestibility alike. We are at the opposite end of the spectrum from Stern's model of mother/infant attunement, which emphasized the close interaction between two human beings attuned to each other's emotionality. Le Bon takes us far away from the intimacy of mother and child, and moves us into the anonymity and indifference of entire crowds. What matters now is not discerning what others are feeling or thinking, but actively joining forces with them in a single mass of human beings headed in the same direction, regardless of what any one person is considering or experiencing (except for a leader if there is one). We have here a model for a group in fusion which is so deeply merged that what individual members of this group—"the crowd"—think or feel becomes almost entirely irrelevant. All that counts now is moving as one group together toward a common aim, be this what it may and however indefinitely formulated it is.[37] We are left with a boldly sketched paradigm of the dynamics of group interactivism that pays little attention to the specifics of emotional experience, concrete bodily enactment, or affective attunement. These latter three dimensions are surely present in crowds as discussed by Le Bon—being integral to their collective dynamism—but they are not given the attention they deserve.

VI

A recent resurgence of fascistic tendencies not only in the United States under Trump but in several countries in Europe, Brazil, and elsewhere exemplifies the intimate relationship between concerted crowd activity, affective transmission, and the role of a vociferous and uncompromising leader. Integral to Hitler's rise to power was an especially virulent instance of the convergence of these three factors. This becomes evident in William Connolly's recent book *Aspirant Fascism in the Age of Trumpism* (2017), in which he demonstrates how there was a dense tangle of factors that converged in Germany in its early fascist period. This book presents "a genealogy of fascism [that] addresses multiple resonances between words, techniques, bodily demeanor, facial expressions, fears, images, music, modes of empathy, bodily filters against empathy, violence, and vilification."[38] No matter how different each of these factors may appear to be from one another, they converge around two primary poles: closely coordinated bodily interactions on the one hand, and what Connolly calls "affective communication" among these bodies on the other—which I am taking as approximately equivalent to what I shall be discussing in chapter 8 under the heading of "affective transmission." The bodies here in question can be considered as resonating boards that achieve a spontaneous "relational attunement" that is synesthetic and not limited to one mode of sensing.

Synesthetic perception occurs, for example, when hearing a musical performance along with seeing it, when both are modes of being touched—moved—by the music at the same time. At traditional musical performances, however, everyone remains in their seat; nor does anyone raise their voice, contrary to what happened in ancient Athenian popular theater and in Hitler's ascendancy. In the street and untethered by the decorum of the theater, the bodies of those who have been drawn into a concerted political demonstration or a pitched rally enter a space in which few holds are barred—especially in a time of economic desperation and political unrest such as was the case in Germany, especially after 1929. The release of intense emotionality across the open spaces of a city, enacted bodily, not only enables concerted political protests but may precipitate riots that easily get out of control, as happened only a few years ago in Charlottesville, Virginia—which witnessed an American version of early Nazi street violence. If the highly charged bodies of those moved by shared grievances combine with affective transmission in a crowd—a transmission that is fueled by shared emotions of anger and resentment—a volatile circumstance arises that is intensified further if a leader articulates these grievances in terse, easy-to-repeat phrases that those assembled not only understand immediately but can easily repeat to themselves vocally or silently: "Heil Hitler!" or "Lock her up!"

The combination of dynamic bodily movements with pithy but telling verbal formulas in the midst of an intense transmission of affects can all too easily become a dynamic commixture that turns into violence: if not on the occasion itself, then in sequel to it. Hitler's carefully crafted speeches to large crowds of admirers after 1932 catalyzed the Nazi movement in ways that were soon to become a massive and lethal war machine. Key words and phrases in these speeches—"Heil!" "Sieg Heil!"—were potent carriers of emotions of hatred and rage that were shared by millions of Germans even if not articulated in so many words. Aristotle's early observations of the power of political oratory were here confirmed, as they are again today in the hate-mongering monosyllabic speeches of Trump in rallies to his base. In Hitler and Trump rallies alike, there is an extraordinary "visceral attunement to fascist rhetoric and violence during times of distress."[39]

Connolly does not hesitate to describe this situation as one of *contagion*. Rather than being a mere "effect" of suggestibility (as Le Bon had held), contagion has a hypnotic force of its own: "those who have been injected with the disciplines of armored males [as with the proto-Nazi *Freikorps* in post–World War I Germany] may find such tendencies [to take action] ignited through crowd contagion when they encounter a leader with the rhetorical brilliance of Hitler."[40] Even if many members of Hitler's audiences had no expressly military background, they did not hesitate to support the Nazi regime and to endorse its sending of troops to support Italy's faltering invasion of countries in north Africa. Connolly's graphic depictions of fascistic rallies stand in contrast with gatherings that are genuinely democratic and non-fascistic. These latter involve "receptive, horizontal modes of affective communication across diverse constituencies [that] help to render such an ethos resilient."[41] Whereas an intensely unified, ideologically monolithic crowd has few if any such "diverse constituencies"—given the insistent sharing of convergent affects of hatred—in the case of what Connolly designates as a "multifaceted" democratic circumstance, affectivity travels across differences rather than reinforcing a fiercely held central identity. In a genuinely democratic crowd scene, there is sameness with difference rather than an identity that excludes any significant difference—where such difference is considered as treasonous.

If an open-ended democracy is to be possible—and Connolly holds that it *must* be possible if we are to avoid a full recrudescence of fascism today—then we should acknowledge a form of crowd behavior that can be designated as an "assemblage" rather than as the sheer mass or mob that is Le Bon's paradigm and that is the basis of fascist violence. I choose the word "assemblage" since it signifies the convergence of similars (via the rooting of -*semblage* in *simlis*, "like") who converge in certain basic concerns and goals—for example, in the formation of a democratic state—even as those assembling may also diverge in their vision of precisely how they can attain this goal. An assemblage allows for a truly multifarious response that respects differences in viewpoints and in recommended tactics; it reaches *across* these differences, acknowledging them all while not unduly privileging any of them. These same differences, rather than being disruptive (and thus calling for immediate suppression, as happened at Trump rallies as well as during Hitler's harangues), are respected as constitutive of the assemblage itself, and are essential to its animation and forward thrust. They are also subject to discursive discussion in what we sometimes blandly call the "adjudication of differences"; active talking-through with an aim of discovering convergent and judicious forms of action is indispensable to the vitality of the assemblage as a whole. Not everyone gets everything they want, but different interests are respected precisely *as different*—as deserving to be heard by others with respect and an effort to understand.

The emergence of such a nascent discursive democracy—speaking not only despite but *from* differences—points to what Fred Evans designates as a "multivoiced body."[42] Such a salutary body politic is based on bodily movements that, when too closely commandeered and fiercely mandated, lead to fascism but that, when allowed a certain latitude in regard to gesture and voice (and both with respect to affect), actively encourage an open variability in the bodily behavior and preferred directionality of members of the assembled group itself. We have reason to believe that something like this happened at the agora in ancient Athens during its best moments, and especially at the aptly named Assembly. For any such proto-democratic crowd activity to emerge, there must be a close alliance between affective attunement and intent listening. Both are matters of lived synchronizing with others' bodies by taking in their gestures and resonating with their voices.

The affective attunement that occurs in such circumstances represents an adult version of the "matching" of bodily expressions that, as we have seen, occurs early on between infants and their caretakers. This matching is itself a synchronizing that benefits from the repetition of gestures and words in a concerted crowd scene—a repetition that, as already with infantile attunement, allows for considerable variation in its realization rather than enforcing sheer imitation. Being in a multivoiced setting requires a willing receptivity to what others are perceived as doing as well as saying, and then carrying forward what is experienced in bodily behaviors and verbal articulations of one's own.

All of this contrasts with the abject contagion characteristic of fascist regimes, where the only communication allowed comes from the mouth of the leader (often reinforced by banners and signs that act merely to repeat, in abbreviated format, what he is already saying): here the communication is expressly and only *one-way*—from an "oracular voice" (in Evans's term) to an enthusiastic but passively receptive audience—and thus fails to count as dialogue, much less as open-ended conversation. The "mobilizing passions" of such a scene include such negative emotions as hatred, resentment, shame, and disgust.[43] In a multifaceted democratic situation, in contrast, we have genuine *polylogue*—a conversation, if not of "mankind," then of those actually present in a given gathering of human beings who interact as presumptive equals even as they differ from each other in education, ethnicity, class, and race—and who are willing to share widely variant emotions and not only those that promote unification on the strictest terms. Something like this was evident in the ongoing protests that followed upon George Floyd's murder in Minneapolis on May 25, 2020: protests that saw the confluence of diverse groups (some focusing on police brutality, others affiliating themselves with Black Lives Matter, and still others with other causes).

In either circumstance—fascistic or proto-democratic—we witness emotions moving not only between individual human beings gathered together, but also across whole swaths of the crowd as well as circulating among them: all this in keeping with an immanent dynamism. Emotions in such settings not only exhibit a conflux of transmissive modes, but also possess a dual potentiality of turning either to fascistic violence or to democratic dialogue. This suggests that emotions themselves are not inherently democratic or fascistic, but in their very volatility they can be deployed for destructive as well as constructive purposes.[44] Precisely because they do not belong to isolated individual subjects, emotions transmitted in such circumstances can move, en masse, in these two major and fateful directions—and doubtless in others as well. The amalgam of transmissive emotion, bodily movement, and verbal articulation constitutes a molten core that, in its very indeterminacy, has radically different potential outcomes.

* * *

In this pivotal chapter we have moved from a consideration of the origins of affective attunement in the mother/child interaction to an analysis of the difference between interaffective attunement and attunement to a given occasion. This was succeeded by a scrutiny of suggestibility and contagion in crowd behavior as envisioned by Gustav Le Bon. From there we moved to a focus on fascistic potentials in mass rallies in contrast with democratic assemblages, allowing us to consider the role of active bodies and verbal utterances in the generation of the affective valence of such circumstances. By these various routes, we saw how emotion is something that is inherently shareable and can be experienced in common, whether in intimate dyads or unruly mobs—or in quotidian settings such as neighborhood supermarkets.

In all these instances, different as they are, emotion shows itself to be genuinely periphanous—and thus something which several and even many people can undergo as a form of social bonding, whether lasting or momentary. This bonding can be put to better or worse purposes, but its saliency and immanent force and power cannot be gainsaid. In each and every case we have examined, we have witnessed emotion as arrayed between and around us: as belonging to an affective field in which human beings are situated together in widely diverse groupings.

8

Following Freud Down Under the Subject

Gustave Le Bon's book *The Crowd* was taken very seriously by Sigmund Freud. He devoted to it an expository chapter in his *Group Psychology and the Analysis of the Ego* (1921) that was in essential agreement with many of its main contentions, especially concerning the role of the unconscious in the dynamics of suggestion considered as a form of group hypnotism. But he was critical of Le Bon's depiction on three major points: its failure to acknowledge the role of repression in the formation of the unconscious; its neglect of groups that are more organized and long-lasting (such as legislative bodies); and, especially, its inadequate treatment of leaders of crowds. Freud observed that Le Bon "does not give the impression of having succeeded in bringing the function of the leader and the importance of [the leader's] prestige completely into harmony with his [otherwise] brilliantly executed picture of the group mind."[1]

Freud agrees with Le Bon that being in a group involves "an intensification of the affects and the inhibition of the intellect," but these are only preliminary phases in a situation that is at once more complicated and more expansive.[2] It is complicated by the fact that a given emotion such as love goes through many "vicissitudes" in the course of a person's life; it does not have a single fixed form, but undergoes considerable modifications in the various ways love manifests itself in discrete behavior and is directed toward others, from family members to group leaders, including differential degrees of identification with these others. The same situation is more expansive in that affects or emotions are phenomenal manifestations of a deeper drive (*Trieb*) that Freud names *Eros*, invoking Plato, and characterizes as "sexual instincts" or as "love-force"—the force supplied by libido, or sexual energy.

Such complication and expansion led Freud to question whether "contagion" and "suggestibility" are, after all, definitive criteria of group psychology. Even if we accept the deep analogy between suggestion and hypnosis (given that both require the positing of an unconscious mind), Freud soon makes clear that for him suggestibility concerns only the surface dynamics of what he designates as love relationships: "We will try our fortune, then, with the supposition that love relationships (or, to use a more neutral expression, emotional ties) also constitute the essence of the group mind. Let us remember that the authorities [such as Le Bon and William McDougall] make no mention of any such relations. What would correspond to them is evidently concealed behind the shelter, the screen, of suggestion."[3] Suggestion, which Freud considers interchangeable with "suggestibility," is a cover for deeper erotic forces that provide both the propulsive force of group behavior and its ultimate motivation. For Freud, it is Eros that "holds together everything in the world."[4] Furthermore, as opposed to the "death drive" (*Todestrieb*), which aims at the dissolution of life into its inorganic constituents, Eros is a profoundly unifying force: "If an individual gives up his distinctiveness in a group and lets its other members influence him by suggestion, it gives one the impression that he does it because he feels the need of being in harmony with them rather than in opposition to them—so that perhaps after all he does it 'for the sake of loving them.'"[5] Freud not only takes us down *under* suggestibility, regarded as a surface phenomenon, but valorizes this deeper layer in a positive fashion by characterizing it as "binding" and "unifying"—both terms he employs in discussing Eros as a primal drive that he designates as the "love drive" (*Liebestrieb*).

Freud's move to metapsychology has the advantage of directly addressing doubts we are likely to have with a term such as "suggestibility." As intuitively attractive as this term may seem, in the end it only points to the phenomenon of being influenced by others: it *names* such influence but does not argue anything significant about its origins and mode of working. Freud's model provides an account of the modus operandi of suggestion: how it comes about through the erotic bonding of the members of a given group—a bonding that need not be overtly sexual, but employs sexual energy or libido in fashioning "emotional ties" between members of the group. The downside in accepting the Freudian account, however, is that it entails buying into Freud's rather elaborate psychogenetic model of human experience. This is to take a significant step toward a *causal* account—one that is unmistakably *explanatory* rather than descriptive. Yet despite his early scientific moorings, Freud is not an unmitigated causalist. Beyond, or beside, his metapsychology there is a genuinely descriptive zeal that is evident not just in his case histories, but even in a highly theoretical work such as *Group Psychology and the Analysis of the Ego*. This zeal leads Freud to his most distinctive contribution in this book: the dynamics of identification with the group leader.

I

The term "identification" in Freudian theory refers to the intense bonding that exists between one person and another to the point of merging the one with the other. In Freud's analysis of group psychology, identification with the group leader channels and consolidates the libido of each group member—which is then reinforced with subsequent secondary identifications that ramify out from this primary identification. Whereas Le Bon had passed over these dynamics, reducing the influence of the leader to his "prestige," Freud tells a more elaborate and convincing story. This concerns how members of a given group identify with the leader and then—in a special twist—with each other as well, thereby increasing the overall amount and intensity of bonding. In this way, they share conjointly their subordination to the leader who is situated above them in an elevated position of esteem as their "superior." Whereas Freud characterizes both processes of identification as happening unconsciously, I suggest that we designate them as "spontaneous" in order to retain a more descriptive tenor. Followers identify spontaneously with a leader and thereby with each other in ways that are all the more forceful for being non-deliberate.

Here is Freud's classic description of this rather complex situation: "[We are] in a position to give the formula for the libidinal constitution of groups . . . namely, those that have a leader and have not been able by means of too much 'organization' to acquire secondarily the characteristics of an individual. *A primary group of this kind is a number of individuals who have put one and the same object in the place of their ego ideal and have consequently identified themselves with one another in their ego.*"[6] What is referred to here as "one and the same object" is the leader of the group, whether this leader came to this position by election, royal succession, or seizure of power. Such a leader is so idealized—lionized, worshipped, or just deeply respected—that he becomes the ego ideal of members of the group: a leader so widely emulated that he gains the status of someone not only admirable but close to perfect in their kind.[7] Between all those who adulate the leader there is a special bonding precisely in and through their common idealization that amounts to an identification with their fellow subjects. In other words, the primary identification with this leader is extended and reinforced by secondary identifications with all those who collectively engage in this first identification. The result is an intensely overdetermined bonding among members of a given group, generating a special kind of cohesion that is compatible with diversity (even if homogeneity often obtains).

This double identification is an intensely emotional process. Freud insists on this in assertions he makes in the chapter titled "Identification" in *Group Psychology and the Analysis of the Ego*: "Identification is known to psychoanalysis as the earliest expression of an emotional tie with another person"; first of all, in a child's "primary identification" with the major caretaker, and subsequently with others: "identification is the earliest and original form of emotional tie."[8] Freud is referring here to the basic mechanism of identification. This occurs first of all prototypically with a parent—typically (but not only) with the father—and then with teachers and other admired figures, including strong leaders. But, as we have just seen, there are also secondary identifications with fellow members of a given group—identifications "in their ego," thanks to their common adulation of a given leader who has become their common ego ideal. This secondary form of identification has the special characteristic of being due to the sharing of a common attribute or "quality" which "lies in the nature of the tie with the leader," that is, the primary identification with the leader as an ego ideal for all followers.[9] This primary identification, which is emotionally intense and specific from the start, is thereby distributed to other members of the group, who bond with each other through this very commonality. Visually expressed, it is as if the identification with the leader is a vertical movement—from the individual group member *up to* this leader—while the identifications with fellow members occur horizontally, *between* them. Where the first mode of identifying is singular (between each individual member and the leader), the second is plural (between the members who are bonded by this primary identification).[10]

Freud insists that the basic character of the "emotional tie" proper to identifications of all kinds is none other than *love*. Hatred is correspondingly affiliated with dis-identification, and when both love and hate are evidenced, the upshot is ambivalence. Le Bon's idea of suggestibility, by contrast with Freud's, is unspecified in terms of its emotionality and, indeed, could be realized in an idea or memory just as well. Freud is clear that identification works only through love, and specifically erotic love.[11] "Love" (*Liebe*) itself is here construed not as a discrete emotion or affect but as something closer to a *state of being*—or better, of *becoming*, since it is always in energetic transformation. Love can be said to *subtend* whoever possesses it, supporting and energizing it *from below*, bearing it up from there, for it is from beneath that its bonding power is exerted. This is not just a matter of "strength in numbers" but of becoming part of a cohesive whole—the group to which one belongs, however contingently and whatever its eventual fate.[12]

This is in contrast with other emotions such as anger and joy, which come forward on the surfaces of expressive bodies rather than being embroiled in subliminal states such as love engenders. These emotions are characteristically episodic, coming and going in accordance with circumstances, whereas love in Freud's sense of the term is comparatively tenacious and has its own history, and thus is well-suited to motivate identifications, primary or secondary. Despite such basic differences in how they operate, however, both erotic and episodic modes of emotionality are experientially transferable in groups and serve to animate them, whether in direct encounters with others or in more indirect ways.

II

Love acts to structure human relationships in detail—as do other inherently constructive emotions (such as empathy), but also destructive emotions such as hatred, envy, and jealousy.[13] Constructive emotions shore up these relationships by increasing trust and confidence, while destructive ones undermine them by leading to a situation where other persons can no longer count on the primary caregiver or leader to provide basic trust. "Basic trust" is Erik Erikson's phrase for what is crucial to instill in very young children; without it, a child lacks the basis for the bonding with others that becomes essential later in life, when an accessible confidence in oneself and others is indispensable. Affective attunement of the bilateral sort discussed by Stern can be considered a phase in the establishment of such trust. When such two-way attuning occurs, each party can be said to be offering emotional reinforcement to the other and thus to be confirming a basic trust in each other. The result is a milieu of mutual trust that is a paradigmatic instance of Ströker's notion of "attuned space." In basic trust the attunement goes both ways—from caregiver to trusting subject, and back from this subject to the other—thus co-constituting a shared affective space.

In the establishment of basic trust and affective attunement, we have to do with situations in which certain primal emotions act to support and structure—or conversely to undermine and de-structure—our lives. Such emotions provide an affective infrastructure that is deeply ingredient in viable being-in-the-world—and whose absence undercuts it and renders it fragile (as we saw in Ahmed's analysis of racial hatred displayed toward the young Audre Lorde in the New York subway).[14] This subjacent emotionality is something of which we are often only preconsciously or subliminally aware. This obtains for many emotions that appear between us and outside us: we may be only dimly conscious of these even if they exceed our own subjectivity: not unlike low-lit stars in the nighttime sky. It is nevertheless *from there*—from their external location—that they transfer their affective being to us.

A useful way of understanding such transfer is found in John Protevi's notion of "protoempathic identification," which takes the notion of identification to a new level. Beneath the working of conscious empathy (as evident in the commiseration and fellow feeling discussed by Scheler), there is a deeper and more spontaneous source of the bonding that is essential in emotional contagion and other forms of group interaction. In Protevi's words, such an identification is not so much with the figure of the other (i.e., a leader) as with others' "affective state," that is, with their emotional tenor: "you feel what another person is feeling."[15] This is *proto*-empathic because it precedes and often underlies intentional empathy as a conscious and concerted act. It is both more general and more pervasive—so much so that it need not eventuate in an act of explicit empathizing at all. Protoempathic identification is at once somatic and social. It is a matter of an "embodied intersubjectivity" in which "there is a linkage of affect, body image, and bodily integrity in the experience."[16] At stake here is the role of the lived body in the sharing of affect.

It is telling that neither Le Bon nor Freud singled out the role of the lived body in their accounts of crowd phenomena. Their emphasis was decidedly on the *mind*, whether the group mind (in Le Bon) or the unconscious mind (in Freud). In contrast, Protevi insists that the body is of singular significance in interactions in groups. The lived bodies of the participants in such situations manifest *in concreto* (and thus literally *realize*) what Freud refers to under the heading of "emotional ties." These ties are woven by interactive bodies that *bear emotion out*, quite literally: taking it out into bodily movements and gestures that make the shared emotion accessible to all who participate in such scenes. For these same bodies are the active agents of protoempathic identification, which animates a concrete intersubjectivity that emerges in the experiences of those who, acting together, make up a crowd. The result of such convergent corporeal activity is what Protevi designates as a "social body" or the "body politic"—both of which depend on the subtle but forceful working of protoempathic identification.[17]

III

The French sociologist Emile Durkheim, a near contemporary of Le Bon who coined the phrase "collective consciousness" (*conscience collective*)—a notion that parallels Le Bon's "collective mind"—assigns a major role to *consciousness* in group behavior, embracing an enlarged notion of what counts as being conscious. All this is well and good, but what if we dive down under consciousness, whether individual or collective? What is the fate of emotions in a strictly unconscious domain? To attempt to answer this question is to move to the level of *unconscious emotions*. Such emotions are directly at stake in Freud's discussion of "identification," which involves "emotional ties" (specifically ties of love) of which we are often not explicitly conscious. In these discussions, Freud invites us to go into an unconscious realm—a realm that Freud early on characterized in these strong terms: "The unconscious is the larger sphere, which includes in it the smaller sphere of the conscious. Everything conscious has an unconscious preliminary stage; whereas what is unconscious may remain at that stage and nevertheless claim to be regarded as having the full value of a psychical process. The unconscious is the true psychical reality."[18]

Setting aside Freud's metaphysical terms "reality" and "true," we have here the assertion of the unconscious as a realm of its own, possessing a unique energetics and dynamics; it operates by "primary processes" (especially condensation and displacement) which have everything to do with the formation of the manifest content of dreams, as well as with the engendering of specific neurotic symptoms. Most crucially for our purposes, the unconscious harbors its own emotional content, as Freud makes clear in his major essay "The Unconscious" (1915), one section of which is labeled "Unconscious Emotions." In this section he denies that such emotions are anything entitative—as if they were discrete items that we could specify as such. As "manifestations" of "instinctual impulses," unconscious emotions are not fixed in form but are always *processive*; in particular, they "correspond with processes of discharge, the final expression of which is perceived as [conscious] feeling."[19] Otherwise expressed, an unconscious emotion signifies "a potential disposition" that, stemming from acts of repression, never on its own reaches a conscious or perceptible state. Repression itself, strictly speaking, is of the *idea* (the representation, *Vorstellung*) attached to the emotion or affect; the result is the "severance" of the affect from "the idea to which it belongs," leaving such an affect to "fulfill its separate destiny."[20] By this last claim, Freud affirms that unconscious emotions pursue their own course, surfacing only when certain occasions call for them but remaining otherwise inaccessible. Once their "ideational component" (that is, what they are *about*) is identified, emotions can be named and discussed as such: as "love," "hate," "anxiety," and so on.[21]

Freud's rather convoluted theory of the genesis of unconscious emotions need not be accepted in its entirety for us to take its major claim seriously: namely, that certain emotions reside in the unconscious as dynamic processes: as *unconscious events*. This is to assert that an entire class of emotions cannot be considered conscious (or even preconscious) in their intrinsic being. They stem from the *unconscious*, construed as their proper locus, however we may wish to understand the reasons for their being down there in the first place, whether as residues of instinctual impulses, or as the result of repression. With the unconscious, then, we stand at the source of the "emotional ties" that are for Freud the basis of the primary and secondary identifications that animate behavior in groups that have leaders. Here two aspects of Freud's metapsychology converge and help us to understand the extraordinary emotional force exerted by political (and other) leaders upon their followers. These followers are bonded not only to their leaders in primary identifications but via secondary identifications with each other, thereby increasing the emotional intensity. The intensity itself stems from the unconscious dynamics of both forms of identification. It is as if the affective attunement and basic trust engendered in early childhood are reincarnated in adult life in the form of such identifications—of which we are, strictly speaking, unaware. Such attunement and trust are all the more efficacious for being unconscious in their generation and preservation.

* * *

Freud's contribution to the ongoing project of this book is complex. On the one hand, he pursues the idea that, thanks to identifications with others, groups take on powerful and unique configurations; on the other hand, he demonstrates that the ontogenetic origin of these same identifications occurs via unconscious emotionality. In the one case, emotions operate through identification with leaders and with fellow followers of these leaders, while in the other case, emotions are located in the unconscious realm. In both cases, decisive steps are taken that support the major thesis of this book, namely, that certain emotions are located *outside* the domain of the isolated conscious subject—that is, the subject privileged by virtually all modernist accounts of emotion from Seneca and Descartes through Hume, Kant, and Durkheim. Instead of thinking that the unconscious realm is somewhere *inside* the subject, it is crucial to realize that it is nowhere to be found there. It is a realm of its own with its independent laws and workings. In this way, it is decisively outside the ambit of the conscious personal subject. We need not go to the length of positing a "collective unconscious" as did Jung: an unconscious whose contents are shared between whole groups of human beings and at the limit by all human beings. Nor need we presume further with Jung that the collective unconscious is ultimately identical with the natural world.[22]

All we have to affirm is that the unconscious is characterized by a radical otherness and that any emotions it contains are outside of conscious cognition.

Freud takes the decisive step of locating emotion outside the conscious subject—where "outside" signifies *outside consciousness.* This outside is found neither in the interpersonal nor in the environmental domains. It is in the unconscious—it *is* the unconscious—regarded as pre-personal and as underlying the inter-personal. Nor can the unconscious be considered as merely contained within the human subject. It is beyond the conscious control of this subject; it is a realm of its own—as much so as is the surrounding social world or the natural environment. Freud is not subjectifying emotion but radically de-subjectifying it by pointing to the unconscious determinants and processes by which emotion emerges beyond the willful control of any conscious subject. For the unconscious is largely if not entirely "unknown" (*unbekannt*) to the subject herself. Thanks to the unconscious underpinnings of identification, human subjects do not have full conscious awareness of their primary identifications with leaders, despite the considerable influence of these identifications, along with secondary identifications, in determining human conduct. And these same subjects are still less aware of their own unconscious emotions: as Freud insists, the unconscious is "as much unknown to us as the reality of the external world" because it is "incompletely presented by the data of consciousness."[23]

This last claim tells us that the outsideness of the unconscious differs in one decisive way from other kinds of outside I have discussed in this part and will soon describe in part 3: it is not anything that we pick up from the world around us. It is nothing we can detect *as such* in a field or atmosphere or even in an ordinary conversation. In short, it is nothing of which we are in the least aware. But that is just the point: this particular otherness is unique in that it will never itself appear in a given place-of-presentation, even though it may influence much that does appear in such a place. But this non-appearance does not make it any less potent as a form of emotionality; if anything, it increases the force and eventual impact of such emotionality, as we can see with the lingering effects of a smoldering jealousy or envy of which we are not ourselves conscious.

What matters most for our purposes is that with Freud's guidance we are able to extend the outsideness of emotion to include its unconscious presence. This presence is formative of primary and secondary identifications—of which we are rarely explicitly conscious—and it has its own modalities in the form of emotions that are themselves unconscious: such as deep-lying resentment that festers and may go unrecognized as such.[24] This means in effect that Freud posits an additional locality for emotions: *in the unconscious,* a domain that is outside the direct influence of the conscious human subject. Emotion is thereby liberated from the daily demands of the ego (and of the superego, an outgrowth of the ego)—and thus from the conscious subject that is the unique locus of emotion for so many early modern thinkers and that is the basis for the exchange of emotions between persons in many group settings (the focus of Scheler and Le Bon, both of whom focus on consciously entertained emotions).

In these various ways, Freud takes us into a dimension that is beneath the consciousness of this same subject and which underlies its interactions with others throughout the course of its life. As such, it represents what is *other* than this subject, for it is located elsewhere, otherwhere than in the arc of consciousness. We need not subscribe to Lacan's invocation of the unconscious as "the Other" (*l'Autre*) in order to valorize the radical otherness of the unconscious and its emotions. Nor is it the only realm of the other in the kingdom of emotions. There are other such realms— such as the natural settings wherein animals interact —in which emotions emerge and present themselves outside ourselves. But the unconscious is a distinctive extra-subjective domain of the emotional in humans and as such calls for our recognition despite its elusiveness and uncognizability by acts of consciousness.

Part 3

Toward a Prospective
Periphenomenology of Emotion

9

Emotional Edges and Interembodiment

This chapter explores two phenomenological foci in juxtaposition: the *edges* of emotion and the role of *embodiment* in emotionally bonded groups. The first has to do with how emotions present characteristic profiles to those who experience them, manifesting a delimited shape; the second has to do with how lived bodies come together in collective gatherings and relate to each other in what I designate as *interembodiment*. As will become clear, these phenomena are interrelated and overlapping. In speaking of *emotional edges*, I intend to invoke how a given emotion reaches an experienced end or terminus, however indeterminate this may be. But emotional edges also characterize the way a given emotion relates to another emotion, colliding with it in some cases, merging with it in others, and folding over it in still others. Interembodiment is the corporeal basis of what phenomenologists in the wake of Husserl call "intersubjectivity." All collective and group formations feature factors of interembodiment—that is, the various ways that bodies relate to each other in such formations.

I

Emotional edges are either *internal* to a given emotion or *external* in terms of its relation with other experiential processes. Emotions often appear amorphous and nameless; they are famously fleeting, notoriously difficult to pin down, changing shape and direction and force continuously—a feature discussed in the next chapter as *elasticity*. Was it genuine grief I felt at the death of a close friend (at the sheer loss) or was it dire desolation (feeling abandoned)—or perhaps both at once? Where does one begin and the other end? Can one ever say *just where* any emotion starts and finishes? It is because this is so difficult to determine that we often can give only an approximate account of the origin and termination of an emotion we are undergoing or have undergone. For the most part, emotions phase in and out of ongoing stretches of our lives, and are rarely the entire content or single focus of our experience except during highly charged moments. Such in/out phasings are edged to the extent that we identify them as "early" or "late" moments of an emotional experience, some of these moments being abrupt, others more smoothly transitional—and all bearing their own edge profiles. Let us focus on two respects in which edge and emotion are closely related: first, that emotions not only have edges but are themselves edge phenomena (a distinction first broached in chapter 5), and second, what I call "emotional front-loading."

Emotions are experienced as edgeless only when—as sometimes happens, as with certain moods—they are entirely diffuse; but most emotions do possess their own distinctive edges, internal and external. This happens with many mundane instances of emotional upset—say, over my partner's seeming neglect at a delicate moment. The opening edge of this upset may be felt at first as a growing apprehension; but then this blossoms quickly into an angry verbal outburst at her when I say suddenly, "How can you do this to me?" These words proceed right out of the incipient edge of my anger. The outburst and its sharp edges are closely interwoven with the earlier phase, in which I sensed myself being neglected when I craved for more attention. The edges of this feeling of neglect are contiguous with those of my overt display of anger: the earlier edges gave way to the later edges in an affective sweep, folding into them, yet they are experientially differentiated. Not only do emotions possess their own experienced edges at various stages of the emergence of a given emotion; they are at one with these edges: indeed, they *are* these edges even as the emotion itself evolves. In this respect, to be emotional is to *be on edge*—an edge that is characteristic of the emotion I am feeling or expressing at the time. The fact that earlier and later phases of a given emotion connect in characteristic ways contributes directly to the emergent identity of the emotion itself, contributing to its distinctive overall gestalt, the form of my anger on this occasion. (This form is both a generic kind—in this case, "anger," of which there are many species—as well as reflecting the way I experience and express that emotion in my own idiosyncratic way.)

Front-loading is my term for what is sometimes described as the "charge" of an emotion, borrowing rather too directly from the model of electricity. It refers to the way that many emotions, rather than reverting to the earlier stages of their formation, *press forward* in being responsive to a given circumstance and especially in an effort to be as emphatic as possible: to *make an emotional point*, as it were. This is not to deny that certain emotions do arise from thinking back on earlier events (for example, a nostalgia felt after ruminating on an earlier, happier phase of one's life), but even when this is so they are often propelled forward into a current intensity that is essential to the full experience of the emotion itself: I feel nostalgic *right now* even though what occasioned this was seeing a photograph from an earlier phase of my life. The nostalgia comes to the fore and presses toward a fulfillment that has its own felt integrity.

Not that front-loading is always smooth or continuous; our emotionality can be interrupted by other events that intervene, including other emotional events: for example, a melancholy that issues from the nostalgia itself in a layering effect. Left to itself, however, an emotion such as nostalgia seeks its own fruition by a kind of internal intentionality of its own. This is a version of what, in the wake of Merleau-Ponty, I have called "operative intentionality."[1]

Such intentionality is the basis of a given emotion's front-loading tendency; it is something intrinsic to the course of the emotion itself, and is a constituent feature of its very dynamism—displaying itself in a scenario whereby *the emotion will out.* Thanks to this dynamism, the emotion moves forward into an intensity that befits the emotional event itself. Not that there is an ideal form of such intensity for a given emotion or kind of emotion; instead, it is a matter of a felt urge to experiential completion that includes not only its trajectory *in me* but also a sensitivity to the way *others-around-me* are experiencing what I am evincing emotionally. In this latter case, it is a matter of noticing how these others are receiving my emotion and responding to it—a response which I take into account even if only peripherally: at the edge of my own emotional edge, so to speak.

In front-loading, it is as if the emotionality in question—be it nostalgia or anger, despair or joy—were informally programmed to unfold as it does, not in so many steps but with a certain inherent force by which it presses toward its own complete expression. It is almost as if the completion were somehow known in advance by the emotion itself—I say "almost" for it is not known in detail, but only in a general format. The way that sadness develops when I undergo it, its pattern of exfoliation as it were, cannot be known in detail in advance; but I do know that it will tend, from my own previous experience of it, to realize a certain characteristic pattern (the usual way I become sad in my way, the way my friend becomes sad in his way). This unfolding pattern shapes the front-loading of the emotion from within, directing its propulsive dynamics of self-realization.

Here two caveats are in order. First, this is not meant to deny that the course of a cluster of emotions may be derailed in several ways: coming to a sudden halt in midstream; petering out before its full expression is realized; or being overtaken by another emotion or set of emotions. But I am speaking here of cases in which a given emotion is allowed to *play itself out,* and in this sense to deliver itself. Second, in referring to a given emotional complex such as "sadness" or "nostalgia" or "anger," I am not claiming that these designators name eidetic types that obtain across whole cultures, different languages, or distinct genders. It would be mistaken to claim that any such constant types obtain across deep-seated differences. Such identifying terms identify a certain minimal nexus of traits recognizable within a shared language and a given historical-cultural lifeworld or continuous tradition. From out of this loosely assembled generic core variations abound and differences proliferate.

II

As already noted, I use the term *interembodiment* to refer to corporeal intersubjectivity as this characterizes collective formations (such as crowds and groups), whether organized or open-ended. All such formations involve a more or less overt display of emotions generated from within a medley of expressive gestures, sounds, and voices. However improvised or tumultuous, the resulting scenes exhibit a coherence of their own by virtue of the fact that emotions move across them, sometimes suspended *over* them and in any case flowing *through* them thanks to the embodiment of those who are present. As a result, emotions are experienced as all around oneself as a member of a crowd that has gathered in a group event. Such emotions are not entirely fluid, however; they have enough shape—or enough edge, in my enriched sense of this term—to be felt as such, even if they are not always easily identifiable. I know that the crowd of which I am a part is feeling anger rather than dismay—and if it is feeling both (as was palpable at the Women's March of 2017), I know the difference between them thanks to their characteristic edges.

The lived body figures into collective situations in several major ways. First, it *bears*—holds and contains—protoempathic identifications, which are felt (and sometimes literally shown) in the sinews and muscles of the bodies of those present to and with each other. Such identifications need not be explicitly intended or fully conscious in such situations, in which conjoint actions of the lived bodies of participants elicit and reflect each other spontaneously. They often figure just below an explicit awareness of their existence. Second, the lived bodies in these situations need not be mute; they often include the exchange of *voices* emitted from the throat and mouth in the literal sense of *vox populi*: the "voice of the people," a voice we first encountered in the Athenian popular theater scene and which continues to spring forth in public gatherings of many kinds. Such public voicings are not merely abstract articulations of ideas; they give vent to deeply felt affective states—felt through the body: not only in my own body, but from the bodies of those around me with whom I resonate on such occasions and with whom I am affectively attuned. The result is again what Fred Evans calls "the multivoiced body."[2] The members of a given group need not "speak with one voice"—this is the extreme case of a single-issue chorus of voices, such as happened at Wilmington in 1898—in order to coordinate and literally in-corporate the many voices of those around them: voices that carry their own distinctive emotional edges.[3]

A third basic form of interembodiment occurs by means of *gestures*. These are expressive means that carry their own affective force, stopping short of articulated words but often being complementary to such words. In such charged settings, gestures can—as we say revealingly—"speak for themselves." In the George Floyd demonstrations in Brooklyn, Manhattan, and elsewhere in the early summer of 2020, there were moments in which a combination of anger and defiance was expressed by kneeling on the ground with one knee, making unmistakable reference to the manner in which George Floyd was killed by a policeman in Minneapolis. Such gestures were fully expressive even if *sans phrase* and were emotionally moving for many present (as well as those watching later on video). Sometimes such gestures were accompanied by words, as when "Let me breathe!" was shouted out while raising one's fist. In such cases as this, gestural expressivity occurred with an embodied dynamism that not only complemented and supplemented overt verbiage, but spoke with a voice of its own that had its own affective edge.

In all such circumstances, the lived body of participants is the *energetic agent* within a collective social body. I am employing "energetic" in the literal sense of being "at work" (from *en-ergon*, where *ergon* means "work"). The lived body is energizing for the person whose body it is—or de-energizing when it is ill or weak. When lived bodies gather in a nexus of interembodiment, their dynamic gestures energize each other, drawing out those present to new levels of efficacy and force (though sometimes resulting in disarray if physical violence erupts). Members of a group of people who are concertedly (and not just casually) assembled feel the "buzz" of being with others, who propel them further along than would have been possible were each member to be acting alone. Such propelling is mutual: those around me offer energy to me and I in turn animate them.

An example of interembodied energizing from my own experience is this:

> When I joined the 2003 protest over the oncoming invasion of Iraq, it was a bitter cold day in February. Had I been alone, or just with a few strag-

glers, I would not have lasted as long as I did or gone nearly so far as I and many others did, striding in a circuitous route in eastern Manhattan that seemed never to end. Once or twice I ducked inside a small store selling coffee, but I rejoined the other protestors soon after, being swept along by the ongoing stream of forward-moving bodies. It was as if my body absorbed energy from their bodies and passed it on to them in turn. Marching together even though not in lockstep, we constituted a coherent social body with a single solidifying purpose: to discourage George W. Bush from invading Iraq. Our individual bodies carried propulsive energies, at once affective and physical, that were widely distributed throughout the moving mass.[4]

When living, moving bodies move forward together in a single synergetic pattern of literal *com-motion*, a special effect often accompanies the movement: a "collective effervescence" in Émile Durkheim's phrase, an expansive brio that arises from the active sharing of affects that emerge between individuals and around them. In contrast with the vivacity of many celebratory or triumphal parades, the affective aura of the Iraq protest effervesced in a rather somber way—as a grim determination to prevent a war foreseen as disastrous by everyone who was protesting. A common dedication to this purpose gave a decided coherence to an occasion that could easily have dissipated into irresolution had there not been a unifying shared intent that lent to the occasion an impetus that allowed it to be a singular event that carried its own insistent message. This event was nothing short of the advent of a unique social body—existing only for that day yet potent in its larger ramifications. Comparable marches happened the same day in other major cities across the United States and Europe. In New York, the marchers made their point, and then moved on. That the Bush administration ignored the protest made it no less significant as the emergence of a dynamic social body with something significant to say about a decision whose consequences were to prove tragic.

This event saw the emergence of a unique *social solidarity*, a term I also take from Durkheim. Social solidarity describes what can happen when the convergent interests or purposes of a coherent group, fueled by what Durkheim called their "common sentiments" (that is, their shared emotions), act as an intensely bonding force between them.[5] In social solidarity—in contrast with the individuating tendencies of persons living their own separate lives—there is a consciousness that is "common to [the] group as a whole, which, consequently, is not ourself [as isolated persons] but *society living and acting within us*."[6] In the midst of such solidarity, one is aware not just of the explicit structure and aims of a given social group (such as that formed by the group of Iraq war protesters I joined), but of the way that the dynamics of this group inhabit one's own consciousness—a consciousness I share with others, not just in detailed intentions, but in terms of certain generic factors such as convergent convictions at a doxic level (that is, having comparable beliefs) and a shared protoempathic identification with the bodies of others participating in the event.

Durkheim contrasts a merely mechanical solidarity in which the individual parts retain their separate identities (*partes extra partes*) with a genuinely "organic solidarity." In such solidarity, "society becomes more capable of collective action, at the same time that each of its elements has more freedom of action."[7] Thanks to such solidarity, there need be no capitulation of the individual to the collective—as happens *in extremis* in fascist rallies—but rather we find a circumstance in which energies and directions are absorbed from the social body in such a way that one's own body can become more meaningfully purposive and gain its own voice. This is just what I experienced in the march of February 15, 2003: my own body was propelled forward by being an affectively and kinetically active part of a mass movement exhibiting organic solidarity yet without requiring abject submission to the collective itself. I willingly became part of an event that can be considered "pro-social."[8] With tens of thousands of fellow marchers, I was in the midst of a moving social body, part of its very fabric. The edges of my moving body joined with the edges of the bodies of others in a shared emotionality whose own intensely felt edges, rendered articulate in words, conveyed the collective message: "DO NOT INVADE IRAQ!"

III

Most of my examples of crowd experience in this book have been taken from the serious side: demonstrations and protests over a particular grievance (the Women's March of 2017, the Iraq protest march of 2003) or from mob actions that had violent intent (the Wilmington riot of 1898). However, not all group formations possess as much gravity as these. Some are much more celebratory and even light-hearted, such as the St. Patrick's Day Parade in New York City and Mardi Gras in New Orleans. In both of these events, there is a shared intent—whether to honor and celebrate the Irish presence in New York (and in the larger American culture) or to observe a major Catholic holiday—all this being done in upbeat ways: with dancing groups, floats, marching bands, and general revelry.

Another such celebratory event is the annual African American Day

Parade in Harlem. I cite from notes taken just after I attended this event on September 15, 2019:

> As we headed over to the parade on the occasion of its fiftieth anniversary, we were struck by the presence in the side streets of rehearsing marching bands whose band members were dressed in rather thick and heavy uniforms, along with people on the sidewalk who were swaying to the music, "getting into it," as if released suddenly to do so. The energies in this literal side-show seemed all but uncontainable. . . . We next situated ourselves at the very front end of the parade on Adam Clayton Powell Blvd., where there was soul rock blasting from several long trucks decked up as floats. People were dancing and keeping time to this even on the less populated western side of the boulevard . . . It seemed that no one was unaffected by the combination of the music and the spectacle, including very young children who were moving their bodies in charming ways, and quite elderly people as well; whites like myself and Mary were drawn in, and could not help but move our own hips and feet back and forth even if not as emphatically as some others around us. . . . All conspired to make this a very lively scene: splendid weather, crowds of spectators, and above all those in the parade itself who were moving adroitly in their diverse regalia, also in keeping with the music. Their movements punctuated and framed the scene, dynamizing it throughout. In one striking episode, an entire group of young drummers, all wearing "Black Lives Matter" T-shirts, turned toward the part of the audience where we and others were standing and addressed us directly on their drums, playing concertedly for at least 8 minutes. At the end of their bombastic but welcome serenade all of the drummers came forward and offered to each of us a friendly hand slap of acknowledgment, creating a momentary community. This unplanned but moving episode epitomized the parade scene as a whole: it was a literal con-celebration.

Integral to this event were two closely related bodily dimensions: attunement and synchronization. Virtually everyone present—in the parade and on the sidelines—was viscerally *attuned* to the melodies and rhythms of the music (some of it recorded, a lot of it sung or played on instruments outright). Not because it was overwhelming in its volume and intensity—even if this was certainly sometimes the case—but rather because of a felt familiarity with the songs or at least their leitmotifs. Whatever differences there may have been in previous experiences of a given piece of music, virtually anyone in hearing range joined in with fellow listeners in a form of unrehearsed receptivity in which people took in the sounds together and resonated with them, thereby creating a scene of lively interembodiment. These sounds were not heard as abstracted music—as when I hum a tune to myself—but as music permeated with emotion: as carrying an affective force in its own right: affective and corporeal attunement here merged. This double attunement was distributed across those who were present at the parade-event. It was *all around* us in the periphanous space everyone there shared.

At the same time, bodily movements were remarkably *synchronized*: "remarkably" because no one was coordinating these movements except for the leaders of individual marching groups. Otherwise there was a genuinely spontaneous synchronization going on into which my partner and myself along with many hundreds of others were drawn powerfully and without hesitation: precipitated into it, as it were. *Syn-chrony* means "time-together," and this was just what was happening: sharing the time together in lively interembodiment. Everyone who could enter the synchronization—and few did not—found themselves moving their bodies in unorchestrated but complementary ways that formed an instantaneous community with the musicians and the marchers. Such synchronicity was the basis of a remarkable bonding action. Sometimes this bonding happened explicitly—as with the small group of drummers who abruptly addressed themselves to our part of the crowd—but mostly it was a matter of a tacit alliance among those present, whether they knew each other or not. Thanks to the attunement and the synchrony, the parade could be considered a genuinely democratic event: heterogeneous in composition, solidary in togetherness, and fecund in the creativity on display.[9]

Both attunement and synchrony can be said to be species of imitation—but only if this does not signify copying something explicitly. Much as Stern excluded outright imitative gestures from the emergence of affective attunement between mother and infant, so in the case of a group event such as the African American Day Parade, we are talking of a more generic and subtle imitation that deserves to be called by its original Greek term, *mimesis*. Mimesis includes many ways by which one thing resembles another, without having to be a matter of outright replication or overt similarity. When diverse musical instruments play "the same" melody, the sounds emanating from these instruments stand in a mimetic relationship with each other: the melody is recognizably the same even as it is conveyed differently by each instrument. We witness this vividly in the case of group improvisation in jazz when a single melody or rhythm—or both—are pursued in subtle variations, as with Miles Davis's album *Kind of Blue* recorded in 1959, with Davis joined by five other musicians, each taking up the main melody in his own distinctive manner.[10] In this way, the same can include the different—indeed, it *requires* the different to be fully what it is.

The situation I witnessed in Harlem on that festive September day displayed its own version of sameness-with-difference. It was the same event throughout but was differentially modulated from moment to moment, phase to phase, one block to the next. Individual persons, as well as whole groups of persons (whether marching or witnessing), moved in ways that were in active mimesis with other persons and other groups. These movements—in sound (instrumental and vocal) and in bodily gesture— did not copy each other but formed a vibrant mimetic whole that exuded consonance across manifest differences of detail. Very few at this extraordinary event were explicitly imitating others, yet all were collected in a single mimetic happening. There was a collective consciousness present, but more significantly, there was a convergence of differences in one and the same celebration. Over at least one mile of Adam Clayton Powell Boulevard, variations in exact motion and emotion, sounding and resounding, pitch and volume, rhythm and speed, and in visual allure—all with their own recognizable edges—were occurring. And yet everything converged in a singular coalescent event that was unique in its enactment: no one African American Day Parade is ever quite the same (and I have attended a number of these).

Such massive mimesis cannot be reduced to agreement at the level of representation (by reproduction in a photograph, for example, or by repetition in overt behavior or in explicitly perceived reality). As Samuel IJsseling puts it in his book *Mimesis*, "the mimetic is not restricted to representation, or rendering, and the recognition of it."[11] The African American Day Parade as those present experienced it was instead a matter of the confluence of differentiated presentations at the level of sight and sound as infused with affect—presentations that configured with one another in ways that were as improvisational as they were planned, creating a memorable mélange. Each of these presentations was made up of appearings and occurrings as heard and viewed by those present; but the whole happening itself was a single place-event that brought together differential but consonant corporealities and emotionalities in an intensely felt and continuously unfolding scene that had its own unique character and shape.

Contributing centrally to this uniqueness was the larger significance of the event itself: this was an affirmation of the vibrancy of African American culture and life in the wake of centuries of enslavement, displacement, incarceration, and impoverishment. My partner and I were very aware that these struggles and sufferings were not our own; we felt fortunate to be present at what was happening and to marvel at the celebratory mood which triumphed on that memorable Saturday in September. We were deeply moved by the vitality of a people who have been massively mistreated—indeed mauled and murdered—and are still reviled and repressed on a daily basis. Despite all this, time was found and place was made to assert an indomitable message of ongoing hope and joy. This hope and joy were experienced and expressed *together*, in an interembodied and synchronic display of collective consciousness, social solidarity, and rising spirits.

IV

Notable in celebrations such as the African American Day Parade, Mardi Gras, and the St. Patrick's Day Parade is not only the lively spirit of those who are official parts of such celebrations, but also the way in which by-standers are swept up into this spirit, *uplifted* and *vivified* by what they witness passing by and before them. Sometimes so taken are they with the spectacle that they leave their sidewalk stance and join the parade itself in an action of literal group fusion. So much is this the case in the Mardi Gras that it becomes difficult to distinguish between those who were part of the parade in its beginning phase and those who joined in freely along the way.[12]

There are also instances that combine a quite definite and serious overall purpose with unplanned and spontaneous actions en route. This was especially evident in a number of Occupy Wall Street processions in New York in 2011 and 2012 that featured innovative posters created for just that occasion, dancing and singing along the way, and a shifting course that sometimes deviated significantly from the originally planned route. As another example of such hybrid actions, take the following vivid description of a street protest in Montreal in 2012 that was objecting to the controversial Loi 78 passed by Quebec's Assemblée Nationale, which imposed severe limits on picketing and protesting:

> We evade riot police by snaking from street to street, improvising the route. I see a dumpster being turned over and lit on fire to block the police from disrupting our march. Spirits are high, and without much talking we cooperate and collaborate with each other with hand sig-nals and chants. In a moment of reflection I think about how the eve-ning's two very different [earlier] events—the punk show and the night march—were both building towards something similar: the reclamation of space and the formation of the commons . . . this re-claiming of the commons was reinforced by the repetition of a familiar call and response chant among North American activists: "Whose streets? Our streets!" We

alternated between French and English. It felt good to chant in unison and I joined the chorus.[13]

Especially striking here is the combination of a quite specific and serious purpose—which invited exact verbal formulation—"Down with Loi 78!"—along with innovation along the way. There was no single leader or group of leaders for this march—at once purposive and light-hearted—which continued for six consecutive nights in the streets of Montreal, each time taking a new route and involving a different set of freely adopted actions. Chanting in unison created cohesion by its very enactment, yet also allowed for variation in the modulation and the volume of one's own voice, constituting its comparative *insistence*.[14] The result was a paradigm of "mutual coalescence" (again in Scheler's term) that allowed for the convergence of members of the group, even as subgroups and individuals took their own directions. The chanting voice was itself a form of *vocalized embodiment*, as well as an articulation of protoempathic bonding among members of the march. Beyond the many ways in which each member of such a protest march took in the bodily actions of other participants visually and kinesthetically, in the auditory register there was an active generation of lively camaraderie in *viva voce*.

Another instance of such protoempathic experience in the auditory/musical sphere occurred in the early months of the coronavirus in Italy and then elsewhere, including New York City. The unorchestrated singing and playing of instruments on outdoor balconies on a nightly basis (to which I alluded earlier in this book) helped to congeal a sense of solidarity in face of the ever-encroaching virus. The fact that most of those playing instruments or singing were rank amateurs, while others joined in by banging on pots and pans or any other handy object, made the occasion all the more moving and memorable. There ensued many variations on this—such as happened in March 2020 in an apartment complex in Bavaria where residents of all ages together sang and played the antifascist anthem "Bella Ciao" in an expression of solidarity with the people of Bergamo, Italy.[15]

The more we move in this direction, the more we approach the welcome extreme case of "dancing in the streets." Such spontaneous dancing need not be for any clearly stateable purpose: neither to honor a given event nor to object to a particular form of economic or political oppression. It can emerge from a conjoint joie de vivre that is enacted by friends, neighbors, and fellow city dwellers who are dancing together—whether from relief or as sheer release. These are displays of a shared exuberance that is deeply celebratory. The ways in which such spontaneous happenings can be regarded as indications of the health and well-being of the dancing populace has been underlined in Barbara Ehrenreich's book *Dancing in the Streets*.[16] The converse case—in which street dancing is discouraged or forbidden—is a significant indicator of a troubled situation, as Ricardo Ainslie shows in his study *No Dancin' in Anson*: because of racial tension in Anson, all public displays of spontaneous behavior were banned.[17]

The cases I have been discussing in this chapter act as reminders that crowd and group behavior do not always arise from gatherings of human beings intent on promoting a particular cause or purpose, nor do they always express a definite demand or protest. When they do, they exhibit a collective version of what Nietzsche called the "spirit of gravity"—a spirit that discourages spontaneity and innovation, as happened with closely orchestrated Nazi rallies and parades. Even so, some explicitly purposeful groups, like those assembled in the Wilmington event, though starting as something organized, can get out of hand and become what we can only characterize as a mob event or "riot," as happened in the attempted takeover of Congress at the US Capitol building on January 6, 2021.[18] Such destructive spontaneity is to be contrasted with an affirmative spontaneity in which certain positive goals and ideals are the primary motivating factors: as with the African American Day Parade of 2019, the early Occupy movement, and the Montreal protests of 2012, all three of which were life-enhancing rather than life-depleting events.

V

We can conclude that when it comes to crowd and group experiences, emotions are shared among actively embodied participants. Interembodiment is essential to the experiences of these participants. As such, it can be considered the basis of a closely linked *interemotionality* that is dynamically ingredient in many group settings. Recognition of the "objective energies" (in Dewey's phrase) of certain embodied emotions—energies that are most acutely expressed in their felt and perceived edges—requires us to reconsider in order to correct a tradition that has been intent on burying emotion within the subject. We must extricate emotions from an ill-advised and premature internment inside human beings: kept inside them rather than recognized as having contours that bear them out in the bodily interactions of those who make up crowds and groups of many kinds. These contours are forms of edge; they allow members of all such gatherings to experience more fully the emotions they undergo in each other's company. They outline the places-of-presentation for such emotions—places that, far from being anything static, are animated by bodies moving synchronously and in attunement with one another.

An emotion like love has a characteristic arc that takes us out of ourselves by allowing us to become related to another person by way of bodily gestures and movements: when we say that we are "drawing close to the beloved," we refer to ways our body desires to bring ourselves into the presence of the other person's body, so that the sentient edges of our bodies can interact and intersect. A different version of such interembodiment happens with felt empathy for the disabled. In such empathy, we extend our bodily awareness out into the orbit of the other's suffering by way of an affective outreach that has its own shape. Such empathy, like love, is a primarily dyadic interembodiment. In larger group settings, our emotions are presented to others by our bodily actions and gestures— while others' emotions are conveyed to us in turn by their own corporeal configurations. Even in the midst of densely populated interpersonal situations, emotions possess characteristic edges that can be recognized by those who are sharing in their experience. They are displayed *by and on our bodies* for others to discern, and *on their bodies* in turn, such that we can acknowledge them and join with them in a con-figured emotionality. As interembodied in the various ways I have traced out in this chapter, emotions can be said to act as the literal *outliers* of human experience: thanks to their effective edges, they take us out into crowds and keep us there as active participants in an evolving (and sometimes devolving) social solidarity.

Lived bodies put emotions into motion—precipitating literal *e-motions*—by breaking free from enclosure in the individual conscious subject where emotions have been held in lockdown for far too long. This release occurs by a re-figurative process in which the presentation of emotion—the place where it is located—is found without rather than within. This dis-enclosure is realized in all the forms of emotional *standing-out* that this book has been tracing, from the ancient Greeks to recent and contemporary thinkers. Such standing-out is something already happening in human (and animal) experience even if it has been ignored or denied in previous conceptions of emotions regarded as the "property" of the conscious subject—as if emotions were privileged possessions held within that subject's heart or mind or brain. Emotions with all their edges move away from strict inherence in the isolated subject and toward a public state in which they fend for themselves by existing and expressing themselves outwardly in interpersonal spaces of many kinds. They get to such spaces by way of an operative intentionality that takes those who are emotionally moved into a larger domain where their emotions are made known to others and those of others to them. This larger domain is constituted by a plurality of placements that constitute diverse affective worlds.

* * *

Emotions brought bodily into such placements are *dis-placements* from any central conscious subject: their place is *somewhere else.* Moreover, the elsewhere of emotions is no single kind of place but many sorts of places—from that of intimate body-to-body proximity to the dense inter- embodiment that ramifies through large crowds. We get to such places by way of a dynamic interembodiment that takes us out of the cage of private consciousness and into entire affective worlds that both surround and exceed us and that are replete with emotions that possess their own profiles as well as their own expressive energies.

The places here at stake are *place-events.* By employing this term, I mean to emphasize that both spatial and temporal parameters character- ize the emotionality of the crowd experiences described in this chapter. These experiences happen in particular settings; but these settings them- selves change with time and constitute *scenes* that are themselves both spatial and temporal. Moreover, this double dimensionality obtains for all emotional occurrences, not just those that take place in crowds. Emotions both present themselves as happening in a given place and as exfoliating through a certain time. If my emphasis has been on the factor of place in the life of emotion, this is not meant to preclude the temporality of all that occurs in this life as it is manifest in the front-loading of emotions, in the synchronization at play in crowd activity, and in more intimate exchanges of emotion; indeed, in the unfolding of any given emotion.

My stress on the importance of place and place-presentation in the display of emotion reflects an ongoing effort on my part to question the pronounced temporocentrism of modern thinkers from Kant to Bergson and early Heidegger. But it cannot be denied that place and its presenta- tion alter their shape and character over time. For place is not reducible to some static expanse; it is itself an *event*: hence my term "place-event."[19] And if place is an event, it must be added that emotion is also an event: it, too, is spatiotemporal in its various forms of manifestation.

10

Elasticity and Transmissibility of Emotion

> E-motion, as sensitive, as revealing of the *sens* of one's world,
> takes an open circulation with the world.
> —Glen Mazis, *Emotion and Embodiment* (207)

The elasticity of emotion is well known. A given emotion can change shape and character frequently, often unexpectedly. Most emotions are highly mutational. My anger can change quickly, suddenly growing more acerbic, or just as suddenly relenting; its course is not entirely under my control. No wonder the classical world, in the first systematic reflection on emotion in the West, focused on anger as a primary emotion—or at least *tried* to make it a focus. Anger itself is notorious for its unsteadiness, its unpredictability. And the changes are not just in its intensity but also in its course, frequency, and target, including the type and number of its objects. Anger can fit into many contexts, unfold at different rates, offer variegated possibilities of attunement, and overall can take various trajectories, exhibiting many different beginnings and endings. The same is true of numerous other emotions, including those that emerge less dramatically. Those emotions that seem slow-moving—such as brooding despair—do alter, only at a tempo less accelerated than highly charged emotions such as anger or jealousy. We are even tempted to say that emotion is nothing but change. For an emotion not to be changeable is for it not to be an emotion.[1]

Elasticity is closely related to *transmissibility*, the special focus of this chapter. Were emotions not so labile, they could not be transmitted as easily or fully as they are. And vice versa, to be as transmissible as they are, emotions have to be able to change course frequently, to alter *location* with comparative ease, thereby facilitating transmission. Such displaceability is an inherent aspect of their volatility: not to be fixed in one carrier, one place, one person. My critique of container models of emotion, above all the idea that they have fixed locations inside the human subject—what Teresa Brennan calls the "illusion of self-containment"[2]—is predicated largely on the basis of the inherent elasticity and correlated transmissibility of emotions. They are not liable to stay put in any ongoing selfsame container, whether of the body, brain, or psyche. My way of asserting this in the present book is that we must *turn emotions inside out*. This means taking them out of the interiority of the human subject—the chest (in Plato), the heart (in Pascal), the psychophysiological ego (in Descartes)—and relocating them outside any such self-enclosure. But to situate emotions outside the subject is not to relocate them to any steady or stable place. This would be merely to reposition them, ignoring their inalienable elasticity, given that a significant factor in this elasticity is an ever-changing locatability.

What I have been calling the "outside" (*dehors*) and the "beyond" (*au-delà*) is no one place but many places. For emotions are *multilocular*—to employ a term Freud applied to the human ego.[3] Multilocularity is closely linked to transmissibility. To be transmitted at all means to be capable of relocation, and in the case of emotions, to be capable of continual *re-implacement*: to be placed, re-placed, and re-placed again in a multitude of locations. These locations are themselves changing: there is no privileged single place or kind of place outside or beyond the subject, but rather an ever-changing set of alternative places, each yielding a differential placement, or what I have designated as the "place-of-presentation." To be transmissible requires at least two places—a place-of-origin and a place-of-destination—even if these places are momentary and are often multiplied by the compresence of many possible places of transmission. Such places are provided by persons, who as fully embodied count as places of interpersonal affective engagement of the sort we have examined in the just-previous chapters; while others are decidedly nonhuman, as with a sublime landscape. These manifold places com-plicate the transmission, offering multiple "folds" (the root meaning of *pli-*, as in the word "complicate") in which a given set of emotions can be situated in passing, bearing in mind that in this scenario *all is transitional*. Of almost every emotion we can say with confidence "this, too, shall pass . . ."

In addition to multiple placement, there is the factor of the *-trans*: the movement across or through space-time between the places through which emotions move, and are thus trans-mitted: "sent across." Transmissible emotions move across places, being subject to continual relocation. We are once again far from anything that could be characterized as *simple location* in Whitehead's sense; there is no single proper place for emotions—least of all inside the human subject. For this reason, emotions are not static entities but (as proposed at the end of the last chapter) *events* in motion: in transit, transitional, continually on the move. Such movement is integral to their elasticity.

Emotions are not the only essentially transitional phenomena that make a decisive difference in human life. Thinking also occurs in transit, especially innovative thinking that moves in new directions.[4] But whereas thoughts move across spaces and in times in ways that are cognitively characterized and packaged—doxic, thetic, conceptual—emotions move more like spontaneously emitted missiles loaded with affect.[5] Yet emotion and thought are both phenomenologically *light* compared with bodily actions that bear weight forward, coping with gravity; both are transmitted by words, gestures, and movements, and neither has a fixed and stable location but leaps with celerity between regions and settings, disparate environments, and diverse sentient beings (not only humans). Both emotion and thought move *all over the place*, and are never fixed in one place. Instead of the *stabilitas loci* (stability of place) prized by the Romans, these two modalities of human experience exhibit *mobilitas loci*, the radical transitionality of placement.

|

Our present question is, what is it for an emotion to be transmitted? Clearly, anything that is transmitted—whether an emotion, a thought, or something physical like a bird—must be light enough to be carried in the transmission. Consider, for example, the condors in the Colca Canyon in Peru who position themselves to be carried upward from the depths of a very deep canyon—all the way from the bottom, where they rest overnight, to the canyon's upper edges and on up into the sky, without flapping their wings, only tilting slightly to direct their path so as not to collide with their companions. These enormous birds weighing hundreds of pounds are transported by updrafts of air from thousands of feet below, though an onlooker might think they were made of paper, so graceful and seemingly effortless is their flight.

The flight of condors is suggestive regarding the movement of emotions between and beyond human beings. Although we easily speak of the "flight of ideas" (*Ideenflucht* in German), emotions take flight as well. They are transmitted by various media comparable to the air currents that levitate the condors: these include natural phenomena such as live bodies, as well as culturally informed phenomena such as words, images, and gestures (all contributing to emotional expressiveness). These diverse media act to *carry* emotions, transporting them from one place to another and providing support for their outbound and inbound flights. Each of these expressive media acts as an effective conveyer of emotional exchange, a site of the promulgation and reception of emotions. Often both occur at once, as in a heated conversation during which it becomes difficult to determine just where emotions are located at any given moment or even exactly whose emotion is at stake. The fugitive emotions exist mainly *between* the agents rather than *in* any of them (as the last several chapters have helped to establish).

It follows that even if human beings as receptive and expressive agents are bearers of emotion, emotion is not primarily located *in* them but *passes through* them, moving in and out of them in disparate ways. Arising from the prospect of an awesome vista, or from an emotion-laden artwork, emotion is not anchored exclusively in human beings but floats free of these beings' conscious intentionalities or willful control.[6] Though floating free, it may call upon the support of semiotically coded entities (images, words, symbols) and may also make use of various habitual bodily gestures to bring them forth. This two-way dependence on semiotic coding and bodily gestures is most conspicuously present in interhuman settings. But the crucial phenomenological fact is that a given emotion can take on a life of its own. This leads us to inquire whether emotions do not in a significant sense transmit themselves, and if so through what medium?

Teresa Brennan's *The Transmission of Affect* is a major study of affect and emotion with a special focus on transmission. Her starting point is comparable to my own in that she critically questions the modernist tendency to ensconce emotion in the human subject: "The fact is that the taken-for-grantedness of the emotionally contained subject is a residual bastion of Eurocentric thinking . . . the transmission of affect means that we are not self-contained in terms of our [emotional] energies." She affirms that our emotions are "not altogether our own."[7] Precisely because of the elasticity and mobility of affects, there is a temptation to enclose them within protective barriers. In the wake of the religious wars of the seventeenth century, during a period of increasing colonialism, she observes, the "increase of affects" that the early modern period brought with it made "the Western individual especially more concerned with securing a private fortress, personal boundaries, against the unsolicited emotional intrusions of the other."[8] But in fact, beginning in infancy and continuing through adult life, "there is no secure distinction between the 'individual' and the 'environment.'"[9] At any age, the fate of affect does not reside in the individual subject. Emotional containment fails at its own game.

Brennan describes the radical exteriority of emotion as "social"; thus her paradigmatic examples of affect transmission are what I have been characterizing as *interpersonal*. This can be seen in a key passage early in her book: "I am using the term 'transmission of affect' to capture a process that is social in origin in that these affects do not only arise within a particular person but also come from without. . . . By the transmission of affect, I mean simply that the emotions or affects of one person, and the enhancing or depressing energies these affects entail, can enter into another [person]."[10] She adds that she is concerned with "an interaction with other people *and an environment*."[11] Although this points in the direction I shall take in this and the subsequent chapter, Brennan ultimately draws back from pursuing the factor of environment as such, explicitly stating that "investigating environmental factors . . . falls outside the scope of this book."[12] She emphasizes how emotions, which she usually prefers to designate as "affects," transmit between people rather than between environmental circumstances and events and the human beings moved emotionally by them. Her study thus contributes primarily to understanding the dynamics of interpersonal affects, and might well have been discussed in the previous chapters, but I invoke her book here because of the broader import of her model, which has significant consequences for the transmission of affect in environmental settings.

Interpersonal transmission does not happen primarily by vision, which objectifies more than it transmits, according to Brennan. Sight is "the sense that renders us discrete, while [affective] transmission breaches individual boundaries."[13] But in the actuality of affective transmission, smell, sound, and touch are key conduits despite their being systematically downplayed in Western modernity. Indeed, the prizing of "objectivity"—with which vision is linked as a natural ally—has meant that transmission of affect has been overlooked in the wake of the general neglect of alternative modalities of sensory awareness of which we are capable.[14]

A case in point is our tacit sense of the affective tenor of a scene we enter, even if there are few visual signals and no words. This tenor can be directly conveyed by olfactory sensation. We comment casually that a situation "doesn't smell right," but we rarely pause to consider that actual aromas may be operative as the effective transmissive medium of emotion. Smell, Brennan affirms, "is critical in how we 'feel the atmosphere' or how we pick up on or react to another's depression when there is no conversation or visual signal through which that information might [otherwise] be conveyed."[15]

Brennan's model of affective transmission is a welcome improvement on earlier theories which asserted that "affective communication" mainly occurs by the mediation of words combined with overt facial expressions. It opens up two advances in particular. First, insofar as multiple pathways of such transmission are valorized, her genuinely multimodal approach to the conveyance of emotion makes possible a more comprehensive understanding of affective transmission, overcoming modern models of emotional communication as primarily visual or verbal. Second, such conveyance does not mean that in affective interaction we are limited to the transmission of a distinct content or "emotional message," but rather we find ourselves in the midst of a richly overdetermined situation in which the felt sense of our immersion has several dimensions, not only two.[16] It is precisely because hearing, smell, and touch do not correspond to distinct "objects" or determinate parameters that they are able to convey nuances of emotionality not otherwise possible. When we say we are "sizing up" the emotionality of a given situation, we don't mean that we are measuring it in some objective manner for which precise wordings or measurements would be fitting, but rather we are "feeling out" the affective tonality of this situation as we are experiencing it. As Brennan puts it laconically, "the things that one feels are affects."[17] One feels them through a variety of sensory channels that, acting as complementary conduits, allow the emotional character of the situation to be taken in.

II

Grouping together hearing, smell, and touch as Brennan does in her effort to circumvent the dominance of vision in modern Western thinking is not to suggest that these three modalities are all equivalent as modes of transmission, nor are they the only conveyers of emotion; certainly *taste*, which she neglects, should be added to her list. Let me point out distinctive features of each of these four individual senses:

1. *Touch* clearly entails actual contact with the transmissive agent: I have to be near it, and it near me, for touch to happen at all; it is from this close contiguity that a specific emotionality is conveyed, whether of affection (appreciative attention, attraction) or disaffection (repulsion, disdain). Touch is also notable for being two-way: when I touch something it "touches" me back, or as Richard Kearney puts it: "If touch is something we do to the world, it is also something the world does to us."[18] One cannot help but recall here the incident (recounted in chapter 6) in which the young Audre Lorde was seated next to a haughty white woman who abruptly jolted away from her on a New York subway train. Here the contact was not skin-to-skin but occurred between two kinds of outer clothing. What repelled the older white woman was not merely that her

coat touched Audre's snowpants but that she felt, with disgust, that Audre was touching her in turn. Also evident in this experience is the fact that touch can happen between any two or more surfaces, fleshly or not.[19]

2. *Smell* can occur at considerable distance, though relatively much less so as compared to sight when it looks across an empty field or at the horizon. The comparative pungency of odors is the equivalent of the felt pressure of touch. But smell has further nuance by way of its wide range of fragrances and odors. These can be considered the aromatic equivalents of colors in the realm of sight. They have the special power of being associated with specific memories, and thus with the emotions associated with these memories—not only perfumes summoning up certain emotionally important individuals, but also a variety of smells that transport us to emotionally charged events, and indeed to whole eras of our past lives that retain an emotional valence over time.

3. *Taste*, closely associated with cooking and eating, also has considerable presence in the emotional realm, as when we say that someone "leaves me with a bitter taste in my mouth." As with smell, there is a special poignancy that attaches to taste and renders it a powerful vehicle of memories. As we see with the character Marcel in Proust's *Remembrance of Things Past*, an entire affectively intense past can be summoned up by merely sipping a "spoonful" of *tilleul*. Proust vividly portrays the way intimate aspects of Marcel's past, along with their complex affective tonalities, come back to him in such an experience rather than being located *in* him as if they were self-contained. Here the taste and aroma of a mere sip of tea unleashes this past emotionality from beyond the limited social moment of "tea-time" in the late afternoon of a given day.

4. *Hearing* happens at varying distances and intervals, and manifests the further complexity that it can take in words as well as inarticulate cries. But for conveying affect, the exact choice of words one hears is often less decisive than a certain rhythm and tempo—the way words configure and resonate with the persons who are hearing them. As in the art of political oratory, more important than what you say is *how* you say it. This is the feature of rhetoric that Aristotle named "emotional display," that is, the pitch and the passion that the orator puts into his speech. (In the epilogue we consider the dangerous downside of such display, with its power of producing unquestioning political allegiance in fascistic regimes.) We hear a vast variety of sounds, drawn to them by their punctuated rhythmicity, as with intriguing bird calls and animal cries. We listen not just to the sheer sounds as such—attractive or frightening as they may be—but to the emotionality they convey to us. For instance, I like to listen to a certain bird cry that emerges every spring in a magnolia tree in my front yard: it possesses an intensity and seductive quality—as if to

say "Come here!" in a syncopated rhythm that has its own allure. There is affective transmission going on here, and I *feel* it even if I cannot say more precisely what is being said, or even see the bird who issues the cry. So too when I hear certain jazz melodies such as "Body and Soul," I feel moved by the gently passionate but insistent notes integrated around a single repeated melody, suggesting emotions associated with love.

In each sensory modality—sometimes in combination, as with taste and smell—I am offered *avenues to emotion*. This is not originally or primarily *my* emotion even if I do experience it myself, and subsequently come to act on it. It is emotion that at least initially *does not belong to me*—it inheres in something else, in another person, a bird, a melody, something I touch, something I smell, something I hear. It *comes from without*, from beyond the enclosure of my mind and body. It is quite literally *extrapersonal*, and this is so even in emotional exchanges with other humans. What matters is that we attend to emotions that alert us to their presence. In all such cases, Brennan observes: "They are there first, before we exist. They pre-exist us."[20] More exactly, *they are inside us only insofar as they are first outside us.* They stream into our lives from beyond our sensorium, even if my body serves as a privileged place of reception for them.

The four sensory modalities just reviewed are indispensable *transmitters of emotion.*[21] If it is true that certain emotions present themselves from without, they need to be conveyed from that externality to the within of our actual apprehension: to our sentience, our "feeling," understood as the subject's own reception and registration of emotion. The various sensory modalities are indispensable in this transmitting role. Thanks to their intermediacy, emotion comes to us in whole cloth and it does so across and through the major sensory channels, which convey it to us as *that very emotion.*

This does not mean that we always accurately take in the emotion thereby transmitted to us: we might fail to grasp its full force and nuance, requiring further experiencing—and often a certain reflection on what we have just undergone. Hearing my colleague's hushed tone of voice in the meeting we are attending, for example, might lead me to think that he is exuding fear; whereas on reading other signals such as body language, I realize this is merely his effort not to be obtrusive. I have even less confidence that I understand the purport of the birdcall mentioned earlier: maybe it was not a seductive ploy but something quite different— say, an expression of loneliness. But the issue is not one of accuracy per se; misconstrual can occur in many other sensory registers as well, including cases of visual misrecognition. What matters is that *something expressly emotional* is being offered to us for our discernment—something to which we attend differently than were we merely observing a certain scene neutrally, taking in its sheer factuality. In the case of an appresented emotion or affect, we are put on the alert, and drawn to pay concerted attention.

There is no blasé emotion, not even in the case of boredom. When I am bored, I exude a certain affect of ennui that puts others on notice of my state, so that they are drawn to attend to how I am conveying this emotion, even if it is in dully undramatic or sullen ways. These ways set my boredom before others, who take it in as a distinctive modality of their experience of me. And this taking-in is largely accomplished by means of the sensory modalities we have just examined. They are the transmitting conveyors, the *via media* of emotion in such circumstances. Without them, no emotion would be detectable by those around me; with them, my emotionality comes to their attention. In their absence, each of us would be a self-enclosed monad rather than an enactive mode whose very essence is to interact with other modes; the interactions reflect differential forms of engagement that are the very basis of our emotional life. When it comes to affective transmission, Spinoza's *Ethics* is a much better guide than Leibniz's *Monadology*.[22]

III

Taking us in still another direction, Brennan speculates on which "concrete mechanisms of transmission" are involved in the transmission of affect. In the case of touch and especially smell, she invokes the relatively recent scientific concept of pheromones. These are definable as "substances secreted by an animal externally with specific effects on the behavior or physiology of another animal of the same species."[23] Pheromones are physical *carriers* of emotion, not emotions themselves, and they are responsible for what is often termed "entrainment" in the scientific literature. Comparable carriers would be sound waves for acoustical phenomena and optical arrays in the case of sight. None of these carriers is itself, as such, smellable, touchable, audible, or seeable; they are wholly hypothetical entities posited to complete a cycle of events considered with regard to causal genesis. While this is a legitimate concern of the natural science of sensation, it has little direct relevance to our *experience* of affect as it is transmitted by the various sensory modalities.

In order to appreciate the experiential dimensions of these modalities, we need to pursue a periphenomenological investigation; that is to say, a description of how affects reach us at the very peripheries of our experiential body: how they insinuate themselves into these peripheries, and more specifically how *their* felt edges impinge on the outer edges of our own experiencing. This is what I have been describing in previous pages focused on the major modes of sensing. Each of these, including vision, is an edge-to-edge operation: the outer rims of sights and sounds, smells and tastes, as well as the contact areas of touch, are taken in by the edges of the bodily surfaces at stake in each of these cases. What lies in between, being strictly nonsensory, is experientially inaccessible. It is a sheer transmissive medium that is populated by *we know not what* because we have no direct access to it. Hence the temptation to populate it with pheromones and the like, filling in the gaps from an all-too-human fear of the void: *horror vacui*. In the end, all that Brennan can say is that "pheromones are literally in the air."[24] Here the term "literally" implies: in the air as scientifically posited causal forces that we cannot smell or see, hear or touch or taste. The vacuum is filled, but in a way that does not clarify the human experience of emotion as something that comes to us rather than being generated within us.

Another factor at play that is not invoked by Brennan is *ecoproprioception*. This is George Quasha's term for the way in which the lived body has a specific sensibility for the larger layout of a given place or environment by way of a kinesthetic awareness of what is happening there, an awareness based on how we sense our bodily self to be moving in relation to that layout. Beyond the basic sensory modalities stressed by Brennan, there is a subtle but pervasive awareness of the scene as a whole (the ecological aspect, with *eco*-derived from *oikos*, "home-place") which we gain from our lived body's self-sensing proprioceptive powers (where *proprius* signifies "own," "proper"). Quasha specifies that this "transitive self-perception . . . introduces people to their own free space."[25] It is transitive as moving beyond oneself toward what populates one's proximal surroundings, a space in which one can move about more or less freely—more so when attuned to what else is there, less so if concentrating on one's own activity. It is a matter of "self experienced as other, as lived environment," a "self-knowing" that is not constricted to one's self but is "continuous with our interaction with environment."[26] Thanks to ecoproprioception we are tacitly *on the lookout* for what is around us. As Quasha puts it: "The implication is that self-knowing and self-managing do not stop with our body, the physiological envelope, but extend afield. One's self-sensing includes direct connection with life surrounding. One *senses with* a range of living otherness. A symbiosis becoming in some measure conscious."[27] This "life surrounding," I would add, constitutes an *affective scene*, and thus ecoproprioception includes an awareness of the affective tenor of the environing world that is conveyed to us by an ongoing felt awareness of our body in relation to that world.[28]

IV

These encompassing environs include other kinds of living beings: nonhumans. If emotion can be transmitted among human beings—the main focus of Brennan and the exclusive focus of Merleau-Ponty, Ahmed, Freud, and still others—we must also acknowledge that such transmission can occur between humans and other species, as well as among nonhuman species themselves. We witness the latter sort of transmission in the intense emotional attachment between young elephants and their mothers—to the point where the premature death of a mother elephant can occasion lasting grief and rage among her children, as Gay Bradshaw has documented in her book *Elephants on the Edge*.[29] The basic fact is that there is significant transmission of emotions across altogether different species, and this occurs more often than we might imagine; indeed, it is so common that we often take it for granted, as between human beings and their beloved pets (including not just dogs and cats but also iguanas, rabbits, birds, fish, and more). Donna J. Haraway has argued in *When Species Meet* (2009) that such animals are not only companions but authentic associates.[30] With them we realize a proto-community that is based on the playful or tense exchange of emotion.

Building on numerous studies of interspecies sociality, Cynthia Willett's *Interspecies Ethics* (2014) makes a convincing case for the way emotion is an active ingredient in cross-species bonding. Her working premise is that "affect attunement is the primary bio-discourse of social creatures . . . [it is] the material stuff of social bonds."[31] Drawing on Daniel Stern's research, as we have, she argues that if human infant and caregiver can become so well attuned without the presence of verbal language, there is reason to expect that comparable forms of attunement occur across different animal species. Such attunement is not restricted to smell, taste, touch, and vision. Depending on the anatomy and physiology of the animals who communicate, attunement may also occur by bodily gestures and movements: "Odors or eye movements, tails, and mobile ears or other muscular motion too can carry expressive force."[32]

However differently matched such "multimodal attunements" may be, affective transmission is essential to the "proto-conversations" that take place between humans and other species—not only with domestic animals but between humans and other primates, humans and bears, and in still other situations.[33] From such studies and others, Willett concludes that there are "multiple channels for biosocial exchange across diverse species . . . [thanks in particular to] a multimodal flow of affect attunement in mixed species societies."[34] Here affect transmission becomes the basis of far more than merely human–animal communication in limited domestic settings. It provides the basis for a form of socialization that, Willett argues, can inspire an expanded vision of "biosocial exchange" exceeding what human societies have been able to achieve by their own efforts.[35] If so, no longer can the human polis provide the paradigm of social-political interaction. What Gary Snyder calls "the Assembly of All Beings" realizes a form of "affect-laden communicative exchange" that is the indispensable basis for a tacit but intense sociality that is biosphere-wide.[36] Such an exchange furnishes "the motivating and intelligent ground for mutual response and responsibility."[37] This ground is found, Willett proposes, in "an affective field structured through biosocial matrices of transmitted meaning."[38]

V

Brennan insists that "affects are preeminently social."[39] This is a welcome thesis in contrast to the claim that they are strictly individual—that they belong or pertain only to us as our emblematic emotional core. It gives us the basis for a positive and persuasive affirmation: namely, that affects or emotions are very often generated *from others*. They stem from the actions, words, and gestures—as well as the smells, sounds, tastes, and contact surfaces—of others with whom we interact. But here we must draw a decisive line. It is one thing to maintain that affects are primarily social in origin and in destination—this is already implied in claims concerning the interpersonal basis of many emotions—but quite another to assert that social affects are exclusively or even mainly human in origin and operation. Willett's work extends the range of socially affective attunement to interspecies interactions of many kinds; thus for her the sociality of affects extends far beyond human interactions. Even so, this is not to say that affects are *exclusively* social, that they are always and only between members of a given species or between members of different species.

There are other modes of affectivity that are not social but what I term "environmental." In other words, sociality is not the only place to find emotion that is located outside the self-enclosed subject. Thanks to ecoproprioception, broadly construed, human beings—and doubtless other species as well—enter into an encompassing awareness of such emotion as it suffuses entire environments. Immediately after claiming that affects are "preeminently social," Brennan herself adds that "they are outside as well as within us."[40] Here I certainly agree, but want to deny that such exteriority of emotions is due solely to sociality. Sociality is only one way—though admittedly a major way—that emotions manifest outside human subjects. There are other significant ways in which descriptive phrases such as "outside," "there first," and "before we are" obtain for affects that we experience. If "environment" is taken as a generic term for the entire domain beyond-the-subject, then the emotional environment has several *regions* of manifestation—including numerous *places-of-presentation.* What Brennan calls the "social environment" is one of these regions, a most crucial one when it comes to interpersonal emotionality and to interspecies affectivity. Yet there are other regions that are environmental but not social, regions subtending what *surrounds us* and lies *beyond us.*

Brennan herself points in this direction when she says that the "air can be thick with anxiety-provoking pheromones."[41] The mention of air is more than metaphoric; it is a word that belongs to the constellation of what I shall refer to as *atmosphere.* Air is broadly distributed among sentient beings, and is essential to their continued life as breathing creatures who inhale and exhale it; hence we are not self-contained beings. Air also conveys light and carries wind and weather; and most importantly is emblematic of what we can call the "affective environment"—the environment viewed in its capacity to serve as a variegated *medium* for the transmission of emotion. Such an environment is equivalent to what Merleau-Ponty calls the "affective milieu."[42] Having alluded to this milieu early in *Phenomenology of Perception*—though saying little about it there—he adds this telling statement later in the book: "Our natural attitude is not to experience our own feelings or to adhere to our own pleasures, but rather to live according to the *emotional categories of our milieu.*"[43]

Some of these categories are social—as Brennan insists, as Willett emphasizes in the case of cross-species attunement, and as Merleau-Ponty himself considers paradigmatic. But some of them are not, and these are characterized by the relationship between human beings (as well as members of other species) and the outlying environment, much of which is neither human nor even primarily human-related. According to Marjolein Oele's model of "e-co-affectivity," what we casually identify as "affects," "feelings," and "emotions" are concretizations and modalizations of a fundamental affectivity that is differentially present in and between all living beings, thanks to their inherent biomorphic materiality.[44] Building on Michel Henry's "material phenomenology," Oele bears out its major tenets by reference to recent research in the life sciences, including botany, animal physiology, geology, and medicine.[45] Her claim is that the evidence from all these fields points to a pan-pervasive affectivity that includes an essential component of *pathos* in Aristotle's sense of the "felt suffering" that all life undergoes, however diversely, in order to become what it is. Life is for Aristotle what it is for Henry: an ongoing scene of "pathetic immediacy in which life experiences itself."[46] Life itself is this literally pathetic embrace.

In contrast with the individualized *ecstasis* that is a predominant existential proclivity in human Dasein on Heidegger's account, Aristotle, Henry, and Oele focus on the pathos of any living thing that includes what Henry calls its "suffering-with" (*pathos-avec*) other living beings. For all these thinkers, it is just there, in the sphere of immanent co-suffering interfaces, that affectivity emerges. This is not to subjectify emotion but to relocate it in "the concrete living places where affectivity happens," that is to say, in the spatial layouts, the experiential fields that provide the many kinds of "affective interface" that make life on earth possible.[47]

Here we are concerned with *affectivity*, not "affect" as such. Where the latter connotes a single emotional state—normally designated with terms such as "delight," "sadness," "fear," or "disdain"—the former names an entire complex state of being or, more exactly, *becoming*. Even though Bergson maintains that becoming is the most basic level of experience for all sensate beings, and as such cannot be adequately characterized by any spatial descriptors (given the primacy of durational time over any spatialized representation of it), I would contend that in the generation of affectivity the role of edges and surfaces as well as interfaces, all essentially spatializing factors, is indispensable. This role is to *bring emotion out* and to *place it in a region* that is coeval with what I designate as *atmosphere*. It is a matter of the outing of emotion.

For many species, skin plays a major role in this heterogenesis. Skin is not only sentient but "sapient": it possesses its own mode of knowing, including knowing how to inhabit places and to help create them. More than this, it is formative of entire worlds: "the making and placing of the boundary that skin is implicates thus the process of building an inside, but it also implies the process of connecting to and distinguishing oneself from an outside world. This outside world is also *produced* in this process: skin extends and mediates outward and touches and changes what it encounters."[48] At the same time, skin is also a site of affectivity precisely because of its status as an interface: "skin is an important affective interface that enables, mediates, and secretes our rational, sensitive, and emotional being."[49] As a dynamic interface, it serves as a uniquely formative shared edge in the living of life on earth. In the words of Michel Serres: "The skin is a variety of contingency: in it, through it, with it, the world and my body touch each other, the feeling and the felt; it defines their common edge."[50]

As a common edge, our skin is both itself *touchable* and puts us *in touch* with the surrounding world—a touching that is not just probative but affectively charged. As a medium for the expression and transmission of emotion on our part, it is also a surface receptive to presentations of affect in our immediate surroundings. The affectivity at stake here is no mere compromise between the sensing and the sensed. As accruing to the skin of a living organism or plant, it is "the exteriority of interiority."[51] This phrase resonates with a model of emotionality as an outwardizing into the circumambience of what is felt inwardly (in the psyche, the heart, the nerves, and so on). It is especially through skin and its gift of touch that emotionality is sensed as situated around us and outside us, out in the environing world as an affective presence that is not simply our own possession and to which we become attuned by way of a spontaneous eco-proprioception that is far more closely related to touch than to vision.[52] But to speak of the outwardizing of emotion is not to say that its proper or original home is within the sentient organism. This organism is part of the process; but affect or emotion, as it comes to be experienced, is felt to be situated on the other side of our epidermis—out there in the circumambient world, confronting us full face.

The term "interfacial edges" refers to interfaces between surfaces: they are instances of edge-to-edge relations. Such interfaces are important not just in the case of inanimate structures, as with joints of doorways or stratified geological formations—where exact "fit" is essential if the collapse of structure is to be avoided—but also in the case of living beings. Animate and sensitive bodies possess interfaces not only with their environments—especially via skin and touch—but also within the living tissues that make up these bodies. In the case of the human body, muscles, tendons, nerves, and arteries form an internal network of such tissues, each possessing its own sensitive interfaces. All such interfaces are zones of mediated sensitivity in which embedded receptors interact with influences in and from the environment.[53]

Plants have their own distinctive varieties of interface in their leaves, blossoms, stems, roots, and rhizomes, all of which interact with the soil and surrounding air. Nonhuman animals have their distinctive versions of organic interfaciality—birds, for example, whose feathers have very sensitive interim spaces that are essential to flying in the air and landing on earth and in trees and bushes, as well as in allopreening with mates: "The condition of possibility for avian touch lies in the untouchable interstitial space between feathers. This untouchable space of absence is the immanent meeting ground of affectivity, a mediated space in which animal identity is born out of difference, and where flourishing, pain, trauma, and demise literally leave their traces. . . . All of which proves avian life to be part of a metaphysics of affective fluidity."[54] Of special note in this revealing statement by Oele is the mention of an "immanent meeting ground of affectivity." Oele contends that affectivity is not felt primarily by an isolated organism—or by a separate part of that organism (say, its heart or lungs)—but above all in the interface between surfaces, both internal and external: surfaces which belong to that organism as well as to other living things. Affectivity is generated from a myriad of interfaces, some of which are found within a given plant or animal, while others lie in the interstices between the living being and its *Umwelt* or surrounding world.

As Oele might put it: *affectivity is co-affectivity is e-co-affectivity.* In my own nomenclature, I would assert that *affectivity is generated by the interrelating of multiple edges at manifold levels of intersecting sensitivity in the generation of place-worlds.* This is to link affect and life in an ever-redoubled fashion: surface-to-surface and edge-to-edge in forms of immediate mediation— *immediate* insofar as it is a matter of surfaces in touch with each other, and *mediated* inasmuch as two or more such edge-specific surfaces conjoin and modulate what might otherwise be considered isolated stimuli impinging on a passive and separated organism.[55]

VI

Thinking in this direction, we soon reach the idea of a *regional topography of emotions*: a diverse layout of places that surround and exceed the affected subject. From this layout there issue affects that are unique to each region of places. All this makes up a refulgent affective environment that serves as a reservoir of emotionality for those affected by it. The term *landscape* describes how the natural or urban environment conveys itself to our direct experience of it as a layout that is configured by differentiated places of many dimensions and types: pastures, hills, riverine settings, public parks, open lots, and the like.[56] These constitute *placescapes* in my own nomenclature, and it is an integral part of my proposal in this book that such placescapes are exemplary instances of affective force fields that do not stem from within our subjectivity and cannot be contained there by our experience of them; nor are they necessarily social in character. A placescape with affective valence constitutes what Gary Snyder calls a "porous world," and it strikingly resembles what Plato calls "the receptacle" (*hypodochē*) in the *Timaeus*, an active assemblage of diverse elements held together in loose array.[57] These placescapes, as places-of-presentation for emotions, do not belong intrinsically to the human subjects who take them in from "outside." They belong *elsewhere*.

When this elsewhere is conveyed to us by our sensory modalities in tandem with our ecoproprioceptive awareness, we have a literally *syn-aesthetic* ("felt-together") experience of affects. These affects are situated in particular places in the surrounding environment—whether in other people's expressive bodies, or in the bodies of other species (as with a raging elephant), or in entire environing circumstances that may not be populated by humans or nonhuman beings—yet which convey an affective tenor of their own (a "mournful" landscape, a "moving" nighttime sky, a "desolate" cityscape). Affectively toned places are gathered together in regions that collect contiguous or similar kinds of places in one coherent grouping, as when a bioregion assembles a congeries of concatenated places within its bounds. A given group of such places makes up a placescape, considered as a field for transmitting emotions that accrue to it, and extending their presence to all who are receptive to these emotions and attuned with them.

A central feature of the topography of emotions is *atmosphere*. We speak revealingly of an "emotional atmosphere" when we walk into a crowded room filled with happy people; indeed, we seek it out when we need cheering up, counting on a kind of emotional contagion or what William James calls a "dynamogenic effect," a transmission of emotion by and through an affective atmosphere. In Scheler's words: "We all know how the cheerful atmosphere in a 'pub' or at a party may 'infect' the newcomers, who may even have been depressed beforehand, so that they are 'swept up' in the prevailing gaiety."[58] Here an emotion exuded by others is picked up and imbibed by ourselves as newcomers. The cheerful affect is not that of any one person but is communal and shared among those present, even if not equally so by each. The affect gathers and animates an interaffective nexus and is transmitted from there to those present; as itself a *com-presence*, it is essential to the generation of the collectively experienced emotion. If we can say that the cheerfulness is distributed in the sociality of the scene—grounded in various uninhibited gestures, sounds, and words—we can also affirm that it is *transferred* from the co-constituted charged atmosphere to the newcomer who takes in the aura of good cheer. As Scheler adds, "it is characteristic of emotional infection that it occurs only as a transference of the *state* of feeling, and does not presuppose any sort of *knowledge* of the joy which others feel."[59]

By "state" Scheler refers to a moment of shared affect that is sustained long enough to allow those caught up in it to experience it together in the same stretch of time while in the same open space, in the *same place*. This occurs by transference—equivalent to what I have been calling "transmission"—where what is transferred is not anything we can be said to know as a separate object; at the most, we can speak here of an implicit or tacit knowing, an affective cognizance.[60] We know tacitly that the emotional state is present even if we cannot pin it down further than to say, in this particular case, that it is "cheerful" and "infectious." With many such states, precise description in so many words is often futile, for what is transferred is not an object or thing but something more like a state of being, or better yet a state of *becoming*, and thus an *event*. For the situation in the pub is essentially dynamic; the affectivity we take in upon entering constitutes a continually changing, emotionally charged atmosphere, a term that becomes increasingly unavoidable in the direction we are now taking. The question now becomes: How to account for such atmospheric effects when they no longer accrue to a social nexus?

Here we reach another kind and level of affective life, one that not only exceeds individual human subjects and their interpersonal exchanges but also surpasses meaningful interactions among species (between humans and nonhumans, and also between nonhumans, apart from any human presence or intervention). This is to affirm the coming-forth of emotion in environmental spheres of affectivity that are not only transpersonal but distinctively transhuman. We are talking of entire emotional atmospheres that have a life of their own and that call for our attention at this culminating moment.

11

Atmosphere and Affective Environment

There remains air, from which thought draws its subsistence.
—Luce Irigaray, *The Forgetting of Air in Martin Heidegger* (13)

Once it is granted that the interiorist theory of emotion demands critique and radical revision, there is need to move beyond the singular subject. But toward what? The two basic options are either toward other living beings (in human and nonhuman relations) or toward the surrounding natural world or environment. The validity of human relations as an affective locus has been affirmed in my treatments of the interpersonal basis of emotion (in Merleau-Ponty, Scheler, Ahmed, Brennan) and in the interembodiment at stake in dyadic and group relations, human and nonhuman (Stern, Le Bon, Freud, Oele, and Willett, among others). But the place of emotion in the circumambient natural world—situated in it and coming from it—remains largely unexplored. It is a matter of "earth emotions," in the telling phrase of Glenn Albrecht.[1] We pursue this now in this final chapter. We begin by exploring the intimate relation between emotion and atmosphere regarded as a basic form of affective environment, and consider how it helps to validate the extrasubjective theory of emotion that this book has pursued throughout.

I

The key issue at stake here is not the ultimate *source* of emotionality. Causal questions of exogeny and endogeny are best discussed by physiologists and neurologists, or by evolutionary anthropologists who attempt to locate the genesis of emotions in humans as an adaptive species, as Charles Darwin does in *The Expression of the Emotions in Man and Animals*

(1872). Our question is rather: in what regions of experience, affective fields, do emotions appear spontaneously, seemingly on their own, away from the subject? My response is that these regions are found in the surrounding natural world, especially in the atmosphere, weather, and air of that world, all of which manifest rhythms and patterns of presentation that resemble those of human emotions. Indeed, do not these three periphenomena deliver distinctive emotions themselves to us—and this despite their manifest nebulosity?

The word "atmosphere" signifies breathing (*atmos*: "steam," "vapor," including the air we breathe) within a certain sphere or globe (*sphaire*). An atmosphere combines a certain medium with an open-ended shape. It is large enough in breadth, depth, and height to sustain all who breathe in it and breathe it in. The earth's atmosphere, the paradigm of all atmospheres, is a scene of suspension and support par excellence, sustaining all those who depend on breathing in its presence—from plants and snakes and humans in its lower range to high-flying birds in its upper reaches. Here another instructive episode from the avian world presented itself recently: two hawks circling each other at great height, soaring ever higher into the upper reaches of the air above Ojai, California. They were moving slowly but surely in an evolving helix, tracing a shape invisible to humans but intimately familiar to them. They were creating their own *sphere of flight* not in accordance with any pre-fixed format or model but by navigation of the current situation, keeping with the wind patterns, the position of the sun, the luminescence of the light, and always with a sharp eye on the earth below. The two birds, flying high and free, created a covalent pattern in the sky, conspiring in a singular event of manifold determination—including factors of wind, air temperature, time of day, season—as I witnessed them from the open patio at the Ojai Retreat Center.[2]

The flight of these hawks is emblematic of the *volatility* of emotions—by which I don't mean their fickleness or mutability but rather their characteristic "pattern of flight" (*volatile* derives from Latin *volare*, "to fly"), the way they move through space and time when flying free. We speak in English of "flying off the handle" to indicate sudden intense anger or fury, or "riding high" to signify being in an elated and triumphant mood. These expressions are neither arbitrary nor merely tributary, but characterize something essential about human emotions: their refusal to be altogether anchored in human subjects, their deep proclivity for detaching from these subjects and assuming flight patterns of their own: *taking off* from inherent physical features of these subjects (heart, brain, blood, skin) and levitating into emotional spaces that they themselves delineate by their own animation. It is not a matter of denying the centralized, weight-bearing dimensions of human subjects—including the various ways we anchor emotions in immanent modes of feeling and forms of lived embodiment—but of appreciating the ascensional moments of emotional experience. Like the two hawks, emotions also return to earth where it becomes feasible to locate and name them; but at times they take flight in movements that are very difficult to map precisely, escaping the modern proclivity for pulling emotions downward and ensnaring them within the human subject.

Although we speak of an "emotional atmosphere" without hesitation, we should not take this phrase as an idle metaphor, nor infer from it that emotions are inherently vague and diffuse.[3] We know this is not always the case: many emotions, notably anger and rage in some of their reaches, have a distinct shape and a definite directedness toward particular people (including sometimes ourselves: as when we are "angry with ourselves") and are more often located between us than within us (as Merleau-Ponty insists). But they are sometimes experienced as beyond us, for example, in the case of "cosmic anger," feeling that the world is angry at us.[4] Whether they are definite or not in how they appear to us, emotions have a capacity to be not only transported across different sensory media—as spelled out earlier—but are sometimes suspended in a medium so broadly pervasive that we can only call it an "atmosphere." Not only is there an affinity between atmospheres and certain emotions—most conspicuously in the case of pervasive moods—but some emotions come forward to us as situated in, and even indistinguishable from, the atmosphere in which they appear. Here we arrive at telling instances of what I have been calling the *periphaneity* of emotions: their showing themselves *around us* in an encircling atmosphere in which they are manifested. This happens more commonly than we might expect, most conspicuously when we find ourselves in a scene that embodies its own emotionality.

At Jalama Beach in Santa Barbara County, I found myself overtaken by a remarkable atmosphere permeated by affirmative joy. This was all the more striking as I was feeling down and dispirited when I first arrived. But after walking on the beach for a while, then drawing back to a bench at its edge, I took in the full spectacle: the fierce incoming tide, the high winds, the brilliance of the midafternoon sun, and the valiant windsurfers making their precarious way between demanding waves with colorful sails darting gaily up and down. No single feature of this scene, not even the sum of its outstanding features, could account for what I experienced: a presentation of sheer exuberance filled with shifting energies and uplifting vectors, "blowing off the top" as one habitué of the beach calls it. All this took place in an atmosphere of sheer *commotion*. In that commotion, indeed *as* that commotion, emerged an emotion that can only be called *exultative*. I was lifted up and out of my dysphoric mood as I absorbed the spirited atmosphere—a celebration of life-in-motion.

Here was a concrete instance of an atmosphere that sallied forth an emotion—that *was itself emotional*. This emotionality emerged from outside my own personal orbit, which in its depressive character was unattuned to anything like it. I was pulled *out of myself*—drawn into a celebratory atmosphere that was irrefusably joyous. It was as if my own emotionality had taken flight, had joined condors and hawks in their peregrinations in open space. But the uplifted emotionality was not my own to keep or to give away; it was part and parcel of the immediate world that had so entirely captivated my attention, *out there*, in the sea and the sky as coeval regions of this world: force fields of affective attraction.

Just as much *out there* was the pervasive melancholy that set in during the coronavirus pandemic. It wasn't just a matter of personal unhappiness or wariness, nor could it be reduced to the frustration of being under lockdown and being sheltered in place for weeks and months that soon became an entire year. Rather, an atmosphere of intangible yet inescapable foreboding hung over many of those in areas of high contagion or on their fringes. There were few visible signs of this dark emotionality other than images on television of highly distressed people, yet it hung over all who were subject to it, portentous and persistent. It was *in the air*, everywhere.

Many further examples could be given of periphanous atmospheres like the exuberant one so evident at Jalama Beach and the melancholic ones in the midst of a pandemic. Such emotion-bearing atmospheres are so common that in their more modest formats we tend to take them for granted: a mellow happiness that attends a family gathering, a certain sadness that hovers over a Midwestern post-industrial town that is in steep decline. We don't have to look far and wide for what comes into our ken from the wide-angle provided by atmospheric emotionality. We live in clouds of emotions that are not ours to begin with, even if we end up taking them in and making them our own, feeling them intensely as if they were our own doing.

II

Atmosphere is closely connected with *weather*, and it is striking how often we refer to emotional phenomena by analogy with weather patterns. We say that a certain friend has endured "a perfect storm" of emotions, and we speak with equal ease of a "stormy disposition"—meaning a tendency to be carried away by negative affects such as jealousy, extreme irritability, or sudden outrage. The common English phrase "a gathering storm" fits well a situation where there is a foreboding of events to come that we expect to find challenging and stressful to deal with emotionally. In contrast with these, we refer to a "breezy disposition" when we mean that a person is light-hearted, somewhat frivolous, and little inclined to be taken over by difficult emotions. As a breeze moves gently from place to place, bringing fresh air on extremely hot days, so certain emotions are experienced as a welcome relief from previous distress. A "ray of hope" suddenly lightens a heavy sense of duress, granting us "something to look forward to" in the midst of daunting difficulties. Just as a ray of light breaks through a bleak skyscape, offering a sense of open space beyond the heavy clouds, pointing the way to a space of mobile possibilities in an otherwise dark prospect, so certain emotions arrive suddenly to relieve a sense of despair that has bogged us down and we experience "a break in the weather," so to speak. Weather can be "heavy," weighing us down with an oppressiveness that surrounds us as if from nowhere; so likewise, emotional states can oppress us, as when we fall subject to an abject state that descends on us from we know not where. Just as weather seems to emerge from beyond our location at a given moment, "descending" on us, so certain emotional states take us over with no clear sense of origin or purpose. We are assailed—just as when we are caught in a drenching rainstorm from which we have no protection.

Our tendency is to think of affectively "down" states as residing *in us*, but this is to ascribe a determinate locus to what has no proper location, to what is experienced as *everywhere and nowhere*. This ubiquity fits most weather patterns as much as it does many depressive emotional configurations. In my analysis, the parallel is neither contingent nor trivial but deeply revealing: the weather, despite being ostensibly situated outside us, is equally felt within us; conversely, emotions that are often thought to reside within us make themselves known outside us: the anger I thought was mine alone is now experienced as all around me. *In* and *out* are not only reversed in chiasmic fashion—crossing each other like the lines that compose an X—but weather and emotions alike show themselves to be imbricated *around us* in several locales, often too many to count or to assess. Instead of being a matter of simple location, their placement is polyplacial and to this extent indeterminate. When caught up in a deep melancholy, for example, I cannot tell just where it is situated; it pervades my entire life-world, spreading throughout my experiential space and ongoing time. It is a black hole, or better a "black sun" that is as much without me as within me.[5] Weather likewise often presents itself as everywhere, either as uniformly present (as on a bright and "perfect" day) or as a collection of converging weather systems (as often observed in the Land of the Great Sky, Montana).

Finally, just as weather is often unpredictable (despite the best efforts at prediction by the Weather Bureau), so emotional states and most notably moods can arrive without notice. We did not expect the sudden storm this morning, but neither did we anticipate the sudden joy we felt. Both seem to "appear from nowhere"—which is not strictly true but is consonant with the multilocularity of emotion and weather alike. Indeed, it is this indeterminate multiplicity of placement concerning not only the place of origin and the destination but especially the modality of appearing that renders both the weather and our emotional life difficult to map in advance. In the case of weather, however, we can take an umbrella "in case it rains," whereas we have few such practical props to help us fend off sudden changes in our emotional lives. The emotional weather system can "take us by storm" and find us defenseless in ways too subtle and sinuous to predict or control.

To be sure, this profound similarity between our emotional life and weather as an atmospheric phenomenon is not an identity. We are addressing matters that are sensuously allied in a basic sameness yet are not identical. As Heidegger argues in his seminar "Identity and Difference," strict identity precludes all difference, whereas sameness *includes* the different within it: it not only tolerates it but depends on it.[6] The affinity between emotions and weather phenomena can be considered a version of what the unwritten doctrine of Plato designates as an "indefinite dyad"—a dyad composed of the same and the different, the odd and the even, the like and the unlike.[7] The very indefiniteness and manifold aspects of the alliance between emotions and weather are a source of strength rather than weakness, constituting a generative scene wherein each member is augmented in its being. Rather than pointing to an identity, then, I am suggesting a sameness that becomes a chiasm in which the phenomena converge and diverge. The sameness is not so much structural as something *sensed*: we sense it instead of literally perceiving it or deducing it from scientific notions of weather or the atmosphere. The sensuous aspects of each—picked up by us when in their midst—may resemble each other but are not identical. We retain a strongly felt sense that there is something comparable between emotions and the atmosphere or weather. Each is a force field of its own: the field of weather being composed of natural epiphenomena (clouds, wind, sunshine) and the field of emotional experience being filled with affective vectors. But these two fields present a convergent sameness of affect despite all their manifest differences.[8]

III

A constituent of atmosphere and weather alike is *air*. In the West it was Anaximenes who first pointed to the importance of air as a basic element: "As our soul, being air, holds us together, so do breath and air surround the whole universe."[9] Besides being a remarkable anticipation of the much more recent notion of the biosphere, this statement holds special interest for us in that it proposes air as an element *surrounding* the world as we know it—or so I construe "the whole universe." Taking note that *environ* means "around," the assertion of Anaximenes is literally environmental. He is claiming that air is the aboriginal sur-rounding element, that which is "round about" us, as we glibly say, not pausing to consider the deeper significance of something as pervasively around us as the air we breathe. We take in air with each breath, and there is always, except in circumstances of suffocation, air enough to breathe. It suffuses our lives, making life itself possible even though it is itself invisible. Hence Anaximenes can add this further thought: "Air is near to the incorporeal; and since we come into being by an efflux from this [element], it has to be both nonlimited and rich so that it never fails."[10] It is telling that human life outside the womb begins with "the first breath." This breath takes in air from the immediately surrounding space in which the newborn gasps for air. The paradox is that although the requisite air must be accessible in the limited space around the infant's highly vulnerable body, regarded as a whole air is nonlimited. All told, air per se has no precise limits, no exact borders, only open boundaries that allow it to be everywhere in the earth's atmosphere, and coextensive with it as a whole.[11]

The nonlimited, *to apeiron*, sometimes translated as "the unbounded," is everywhere. As Anaximander, a contemporary of Anaximenes, put it: "The Non-Limited is the original material of existing things; further, the source from which existing things derive their existence is also that to which they return at their destruction, according to necessity. . . . [The Non-Limited] is immortal and indestructible."[12] Air, then, is a nonlimited resource on which all living-breathing beings depend. This is not only an axiom of the natural philosophy of the earliest recorded thinkers in the West, but a profound peri-phenomenological truth. We live from the breathable air that surrounds us, which acts as an indispensable medium for the flourishing of life on earth—and its deficit incurs the suffering and demise of this life.

To the axiomatic assertions of Anaximenes and Anaximander that air is the nonlimited element, we need to add that air is also essential to the presentation of certain emotions, being their means of conveyance. This happens when we sense the presence of a certain emotion "in the air," that "hangs there," as we say. When we feel a "sense of impending doom"—as many have experienced during the coronavirus pandemic—it is as if the presence of this doom is suspended in the air, amassing over us as a doom-to-come.[13] On a lighter note, when we anticipate a celebration— say, a birthday or graduation—we experience an affirmative happiness hovering around us as we anticipate the event. This affect "floats in the air," borne up by an invisible medium that has all the characteristics of the air we breathe: lightness, luminosity, buoyancy, upward movement.[14]

Luce Irigaray, in *The Forgetting of Air in Martin Heidegger*, decries the obsession of Western thinkers with determinate presence, overlooking another whole dimension for which air is emblematic: that of "clearing" (*Lichtung*), a notion she borrows from Heidegger even as she claims that he fails to adequately allow for the factor of air, favoring earth (*Erde*) instead. In this he follows a basic proclivity on the part of Western think- ers to conceive of being as a "solid crust." But "philosophy dies—without air," for it needs the clearing of a field or open space "where air would still give itself."[15] Air is "diaphanous, translucent, transparent," and always "situated in a clearing." This clearing of and by air is even "the whole of our habitation as mortals." "Is there a dwelling more vast, more spacious, or even more generally peaceful than in air?" Irigaray asks. "The clearing of air is a clearing for appearing and disappearing, for presence and ab- sence." Despite this priority, air is all too easily overlooked: "This element, irreducibly constitutive of the whole, compels neither the faculty of per- ception nor that of knowledge to recognize it. Always there, it allows itself to be forgotten."[16] We can say much the same for emotions: those that are not clearly grounded in human subjectivity have allowed themselves to be forgotten. Those that are "up in the air," that "float above us"— coming from beyond, from a clearing not of our conscious devising—are those that have been most overlooked by philosophers in modern times. Determinate presence predominates in the modern subject's pursuit of knowable substance, so that the clearing which air provides for emotional presentation is passed over, its radicality unappreciated, with the result that "air remains the unthought resource of Being."[17]

We do not have to subscribe to Anaximenes's or Irigaray's insis- tent promotion of air to grasp the importance of the acrial dimension of emotional experience, beginning with the inherent emotionality of life-bestowing breathing and extending into such diverse phenomena as exuberant cloudscapes and turbulent seascapes, in all of which air is an essential medium, bringing us into various affective layouts when we are in their presence. In such cases emotions are *air-borne*, experientially if not literally. Here we are a long way from Scheler's insistence that emo- tions are borne by persons as the carriers (*Träger*) of value. The very air that persons inhale and exhale transports emotion into and out of them, and it does so as situated up and away from where they stand, drawing them into the atmosphere regarded as the Encompassing.[18] Air is the elemental basis of atmosphere, just as weather is an amalgam of air and atmosphere. Air, atmosphere, and weather form a virtual triumvirate of elemental presences that present affective force fields that manifest emotion around and above us. These fields *offer* emotions to us—emotions which we can acknowledge and incorporate into our lives, or else refuse. Nothing forces us to accept these emotions or act upon them; but they are *placed before us.*

IV

Here a skeptical reader might ask: Have I not been describing something closer to *mood* than emotion, especially if emotion is defined in terms of Massumi's formulation as "the capture of affect in the interiority of the subject"?[19] In contrast with emotion thus conceived, mood is more diffuse and generic, and is certainly not limited to the subject's interior life. Moods are both pervasive and suffusive. Consider how we utter without further reflection phrases like "the mood of the place was somber" or "the mood on election night was ebullient." We imply that the mood was not limited to isolated individuals, but was widely shared and experienced by virtually everyone present. This describes what I experienced at my local supermarket that Saturday in March 2020: a shared mood of collective uneasiness.

Heidegger points to features of mood that converge with what I have been describing as emotion beyond-the-subject, while giving to it an ontological twist. His basic definition of mood in *Being and Time* reads: "A mood assails us . . . It arises out of Being-in-the-world, as a way of such Being. . . . *The mood has already disclosed, in every case, Being-in-the-world as a whole, and makes it possible first of all to direct oneself towards something.* Having a mood is not related to the psychical in the first instance and is not itself an inner condition which then reaches forth in an enigmatical way and puts its mark on things and persons."[20] Moods involve a "primitive disclosure" in which "Dasein is brought before its own being as 'there.'"[21] Rather than turning us inward, they direct us to our being-in-the-world as sheer manifestation: "The pure 'that it is' shows itself, but the 'whence' and the 'whither' remain in darkness. . . . The Being of the 'there' is disclosed moodwise in its 'that-it-is' [*seinem Dass*]."[22] In other words, moods show Dasein in "its Being-delivered-over-to-[its] 'there.'"[23] In sum, a "mood brings Dasein before the that-it-is of its 'there,' which, as such, stares it in the face with the inexorability of an enigma."[24]

In short, moods take us out into the world, into its circumambience, its surrounding. They draw us there, and to this extent bring us out of the closed-in character of daily life. Here Heidegger converges with the overall path I have been seeking to forge in this book. He proceeds to add a special twist by asserting that moods also take us *before ourselves*: "In a state-of-mind [*Befindlichkeit*] Dasein is *always brought before itself*, and has always found itself, not in the sense of coming across itself by perceiving itself, but in the sense of finding itself in the mood that it has."[25] Note that here Heidegger is not pointing to the self of introspection, the "inner self," but to *a self that is located in the very mood it experiences*. This amounts to what we can call *a self-outside-itself*—outside itself in its own mood. This self-discovery is said to be "*prior* to all cognition and volition, and *beyond* their range of disclosure."[26] The self at stake here is no ego or inner psyche, it is another kind or sense of self: the self as self-transcending. Such a self is not just subject to moods but comes to know itself in them.

For the most part, human beings engage in "thrownness" (*Geworfenheit*)—that is, they submit "to that world which is already disclosed with its own Being; [we have here] the existential kind of being in which Dasein constantly surrenders itself to the 'world' and lets the 'world' 'matter' to it *in such a way that Dasein evades its very self* [i.e., in being thrown]."[27] Notice this last twist. Our thrownness amounts to losing our authentic self—our "very self" that can be found in moods that are not preoccupied with the ready-to-hand or present-to-hand entities that divert us in thrownness. The exit from thrownness that mood offers is important and even essential to identifying and affirming our authentic self. This is not to say, however, that moods always deliver such a self: at best, they offer a temporary reprieve from the fallenness of everyday immersion in the world. But they do offer something special: the prospect of discovering a self outside our quotidian self, a self-beyond-the self. This is to continue the thesis of outsideness, now in relation to selfhood itself.[28]

However much he may have overlooked the significance of air, Heidegger in *Being and Time* is an important ally. If we set aside his obsession with an authentic self, much of what he says about mood is true of emotion in the basic direction I am pursuing here: above all, that emotion is disclosive of the surrounding world, whether this is the interpersonal world or the larger atmospheric world. Heidegger adds, moreover, that an important part of what is disclosed in mood is a self we could not otherwise reach. If this is true, then we need not cordon off emotion from mood. Rather, mood must be regarded as a species of emotion that is as much about the self as about the surrounding world. Such a self is neither the restricted self of early modernity nor Freud's unconscious self, but an expansive self that finds its outer reaches in mood rather than in cogitation on sensory givens or in the analysis of dreams or neurotic symptoms. In this way, we avoid the entrapment of thinkers like Descartes or Seneca and move directly to a life-world (*Lebenswelt* in Husserl's term) that includes an ampliative self along with environing places, air, and atmosphere. Mood, and emotion more generally, allow us to gain access to realms of experience that are not otherwise accessible. They open us up, they open us out.[29]

V

We now move to an essential contribution by Eugene T. Gendlin, the eminent philosophical psychologist, and a close reader of Heidegger who draws from the German thinker's treatment of mood in proposing a schema that is specifically environmental.[30] He offers an expansion not of the self as such but an *expansion into the environment*. Especially important for our purposes here is his claim: "The environment is directly involved when we act. But the environment should not be considered *external*. It is not in the here-there space of perception."[31] Gendlin distinguishes environment #1, in which body and environment are separate entities, from environment #2, in which the body "implies" the environment while the latter, in turn, is said to "occur-into" bodily processes. This two-way interaction is a matter of "body-environment interaction" in which "the body lives *directly* in each of our situations."[32] This leads to Gendlin's basic claim that "we *are* interactions with the environment—other people, the world, the universe—and we can sense ourselves to be just such an interaction." In short, "we are environmental interaction in the universe."[33]

Certain emotional states bear out this radical environmental interactionism quite compellingly. We already had a presentiment of this when considering Kant on the sublime: the sublime, we concluded, is located just as much if not more in the landscape by which I am moved as it is in myself as its witness. To this we can now add the phenomenon of emotional contagion as discussed by Le Bon and Scheler. In such contagion there is an emotional transmission that is multiply located, not just in myself but in those around me (much as I experienced at the Women's March and the African American Day Parade). This kind of "sociality of affect" obtains not only in crowds but also in more intimate settings. Concerning all such instances we can say, in the light of Gendlin's schema, that we *are* the very interactions that qualify the emotionality as environmental, as pertaining not just to you or me but *to us*, and pertaining more radically still to the entire setting that includes us and others who are present in it. This setting is the affective environment in which we are ensconced and by which we are surrounded in what Heidegger calls "the aroundness of the environment" (*das Umhafte der Umwelt*).[34] Environment understood as what includes and surrounds us thus characterizes our emotional lives far more extensively than we realize when we consider ourselves as separate individuals—and certainly far more so than early modern accounts of emotion permit or envision.

If we allow with Gendlin that we *are* our environment in a meaningful sense, this holds true for our emotional lives, which concern not only the human subject and the way this subject inhabits its world, but also the ways this subject, as emotional, *is its world*. This radical thesis goes beyond any relational model; it is still more radical than is suggested in Gendlin's own language of "interaction." In this spirit, we shall have to go beyond interpersonal models of emotion as proposed by Merleau-Ponty, Scheler, Ahmed, Stern, Le Bon, and Freud toward a radically *fusionist* model. Such a model maintains that in being emotional, the way we are merged with our surroundings, and indeed melded with them—and they with us—becomes patent. Emotions not only take us into encompassing environments, nor do they merely relate us with them, *they are themselves environments*, allowing us to *be there* in ontologically unique ways. At stake here is more than emotion's *pervasion* of the life-world or of an expanded self in moods; it is a matter of the life-world existing *as emotional*. In being emotional myself, I become affectively co-constituted with this world and vice versa—even if differences remain in the characterization of each in relation to the other.

One of these differences is the role of the body in this emerging paradigm. The body is the *enactor* of the co-constitution of emotion and environment. This is not a matter of the physiological body—the medical body—but of the *lived* body. This body is for Gendlin not only a facilitator of the emotion–environment dyad by way of skillful actions and appropriate habits (as stressed by Merleau-Ponty), but the bearer of meaning, of "felt sense," in Gendlin's preferred term for the way the body is a uniquely perceptive-expressive agent. The body provides an anchor of sorts, not merely because it is physical but because of the agential powers by which it enacts multiple projects in the world. Some of these projects are emotions, which can be said to *pass through* the body-subject rather than being locatable in it (e.g., in the heart or brain). Although Gendlin rarely singles out emotion as such for discussion, it follows from his conception of the lived body that integral to being emotional is being bodily-expressive: *the body bears emotionality out into the world*. The body is not just the intermediary between emotion and environment, but the very agent enacting their convergence.

CHAPTER 11

I propose that we accept Gendlin's and Merleau-Ponty's emphasis on the lived body while adding, in light of Gendlin's notion of environment #2, that emotionality as it is lived bodily qualifies the life-world as we experience it. The lived body itself is the pre-personal subjective pole of this world. As in the case of emotion, the body needs to be de-subjectified. Though it is the enactive agent of the worldifying subject, it is not itself subjective. We should think of the body in radically de-subjectified terms, as in this telling statement of Massumi: "The body is that region of in-mixing from which subjectivity emerges. It is the coming together of the world, for experience, in a here-and-now prior to any possibility of assigning categories like subject or object."[35]

We can say much the same of emotion: it is something pre-objective and pre-subjective—even if we are continually tempted to trace it back to physical states and psychic proclivities in a quasi-explanatory maneuver. The path of explanation takes us quickly to causation, however, and thus to the endogenous approach we first encountered in Descartes, and still encounter today in neurological theories of emotion. Instead, we should think of emotion as a concentrated expression of the surrounding world at a given moment, its condensation into gestures and affective states that we then label as "fury," "delight," "wonder," and so on. These are conventional linguistic tags for what we are experiencing here and now in an affective space that should be designated as environmental rather than personal. Emotions are primarily situated in the space around us, in our environs, rather than in us. It is the interaction with this environment that Gendlin declares to *be* ourselves, and (I insist on adding) *ourselves as emotional*: as experiencing emotions that stem from the placescapes around us. Gendlin's radical conception of environment #2 thus provides a schema for understanding how and where emotions emerge and play out—and indeed, for understanding where we ourselves emerge and play out the course of our lives on earth. As emotional beings, we exist on the far side of anything merely private or subjective; as well as on the near side of what surrounds us—so near that we merge with it. Not only do we exist *in* environments, we *are* our environments, and our environments *are* us bodily and emotionally.

VI

The foregoing reflections lead to six final points of clarification.

1. The term *environment* is sufficiently encompassing to include much if not all that this chapter has addressed in terms of "world," "life-

world," "atmosphere," "weather," "air," "surroundings," "peripheries," and the like, all of which can be said to be *concretions*, individuated singularizations of environment construed as an open genus of many affiliated yet differentially specified spheres, each yielding its own distinctive kind of experience, including emotional experience.

2. Environment in the enriched sense formulated by Gendlin, and implicit in Heidegger and Merleau-Ponty, is not a matter of space but of *place*. For environment is not just an extended Cartesian space, but a congeries of interrelated particular places. We return here to what was first discussed in part 1 as *places-of-presentation*, a term that implies the real possibility of location in multiple places; the emotion of the sublime, for instance, can emerge in the presence of quite different landscapes or seascapes. There are no wholly isolated places, moreover; each place is contiguous with proximal places and is related, directly or indirectly, to further, more distant places. Each such place is capable of *bearing emotion out*: situating it outside the very subjects who take it in.

3. The adverb "outside," on which I have laid such stress, is not an independent variable, a free-floating signifier. Not only is the "inside" always situated within places of greater extent (the heart inside the body, a specific psychical state in the greater psyche), but such places themselves give out onto a more capacious arena. My bodily state registers and adapts to the weather on any given day, a weather event that itself belongs to a larger weather pattern, which is in turn a feature of the earth's biosphere. A similar pattern of ever more inclusive places holds for what I have been calling "atmosphere." This means that there is no definitive or final container for physical or emotional phenomena. Much as the two hawks in Ojai were engaging in a flight pattern that reflected the air currents of the valley below, so our emotions trace out identifiable shapes and volumes that belong to ongoing, ever-more-encompassing configurations of our emotional life. Our emotional predispositions and tendencies are an integral part of what we call our "character," a relatively stable but not permanent disposition. But this is only a starting point in the full outreach of emotions, an outreach that extends far beyond the delimited perimeter of human character regarded as something reliable and resilient. To claim that emotions have their proper place outside the human subject, however, is not to say that they have such a place in a determinate location somewhere else. It is to say that they belong to certain capacious and often quite indeterminate locational volumes—places from which they present themselves on specific occasions. Just as a contemporary social theorist can talk of "place-bearing" common spaces, so we can talk of *emotion-bearing places*.[36]

4. Gendlin's environment #2 can be considered the broadest basis

of affective transmission. It is the overall scene of transmitted emotion, the polymorphic placialized space of such transmission. Emotions are transmitted *by* and *through* the surrounding environment regarded as encircling us while actively including us as integral components of its scope, its being—even as it is itself included in our experience as its penumbral edge. The dense web of emotional life is both subtended and encompassed by this environment, which is continuous with our existence on earth. As Oele insists, this life and the environment that sustains it are co-affective and are mediated by our body, including our skin, which is not only sensitive but connects us with whole worlds of experience: *placeworlds*, as I prefer to call them.

5. Beyond the encompassing presence of the environment, there is an entire series of edge-phenomena that qualify the life of the emotions. The many places that emotions occupy in the environment have their own characteristic edges that call for discernment and recognition. Emotions regarded as environmental edge-phenomena first emerge in initial arenas and then populate subsequent zones until they fade away—with many vicissitudes along the way. Emotions, as I have insisted, themselves possess recognizable edges. We are tempted to speak of outrage as having a "sharp edge," of joy as exhibiting an "expansive edge." These are not just casual metaphors but ways of expressing how emotions, arising from the environments that surround us, have their own characteristic edges by which they are experienced as well as classified, even as they situate themselves in settings that possess their own placial edges. Emotions, we may conclude, both bear and produce edges: a theme to which we will return in the epilogue.

6. Emotions may have edges but they are not thinglike; as I have emphasized earlier, they are *events.* Whitehead was already clear about this: emotions, or in his vocabulary "feelings," are regarded as the leading phase of what he called "actual occasions"—his technical term for what we ordinarily designate as "events." Actual occasions are happenings, that is to say, dynamic movements of experience as it takes its own course. They are not just movements in space and time but becomings of entire organisms, including their emotional sensibilities regarded not as features of a closely held subjectivity, but as reflecting what they take in from the near and far environments which surround them and with which they are continuous, and finally at one.

***

Emotions are not only events, they are *impersonal* events. I borrow the word "impersonal" from John Dewey's *Art as Experience*: "The resultant emotion is 'impersonal' because it is attached not to personal fortune but to the object to the construction of which the self has surrendered itself in devotion. Appreciation [of art] is equally impersonal in its emotional quality because it also involves construction and organization of objective energies."[37] What Dewey calls "objective energies" coheres with Gendlin's sense of the surrounding environment in which human beings find themselves enlivened by what lies all around them and with which they merge, as well as with Oele's notion of an e-co-affectivity that is immanent to this same encompassing environment. For Dewey, the term "objective" does not signify what science shows by empirical studies or what it models by theoretical constructs; rather, it refers to what cannot be reduced to the machinations of human subjectivity but comes in upon such subjectivity from outside the orbit of solely "personal" selves. This is to draw tacitly on the etymological root of the word "objective"; that is, "thrown before" or presented (e.g., to mind or thought or body). Dewey adds that "emotion in its ordinary sense is something called out by objects, physical and personal; it is a response to an objective situation . . . [It] is an indication of intimate participation, in a more or less excited way, in some scene of nature or life; it is, so to speak, an attitude or disposition which is a function of objective things."[38]

Dewey's claims for emotional objectivity converge closely with what I have been maintaining in this final chapter: that the "objectivity" of emotion is inherent in the settings provided by atmosphere, air, weather, and more generally the environment. For it is in these settings that we experience emotions that are *not our own*. They devolve from various place-worlds, inhabiting and animating them, and are transmitted to our bodies as receptive to them, taking them in rather than dishing them out. They ingress into our lives from these worlds rather than stemming from the inner realm of our subjective being. Whatever their contingent rooting in previous and ongoing experience, they come to us already turned inside *out*.

Epilogue

Outwardizing Emotion

> The edge has a quality of motion that only unnamed emotion
> can learn from.
> —George Quasha, "Dangling Fructifiers"

The primary stake of this book is unseating the sovereign emotional subject, the self-directed egological subject who claims that emotions belong to *me*, that *they are mine* to have in the first place and mine to determine henceforth. It is as if this subject claimed a right to be in possession of whatever feelings and emotions occur in it; and if not to be their literal origin, then to take them over and redirect them, to master them from here on out, even if their advent was not willed to begin with. If I discover I cannot do this by myself with the aid of self-disciplinary or meditative practices, then I can seek therapeutic assistance with the aim of gaining better control of my emotional life. The premise is that the central human subject is autonomous and self-determining, and that anything that inhibits its free action should be eliminated or at least reduced in its force. This reflects a preoccupation with "negative freedom," in Isaiah Berlin's apposite term: freedom *from* whatever threatens to hinder or overpower me, including very strong emotions that lead me astray, blocking the way to clearly envisioned aims and concrete plans for efficient action.

I

Proceeding on these assumptions, having a "perfect emotional storm" is taken as an epitome of unfreedom—something we should strive to preclude or get over so as to return to having a firm grip on oneself, being the "master" of one's immediate destiny. Plato's recourse to "reason" (*nous*) and Seneca's invocation of "deliberation" are telling signs of efforts to reinforce the virtue and value of reclaiming a central self as the seat of a controlled emotional life: a self that flourishes from disciplined practices in which affectivity is not allowed to "get the better of me," and where what is for the best is accomplished by my powers of self-control. Others, notably Descartes, sought to give a physiological basis to central command centers to be found in the brain and heart as subserved by animal spirits. In such a model, not only does my egological self affirm my sovereignty, but I am assured of the practical bodily means of putting such sovereignty into practice thanks to an endogenously generated system of causal powers. In this way, a life that does not allow itself to get out of control emotionally becomes viable, for when all is said and done my emotions *are mine*; I *possess* them, so that I should be able to direct them as I wish.

But if instead we affirm that emotions are *not* the exclusive property of the self-controlling subject, we can proceed very differently by asking ourselves: what if they have a life of their own, a life that I as a conscious subject cannot simply "control"? And what if I myself can realize a certain positive freedom—a freedom *to* (do X) that is not a disguised form of freedom *from* (being overwhelmed by Y)—by acknowledging this life as having an integrity and value of its own? What if I recognize emotions neither as my minions nor as dominating me, but as liberating forces that can augment and enhance my own free movement in the course of my life? If something like this is possible, as Spinoza foresaw, then I gain rather than lose by affiliating myself with emotion: I gain outreach into a wider world where my not being in full control does not mean that all is lost. Rather, I am literally *self-educated*, drawn out of myself (*e-ducare*) into experiential reaches I could not otherwise attain. My own sense of self is extended by becoming open to the extrasubjective regionality of emotion. I become more *em-pathic* in a sense that exceeds mere sympathy with others' suffering; I *feel into* the emotionality of other people, animals, plants, and the earth itself. In rejoining them, I *go out of myself*, my putatively sovereign inner self, and enter into the *periphanous* dimensions of experience as configured by its outer emotional edges.

This is to honor and learn not from what is controlled by an autonomous central self, but rather from what draws me out of myself. This self—*my* self—remains an indispensable element of my experience as it becomes aware of certain emotions, registering and remembering them. But this self is far more limited in its significance than modern egological models of the human person allow or admit. It is a way station within the larger circuit of an ecologically sensitive emotionality that far exceeds the scope of any private self. Once more, this is not to deny that many emotional states are experienced from within, at the level of what I have designated as "feeling." Feelings issue from and circulate around myself as a psychophysical subject; they cluster and congregate there, as if magnetized to this subject. But there are other affective states that exhibit the emotional equivalent of what was traditionally called "intromission" in the case of vision: that is, when light rays *reach us from without*. Thanks to their intromissive character, such states can be said to possess a *reversed emotional directionality*—proceeding not from within our unique subjectivity but from outside, directed at our receptive surfaces.

Emotions embody a distinctive form of *operative intentionality*, a concept that has been invoked at several key moments in this book. I take such intentionality to imply that our emotions, considered in their propulsive dynamics, are congeneric with what surrounds us—namely, an *affective environment* regarded as a congeries of places. In Merleau-Ponty's words, operative intentionality is "the intentionality that establishes the natural and pre-predicative unity of the world and of our life, the intentionality that appears in our desires, our evaluations, and our landscape more clearly than it does in objective knowledge."[1] Especially striking in this statement is the mention of "desires" in close conjunction with "landscape," which I take to be equivalent to the affective field that surrounds the subject on all sides and from which specific emotions proceed (and into which they recede). This landscape, being far more than a mere background, is an active presence in its own right, manifesting attractive and repulsive qualities of its own. In our ongoing emotional lives, we *operate within this landscape*, coming and going there in multiple ways. Switching metaphors, it is as if our emotions reach us from an immense seascape across which we surf with more or less aplomb—sometimes upright on our surfboard, sometimes sinking under the waves, and sometimes clambering to get back on the board.[2]

Taking this route, autonomy gives way to outright and explicit *heteronomy*, literally 'law of the other'. The situation is out of our conscious control, but far from this being something regrettable, it opens up new levels of experience and insight—expanding subjectivity rather than constricting it, and effecting a radical decentralization of the conscious self. Understood in their larger reaches, emotions effect a displacement of the psychophysical and personal subject, taking this subject *elsewhere*—an elsewhere where it can become itself precisely by leaving itself and becoming other than itself—thus making it *more than itself*. This is what happens when we turn emotion inside out, venturing out from the sequestered human subject, being with others of many kinds and types, including other species as well as inanimate things: out into the wider world of all that surrounds us periphanously, out into the myriad affective interfaces of environing place-worlds with their pervasive atmospheres.

II

Here we head toward a regional topography of emotionality, finding ways
in which emotions can be discerned as rhizomatic as well as multilocular.[3]
I have been arguing that emotions are situated around, above, below,
across, under, and in other directionalities that open outside the subject,
sometimes shared with others, at other times unreciprocated, arising on
their own ("I don't know where this sudden sadness came from"). If so,
emotions are not only multiply located but *multidirectionally oriented,* as
in the case of a rhizome, with their operative intentionality propelling
numerous differential vectors. They often head in different directions,
not only one at a time but sometimes several at once, as when I have
"mixed emotions" regarding a person or circumstance, with various
emotions folding in upon one another. My emotional intentionality is
hybridized in ways I cannot predict, much less control. When I do attempt
to control demanding or disconcerting emotions, I find this difficult to
accomplish, given that emotions *have their own force* and are liable to the
incursions in view of unplanned and conflicting "emotional outbursts" as
well as many less dramatic diversions. Such an effort at control can only
be approximated at best, and it is not clear in any case that this should be
our primary aim.[4]

What then should be the main goal in our affective life? It is to be
receptive to what emotions tell us, paying special attention to how and
where they appear, and oftentimes just when as well. This means looking
out for them as they emerge in interpersonal, group, and environmental
settings. For we have more to learn by attending to what they have to say
in and from these settings than by looking within ourselves. When we do
grasp their message, we liberate ourselves from the *huis clos,* the closed
doors of introspection that signify "no exit." Emotions teach us how to
exit from ourselves—from our abjectly driven or distracted lives—so as to
enter a domain of increased insight as we navigate the open seas of unan-
chored affect. In those seas, we may not know exactly where we are going;
but we do have a felt sense that we are going somewhere worth exploring.

However ambiguous or incoherent they often are, emotions point
the way to a distinctively *affective liberation,* fugitive as this may be on a
given occasion and however obliquely we may try to realize it. Instead
of evading or regretting emotions—or denying them in bad faith—we
must trust them to take us somewhere other than where we would have
gone without them: their energy and intelligence come forward to direct us otherwise than were we to follow custom, common sense, regret,
or rigid reason. They take us out of ourselves—out of our self-imposed

private circuits—into a more encompassing whole that is the place-world in which we reside, connecting and reconnecting with this world in new and surprising ways. They give us unmatched insight into where we are going as well as where we are coming from. They take us there—*out there*—instead of leaving us only *in here*. This is a gain of enhanced life we cannot afford to forgo, however much we may be tempted to flee a dark and difficult emotional episode.

I am here underscoring the dynamism that is peculiar to emotion, which has its *own élan*, its own force, its own propulsion. Such emotional dynamism is akin to what Coleridge called "primary imagination" in his effort to distinguish spontaneous creativity from what is planned or programmed in constrictive ways. This is a creativity that comes from somewhere other than the conscious or deliberate intentionality of the human subject. Similarly, ongoing experience exhibits a primary emotionality whose source is not in the human subject but somewhere else: often between subjects but also beyond them.[5] This is not to assert that emotions possess fixed or proper places outside the subject: determinate locales that serve to anchor them. Part of the *genius loci* of emotions is that their *loci*—their locales—are radically fluid. This is reflected in the way we speak of the "explosiveness" of certain emotions, alluding to how they erupt spontaneously, seeming to come from *any which where*. By speaking of a regional topography of emotion, I point to a circumstance in which emotions may assume varying locations within an open-ended array of heterogeneous locales, rather than being confined to the sort of determinate and delimited positions that Coleridge designated as "fixities and definites." Such an informal mapping *topofies* the fate of emotions outside the subject, invoking localizations from which emotions emerge and situate themselves in ever-transforming dynamic displays.

The fascination and frustration of writing about emotion—an effort at once elusive and alluring—stems in large part from having to confront a shifting scene of heterogeneously located *topoi* of our ever-mutating emotional lives. We seek to pin down their places-of-origin and their flight patterns precisely because we often do not know just where certain emotions are coming from, much less where they are leading us. Many who have written on emotion have overcompensated by claiming privileged and abiding sources for the emotions that course through our lives, whether these sources are regarded as "animal spirits," the physiological or metaphoric heart, or certain sectors of the brain. Plato himself knew better than this: in speaking of *thumos*, the phenomenological "chest" where courage resides, he in effect refused such pinpointing and valorized an entire region of the lived body—a region that is the anatomical analogue to what he designated as *chora* or "open space" rather than a strict *topos* or discrete site. It is no wonder that Aristotle, suspicious of the indefiniteness of *chora*, preferred to speak of *topos*, a proper place that is defined in terms of strict enclosure.[6] For many emotions, however, there can only be *im-proper places*, that is to say, momentary locales in open-boundaried regions that are loose assemblages of ever-changing placements of these same emotions. Where exactly was the exuberance I experienced at Jalama Beach? It was not in any one spot but in the whole encompassing scene as witnessed from its edge. Punctuated by sparkling sea waves, intrepid wind surfers, and colorful free-flying sails, the exuberance was at once everywhere and nowhere: everywhere overall and nowhere in particular.

III

There is no emotional Heaven from which the emotions we experience descend; rather, we encounter the extraversion of emotion in the larger environment or placescape of which we are part. The densely interwoven texture of such an encompassing scene as I experienced at Jalama Beach folded into the receptive mass of my experiencing body. The edges of this scene were interwoven with the edges of my jubilant emotionality. The result was an edge-to-edge event—the edges of what I perceived intercalating with the edges of my exuberance. Not just in extraordinary situations, however, but in everyday life we live in the con-texture that such convergent and divergent edges co-create. There we live outside ourselves, even if we are often tempted to assume that we live inside the inner world of our own self-delimited domain of personal feelings and thoughts and memories. The periphenomenological truth is that as emotional beings we live beyond this inner world—a beyond that is patterned and transmitted by the moving contours of our emotions as they play in and out of the shifting scenarios of daily life.

A given emotional experience is *self-eclipsing*, bringing us to the edge of another emotion, another set of thoughts, a particular action, or a period of comparative quiescence that lies on the other side of this experience. At stake here are what I call "active edges," edges that move beyond themselves, out of themselves.[7] There certainly are instances in which we just "stew in our emotional juices," caught up in them, edges and all—when we are fully engrossed in the experiencing of a given emotion itself. This occurs when emotion is self-invested, as when my anger flares and preoccupies me. What is striking is how, after such moments of self-investment, we often find ourselves moving to the other side of the emotion we have just experienced and expressed. This is not only a matter of pausing and taking stock—a moment of "deliberation" in Seneca's sense—but of *moving to the other side of the emotion itself*, its downward slope as it were: a phasing down that follows upon the emotion's initial front-loading or gearing up. This is often experienced as a diminution of the emotional force we experienced earlier. At the same time, an emotion can itself come to an abrupt halt, with its outer edge suddenly intervening, bringing closure. The temporal destinies of emotions are highly diverse.

This is not just a matter of the displacement or sublimation of psychical energies, as Freud might claim. Energetic models that claim scientific validity often posit a continuity of flow that is false or inadequate to the emotional disruptions, foreclosures, and interruptions that frequently figure in human experience. An emotion's waning can give way to very different emotions with their own distinctive contours. Even if repetitions of certain characteristic edges of emotions we have undergone seem to occur, these are never exactly the same, since the circumstances and settings as well as the felt tenor of the emotionality will have changed.

IV

I have given the foregoing condensed description of the course of emotional experience in order to indicate that wherever and however we receive an emotion—whether from being in the company of others or from an encompassing atmosphere—there is an aftermath that has its own twists and turns. It is not a matter of passively receiving prefabricated affects and emotions in whole cloth but of a situation that gives rise to an entire congeries of events, each with its own distinctive pattern and each integral to the emotionality of the unfolding circumstance. At every stage of this sequel, edges are at stake: affective edges that spell out the history of a given emotion or set of associated emotions. In the unfolding of this history, edges are everywhere evident. They act to prefigure, configure, and close out this history, endowing it with its unique profile.

We encounter here the temporal dimensionality of emotional life—its unfolding in time in the wake of its first emerging in the place-presentations of its initial reception. In this book I have emphasized the neglected importance of this latter source; but the placial origins of emotion are interwoven with their durational spread, which allows emotions to have distinctive trajectories over time and in history. In the end, emotions as *events* are composed of both placial and temporal parameters, each interwoven with the other in ongoing affective life.

* * *

"Hegel said that philosophy consists in turning the world inside out. Let us say rather that this world is here and now inside out."[8] This statement of Henry Corbin captures the gist of what I have been maintaining about emotionality. Emotions are not only shared with others but situated beyond this very sharing; they are not only in the radical underside of the unconscious, but also in the alongside of members of crowds who surround us and carry us with them in the solidarity of interembodiment. They arise in a field of e-co-affectivity, an encompassing edge-world that constitutes the placial-temporal environment in which we are always already immersed. Living beyond the privatism of personal emotionality, we are engaged in a circumambience in which emotions show themselves to us outright: here indeed the world comes to us as already inside out. For it is outside ourselves that we *find emotion out*.

Gerhard Richter (German, 1932–), *Birkenau (937-2)*, 2014. Oil on canvas, 260 × 200 cm. Copyright © Gerhard Richter. Gerhard-Richter-Kunststiftung, Cologne.

Appendix

Art and Affect in the Wake of the Holocaust

> My paintings aren't about art issues. They're about feeling that comes to me from the outside, from landscape. . . . I get feelings from the outside.
> —Joan Mitchell

The two paintings I shall discuss here could not be more different in what they present to the naked eye—Gerhard Richter's being entirely abstract, Anselm Kiefer's ostensibly representational—but they are united not only by their common testament to the horrors of the Holocaust but by their invitation to viewers to enter into an emotional engagement with these artworks regarded as deferred and displaced witnesses to those horrors. They speak to viewers—that is, to *us*—by their unmistakable allusion to a deeply tragic moment in world history, inviting us to recognize more fully how destructive and disastrous this moment was for Jews, Roma, homosexuals, and the mentally and physically disabled. In short, they draw us as second-order witnesses into an affective attunement with the emotions they appresent thanks to the material implications which such paintings enact.[1]

I

Gerhard Richter's recent series of paintings titled *Birkenau* bears the name of the major death camp facility at Auschwitz. This title refers directly to the gas chambers where more than one million Jews were murdered in the last four years of the Second World War. Auschwitz-Birkenau was where the emerging fascism of the 1920s and 1930s came to its most gruesome and tragic expression—as well as being integral to Hitler's ambitions as the commander of the Third Reich. As an integral part of what he and his generals labeled as the Final Solution, what happened at Birkenau can only be described as apocalyptic.[2] Richter's series of paintings, which are altogether abstract, contain no images of prisoners or the gas chambers in which they perished. Here I single out just one of these works. Despite being unreadable as anything recognizable, the harsh blacks and grays in *Birkenau* are suggestive of tragic events that cast a pall from which there is no evident exit. It is almost as if this is a view from inside a gas chamber that has no egress. The interspersed white areas offer no real relief but only serve to heighten the sense of foreboding in the painting as a whole. The intense red (fading into pink) in the middle of the painting, though quite abstract, suggests blood smeared onto the painting. None of this invokes emotion in any easily identifiable way. But a comment at the bottom of the *New Yorker* page on which I first saw this painting reads: "Richter's series 'Birkenau,' from 2014, exposes a thread of sorrow and guilt."[3] What can this mean? What kind of thread is this?

Sorrow and guilt (and, I would suggest, sadness, sense of loss, and despair) are certainly not represented as such here, much less named by the artist, who chooses a title that designates an infamous but integral part of the Final Solution. Yet something emotional is somehow present in this painting. How so? How is such a painting *emotional* even if it does not depict given emotions as such, and certainly not in any readily detectable way (e.g., by showing human figures that are evincing identifiable emotions)?

I would suggest that *material implication* is at stake in this circumstance—employing this term not in a logical but an apperceptual sense: as allowing something to be seen spontaneously without regard to issues of representation. Whatever emotion is presented here is conveyed by the materiality of the paint—its perceived color, the way it is laid onto the canvas with decisive if irregular brushstrokes, the pattern made by the various parts of the painting. None of these elements taken by itself alone conveys sadness or the other emotions I have named; rather, it is their conjoint presence in the very materiality of the paint that suggests any and all such emotions: this is the "thread of sorrow and guilt" to which the *New Yorker* caption refers and which composes the fabric of the painting as a whole. The felt heaviness of sadness, for instance, is materialized by the precarious conjunction of the shadowy shapes in Richter's painting— shapes that together compose an emblematic image of incarceration in a congeries of cell-like modules from which there will be no release short of death. Despair comes across as a hopelessness exuded by a painting that offers no release, no promise, no future. Unlike a landscape with open horizons, this painting closes itself down at its edges, both internal and external: nothing further is adumbrated beyond what we are allowed to see—and *that* is bare and bleak. Furthermore, a poignant sense of loss is conveyed by the very fact that no human figure is so much as glimpsed in this painting. It is as if the brusque layering of paint acts to eliminate human presence, "paints it out"—in grim parallel with the incineration of corpses at Birkenau. This same insistent layering at once obscures whatever might lie beneath it and yet intimates that something foreboding is coming forward from below: a below that is adumbrated by the black areas of the work.

Not only is there *no one* present in this painting: *nothing* is there. Any hint at living presence is absent; everything has died away. All that is left are traces in the guise of brushstrokes—traces of we know not what exactly, but which we somehow suspect, given the title, might be the remnants of burned corpses. The layering of these traces suggests descent—a movement down and back into a somber inferno: into the Circles of Hell. The more we think in this darkening direction, the more we can imagine the black and gray areas of the painting to be tantamount to human ashes mixed in with oil paint. All this happens in and through the paint's very materiality—which provides not only a visual spectacle but actively solicits our touch, inviting us to reach out and stroke the shadowy surface with our phantom fingers. But to literally touch anything related to an event as hellish as Birkenau is not something many would ever want to do literally: *noli me tangere.*

The sadness and the sorrow, along with a sense of loss and felt despair occasioned by perceiving this painting, are not explicitly announced or signified as such. They are materially *implied* in the various ways I have just suggested and doubtless in other ways as well. This means that they are *suspended before us* as viewers of this painting: suspended as folded into it (as *im-plied* literally means). They are also implicitly *heard*: as the visual equivalents of a *missa solemnis*; a literal "black mass" as it were. "Sadness" is not presented as such but is instead ap-presented: it is presented *to* us as a spectacle of death in paint. How can we not feel sad when we try to face up to the import of such a painting? And how can we not also experience a sense of loss? (I say *sense of* loss rather than literal loss, for the literal loss is incalculable, given that the number of corpses burned in the ovens at Birkenau alone was at least in the high hundreds of thousands.) And certainly despair—a word that means "loss of hope"—is experienced in the very bleakness of the work itself: black on black, dark on dark, death on death. There is no way away from death as conveyed here in full affective presence.

The four-fold emotionality I have just singled out (sadness, sorrow, sense of loss, despair)—and there are doubtless other folds, other threads, other edges as experienced by different viewers—is not located *in us* but is held *before us* in the painting we see reproduced here. This painting may elicit *feelings* of sadness and sorrow, of a sense of loss and despair in us; but the depth of the corresponding emotions stems from the painting's densely interwoven material implications and, back behind these, the sinister history of what happened at Birkenau. All such emotions reach us from an elsewhere: an infernal scene we never ourselves witnessed. As set before us in this artwork, they reach us as sheer affects—where *affect* signifies directly impinging and darkly charged incursions on our sensibility, even if not yet occurring as fully articulated emotions (which would come from reflection on the deeper import of these affects).

Precisely because today's viewers were not present at Birkenau—there are very few survivors of the death camps still alive now—we can consider Richter's painting to be a *stand-in witness* of what happened there. Invoking Robert Harvey's suggestive concept, it can be considered a *témoin d'artifice*—a "prosthetic witness"—of an event that Richter himself never witnessed even if he came to learn about it while still very young.[4] For the painter as for us as its viewers—displaced as we are from the Dantesque tragedy itself—the painting stands in as testimony to the horror of the Holocaust that was (in Adorno's telling phrase) "worse than death." In the absence of any direct witnessing, the painting offers testimony to what happened at Birkenau—and it does so by way of the implications that inhere in its painted surface. This happens not by claiming a stance of literal perception (as with a photograph of the ovens), or even by means of a vivid imagination of what went on there, but thanks to the way that the material shapes in the painting itself serve to act as indirect witnesses *in their very inarticulate but affective force*.[5]

This affective force—incited by the somber reality of *Birkenau*—is what is generated from confronting such horror: not in the first person but by way of an artwork that stands in proxy to scenes of unspeakable suffering. In such lateral witnessing, Richter's painting acts as the prosthesis (literally, "positing before") that conveys to us such affectivity by way of material implication. Artificial as it is, it conveys to us the "objective energies" (Dewey) of raw emotions that are a felt response to what happened at Birkenau. This painting is a substitute for actual witnessing, yet it remains effective as transmitting the felt emotionality of this abysmal situation—transmitting it to our felt insides from the surface of the painting: from its outside, from the affective presence of its very surface. In Joan Mitchell's words, "[it's] about feeling that comes to [us] from the outside."[6] Such feeling comes from outside us as viewers thanks to the fact that the painting serves as an artifact of prosthetic witnessing. Indirect as its trajectory is, this emotionality is brought before us, condensed and intensified, in the single haunting image that *Birkenau* thrusts upon us.

II

Anselm Kiefer, another German artist who grew up in the shadow of the Holocaust, is the painter of *Bohemia Lies by the Sea*, now on display at the Metropolitan Museum in New York. This is a very different work, beginning with the fact that it presents us with a recognizable countryside scene. Rather than the intense abstraction of *Birkenau*, now we have arrayed before us an open field festooned with innumerable poppies, a flower that signifies springtime (but having more complex connotations as well, given its role in the production of opioids). At first glance, we might think that we are seeing an expansive scene of hope and possibility: the very opposite of sadness and despair. But a closer look reveals that something else is happening here, as is suggested in the title of the painting: *Bohemia Lies by the Sea*. In geographic reality, Bohemia (an ancient region of eastern Europe) does *not* lie by the sea—quite to the contrary. This alerts us that something on the strange side is being presented here, as we also discern when we imagine the soil from which the poppies spring. In its dark density and precisely as largely hidden, this soil is at once brooding and foreboding. Reinforcing this ominous sense is the country road that runs awkwardly and starkly athwart the painting, disrupting its apparent tranquility. This road is crooked, unpaved, and full of ruts. It is as if it is the very image of "the rough road of life," in the banal English expression. We also notice that it disappears in the distance, suggesting a future that is portentous, likely to engage the traveler in demanding trials and tribulations to come. Nevertheless, our gaze has little choice but to take this compelling *via rupta*. We do not have the option of another "road not taken," as in a stanza of Robert Frost's poem of this title:

> I shall be telling this with a sigh
> Somewhere ages and ages hence:
> Two roads diverged in a wood, and I—
> I took the one less traveled by,
> And that has made all the difference.

Very few contemporary viewers have any real idea of what taking the way to the Holocaust was like; for most viewers, fortunately, it is a road they did not have to traverse. But Kiefer is not tendering consolation to us, nor is he indicating hope. His painting is a massive, if coded, portrayal of the aftermath of the Holocaust. For he is thrusting upon the viewer the visual equivalent of a mass grave. The longer one looks at the painting, the more the awareness dawns that the poppies have sprung up over an immense burial ground, covering it up but also revealing it: revealing it *by* covering it up. Given the vast vista offered by the painting, there is reason to believe

Anselm Kiefer (German, 1945–), *Bohemia Lies by the Sea*, 1996. Oil, emulsion, shellac, charcoal, and powdered paint on burlap. Overall dimensions: 75¼ × 221" (191.1 x 561.3 cm), consisting of two panels, each: 75¼ × 110½" (191.1 x 280.7 cm).

that if it does present the field of flowers as a covert cemetery, then this field must contain numerous buried corpses in unmarked graves.[7]

And the emotionality in *Bohemia Lies by the Sea*? This is not easy to name, but I would suggest that *melancholy* comes closest to designating it. Just as we say that melancholy "weighs on the soul," moving our felt center of gravity downward—hence its close alliance with *de-pression* (literally, "pressing down")—so we also feel this downward pull in our body as well. Standing before Kiefer's gigantic work, we sense its full ponderous force—so much so that we cannot help but ask ourselves: how was this work ever suspended from the wall? How does it stay there rather than falling onto the floor? It is as if the sheer immensity and physical weight of Kiefer's painting acts as a material analogue of the enormity of the crimes committed during the Holocaust. Just as the painting invites us to go *under* the poppies to the ground below as well as thrusting us *onto* the irregular road in the middle, so we are drawn into a downward spiral emotionally, deposited on a path of despair.

Purchase, Lila Acheson Wallace Gift and Joseph H. Hazen Foundation Purchase Fund, 1997 (1997.4ab). Copyright © Anselm Kiefer. Image copyright © The Metropolitan Museum of Art. Image source: Art Resource, NY.

Much as it hangs precariously on the wall at the Metropolitan, so Kiefer's massive work *takes us down* emotionally: down into a melancholic zone from which there appears to be no exit. Those who are buried in the earth underlying this painting's manifest image will never again see the light of day. Neither the poppies on top of this tacit burial ground nor the distant horizon offer any prospect of relief for the victims of the Holocaust—who are forever beyond relief—nor is there any consolation for ourselves as the silent witnesses of this scene. Where normally a horizon signifies a promise of good or better things to come, in this painting the horizon is burdened by a very dark sky that presses down upon it. Just as it often feels as if there is no escape from a protracted period of melancholy, so there seems to be little or no exit from this painting, which dominates our vision so thoroughly that there does not seem to be any way out—unless we turn around and walk right away from it, which few in fact do, being transfixed by the sheer affective and visual force of the work. By staying and looking, we allow ourselves to enter into the melancholic emotionality of this virtually alchemical work. And if we do experience this melancholy, it is by way of the same dynamism of material implication and indirect witnessing that is at work in *Birkenau*—now happening in a more explicit way as we allow ourselves to be drawn into the solemn insinuations of the scene it offers.

The way *Bohemia Lies by the Sea* induces melancholy in us is not in a single abstract image as with *Birkenau*, but by conveying a vectorial force that moves downward into the earth—both the earth under the flower field and the earth under the museum in which we view it. (The painting is on an upper floor, but standing before it we feel ourselves thrust downwards toward the ground floor.) This force is felt emotionally as well as visually, and it draws our lived bodies downwards. If sinking into a psychological depression often occurs in subtle and indirect ways, Kiefer's masterwork draws us down quite directly and forcibly. As the darker import of the painting is borne in upon us, we feel ourselves dragged down, visually and viscerally, into an emotional abyss: an underworld in which there is little trace of hope as we take in its full foreboding.

The emotionality we experience in viewing *Bohemia Lies by the Sea* is not held within our subjectivity, but is felt as stemming from the painting itself regarded as attesting to the Holocaust and its immediate aftermath. The painting offers silent testimony in the form of an image of mass interment in the earth. Through its very artifice—this is, after all, a work of *art*—it transmits to us somber emotions elicited by actively imagined scenes of executed and buried minorities. The melancholic emotionality conveyed by this transmission is outside us in two senses: a vertical outside as appresented in the work itself once we look up into its dark subject matter, and a horizontal outside that is down below us in the earth: in a spread-out region that underlies any conscious subject. In the latter case, we enter a place that is the painterly analogue of the Freudian unconscious. Just as dreams and neurotic symptoms draw upon the primary processes of the Freudian unconscious in their generation, so Kiefer's painting takes us from a seemingly pristine and innocent first viewing—as if of a lively field of flowers—down into the primary processes of a stark and unrelieved melancholia that links us as its viewers with the disastrous reality that was the Holocaust. Thanks to this painting regarded as a *témoin d'artifice*, we are brought before and into an intensely felt emotionality we might not have experienced in merely hearing or reading about the Holocaust.

III

The two paintings just discussed together realize something quite extraordinary: an implicit *affective compact* with viewers, a bonding that derives from appreciating just how quietly forceful is the appresentation of emotion in each case. The bonding at work in this compact goes beyond any merely consensual agreement; it has to do with how the viewer realizes that not only she but many others are capable of undergoing the emotions that the paintings convey: sadness, despair, sense of loss, and melancholy. These emotions are both *intensified* and *consolidated* in such convergent experiencing. The artistic genius of Kiefer and Richter, however differently realized, has allowed them to create works that induce such emotions. To induce is not to guarantee, much less to require; but it is to make it difficult to refuse—visually, viscerally, and emotionally—the deeply felt experiencing these paintings are capable of engendering in ourselves as contemporary viewers.

At stake here are two ways of going beyond the inner and outer edges of an emotional event: the after-play of this event as self-eclipsing, and the advent of a new experience that emanates from the after-play itself. Both ways have their own inherent energies, but their trajectories diverge from the primal event that is their origin—uniquely and powerfully so. Some such after-play and advent must have happened in the case of the two artists whose paintings I have considered in this appendix. As mentioned, Gerhard Richter and Anselm Kiefer both grew up at the very end of World War II. Richter, born in 1932, experienced the last phase of this war as a young boy who was forced to become a member of the junior auxiliary of the Hitler-Jugend, while Kiefer was born in 1945, at the very close of the war. They have both testified to how much they were disturbed by learning more fully of the Holocaust and what a struggle it was for them to come to terms with it as young artists. The emotions generated in them—very likely a mixture of chagrin, guilt, shame, and horror—gave rise, however circuitously, to paintings that constitute a testimonial to the nightmare of the Holocaust.

The turbulent emotions of these two artists were not only experienced as such but gave birth to artworks that can inspire kindred emotions in ourselves as their viewers. This is to suggest that the aftermath of their bare emotions—the sequel to their felt intensity—eventuated in actions of significant artistic creation. Kiefer and Richter went beyond an initial emotional response not by transcending it but by following out its course and entering a transitional space where acts of painting could emerge. They took the edges of their original emotionality to the limit, and then pursued a path that led onward from its retentional residues into a new kind of event: that of creating artworks that serve as indirect witnesses to the horrors of the Holocaust.

As viewers, we in turn become witnesses at second or third remove of events we never underwent ourselves but can now take in, thanks to the affective transmission accomplished by these artworks. This is to join in the wide wake of the primal emotionality felt by these artists—and many others who knew the Holocaust from close up—by moving from the downward slope of its fading memory into the living presence of artworks that allow us to experience now, even today, the equivalent of such emotionality with an acute albeit deferred force.[8]

Notes

Introduction

1. See, for example, Lisa Feldman Barrett, *How Emotions Are Made: The Secret Life of the Brain* (New York: Houghton Mifflin, 2018). Barrett claims that emotions are "constructed" from *concepts* that are generated in the brain: "an emotion is your brain's *creation* of what your bodily sensations mean" (30; her italics). In her view, emotions are *made* in the brain, which is thus their proper home-place. Not only in neurological accounts of human experience but in other contemporary approaches to emotion, there is a strong echo of seventeenth-century accounts of the individual as self-contained. Recent theorists of crowd behavior, for example, insist on the role of the "rational individual" in group experience. Reviewing their work, Teresa Brennan remarks that "the turn away from affect in the recent work on group psychology is related to the turn toward the self-contained individual" (Teresa Brennan, *The Transmission of Affect* [Ithaca, NY: Cornell University Press, 2004], 62). Even if the role of affect is downplayed in the emphasis on the rational individual, its reduced presence is still located *in* that individual, contained inside him or her, falling into what Brennan calls "the illusion of self-containment" (ibid., 73): an illusion shared with neurological accounts like that of Barrett.

2. Maurice Merleau-Ponty, *Phenomenology of Perception*, trans. Donald A. Landes (New York: Routledge, 2012), 430.

3. See Martin Heidegger, *Being and Time*, trans. J. Macquarrie and F. Robinson (New York: Harper, 1962), 58.

4. Anthony Steinbock suggested the locutions "periphanous" and the related "periphaneity," which replace my earlier term "exophanous," which I shall employ only very rarely.

5. Heidegger, *Being and Time*, 68.

6. "Periphenomenology" is the term I have coined for a kind of phenomenological inquiry that focuses specifically on the peripheries of the life-world, as well as on the edges of our own ongoing experience of that same world. For a concerted discussion of the periphenomenological approach, see *The World on Edge* (Bloomington: Indiana University Press, 2017), 53–56, 315–16; and *The World at a Glance* (Bloomington: Indiana University Press, 2010), 438–39. The current volume is in effect the third in a series of studies employing a concerted periphenomenological approach.

7. Edmund Burke, *A Philosophical Enquiry into the Origin of Our Ideas of the Sublime and Beautiful* (Oxford: Oxford University Press, 1990), 150.

8. See Max Scheler, *Formalism in Ethics and Non-Formal Theory of Values*, trans. Manfred Frings (Evanston, IL: Northwestern University Press, 1973); and *The Nature of Sympathy*, trans. Peter Heath (Abingdon, UK: Routledge, 2017). I draw upon Scheler's account of emotion in chapter 5.

9. The citation in the previous sentence is from Jean-Paul Sartre, "A Fundamental Idea of Husserl's: Intentionality," in *We Have Only This Life to Live: The Selected Essays of Jean-Paul Sartre, 1939–1975*, ed. Ronald Aronson and Adrian van den Hoven, trans. Chris Turner (New York: New York Review of Books, 2013), 4. I thank Bob Stone for pointing me to this translation. Yet, let us note, Sartre also asserts about emotions as such that they "cannot come to human reality *from the outside*" (italics in original; Sartre, "Emotion," in *Phenomenology: The Philosophy of Edmund Husserl and Its Interpretation*, ed. Joseph J. Kockelmans, trans. B. Frechtman [New York: Anchor, 1967], 482). This is the very converse of what I maintain in this book.

10. Andy Fisher, *Radical Ecopsychology*, 2nd ed. (Albany: State University of New York Press, 2013), 9; see also 10–12.

11. David Abram, *The Spell of the Sensuous* (New York: Pantheon, 1996), 262.

12. Merleau-Ponty, *Phenomenology of Perception*, lxxiv. Merleau-Ponty is here intentionally inverting Saint Augustine's dictum, cited by Husserl: "Turn within, for truth dwells in the inner man." It is noteworthy that both Abram and Fisher are deeply indebted to Merleau-Ponty, who stressed the interpersonal context of many major emotions, including anger, as discussed further in chapter 5.

13. Fisher hints at the implications for emotion in *Radical Ecopsychology* (14ff., 56ff.), but does not develop a systematic view. Abram does not address these implications, given his exclusive emphasis on the relationship between psyche, body, and the natural environment.

14. See Gilles Deleuze and Felix Guattari, *A Thousand Plateaus: Capitalism and Schizophrenia*, trans. Brian Massumi (Minneapolis: University of Minnesota Press, 1987), xvi, 258–62, 400. See also Gilles Deleuze, *Cinema I: The Movement-Image*, trans. H. Tomlinson and B. Habberjam (Minneapolis: University of Minnesota Press, 1986), chapter 6, "The Affection-Image."

15. Edward S. Casey, *The World on Edge* (Bloomington: Indiana University Press, 2017).

16. I thank Cynthia Willett for her insistence on the difference between "affect" and "emotion." For more on this distinction, see the work of Silvan Tomkins as presented in Adam J. Frank and Elizabeth A. Wilson, *A Silvan Tomkins Handbook: Foundations for Affect Theory* (Minneapolis: University of Minnesota Press, 2020), 5–6, 31–37, 59–60.

Chapter 1

1. See, for example, William V. Harris, *Restraining Rage: The Ideology of Anger Control in Classical Antiquity* (Cambridge, MA: Harvard University Press, 2001);

Robert Kaster, *Emotion, Restraint, and Community in Ancient Rome* (Oxford: Oxford University Press, 2005); David Konstan, *The Emotions of the Ancient Greeks: Studies in Aristotle and Classical Literature* (Toronto: University of Toronto Press, 2006); and Glen Most and Susanna Braund, eds., *Ancient Anger* (Cambridge: Cambridge University Press, 2003).

2. Maurice Merleau-Ponty, *The World of Perception*, trans. Thomas Baldwin (New York: Routledge, 2004), 83–84. We shall return to this statement and others of Merleau-Ponty in chapter 5.

3. Plato, *Laws*, trans. Trevor J. Saunders (New York: Penguin, 1973), 700a–e.

4. See R. G. Collingwood, *Principles of Art* (Oxford: Oxford University Press, 1938), chapter 1.

5. Plato, *Laws*, 700e–701b.

6. Plato, *Laws*, 812c; my italics.

7. Travis Holloway, "How to Perform a Democracy: A Genealogy of Bare Voices," *Epoché* 21, no. 2 (Spring 2017): 351–70.

8. Plato, *Republic*, 400d–401b.

9. On self-control, see Plato, *Republic*, 395c, where the discussion concerns which theatrical characters young men should be allowed to embody: "men of courage, self-control [*sophrones*], piety, freedom of spirit and other qualities." This is echoed and reinforced at 402c: "the qualities of discipline, courage, generosity, and greatness of mind, and others akin to them." Note also: "in all showing no conceit, but moderation and common sense and willingness to accept the outcome" (399b–c).

10. The dark horse is "a companion of excess" (*Phaedrus* 253e 3); when held back by the charioteer, it engages in "angry abuse" (ibid., 254c 8). Desire (*eros*) becomes irrational when it has "gained control over my judgment" (238c 7); enacted as love, it is subject to "frenzied compulsion" (240d 1).

11. Aristotle, *De anima* 403a 24–28, 403b 17–20; cited from *Aristotle, De Anima: Books II and III*, trans. D. W. Hamlyn (Oxford: Oxford University Press, 1993).

12. Aristotle, *De anima*, 408b 9–15; my italics.

13. See, for example, Roy Schafer, *A New Language for Psychoanalysis* (New Haven, CT: Yale University Press, 1976).

14. Aristotle, *De anima*, 408b 26–30.

15. Aristotle, *Nicomachean Ethics* 1125b 32–36, in the edition edited and translated by R. Crisp (Cambridge: Cambridge University Press, 2013); my italics.

16. Aristotle, *Nicomachean Ethics*, 1126a 3–6 and 9–11.

17. Aristotle, *Nicomachean Ethics*, 1126a 33–34, 1126b 3–9.

18. The full statement is this: "the mean is nameless, and the extremes pretty much so [too]" (Aristotle, *Nicomachean Ethics*, 1125b 26–27).

19. For an example of this, consider the institution of slavery in the United States beginning in the early seventeenth century, and still very much present in the form of forced labor in federal prisons today. Justifiable anger may well seethe among contemporary African Americans even if specific perpetrators cannot always be identified; we have to do here with what Hannah Bacon calls "durational trauma" which can readily occasion outbursts of anger or fits of depression in the present. See Hannah Bacon, "Bearing With: An Intersubjective Ethics and Politics of Durational Trauma," PhD thesis, Stony Brook University, 2020.

20. Aristotle, *The Art of Rhetoric*, trans. H. C. Lawson-Tancred (New York: Penguin, 1991), 1355b.

21. Compared with the citation of examples, enthymeme is "the most powerful of proofs" in rhetorical speech (see Aristotle, *Art of Rhetoric*, 1355a).

22. Aristotle, *Art of Rhetoric*, 1378a.

23. Aristotle, *Art of Rhetoric*, 1378b.

24. Aristotle, *Art of Rhetoric*, 1378b.

25. Aristotle, *Art of Rhetoric*, 1378a.

26. Aristotle, *Art of Rhetoric*, 1378a; italics in original.

27. Emotion analyzed in terms of the four causes would have looked something like this: the "state" or actual experience is the material cause, the instigating "people" (e.g., the orators) would be the efficient cause, and the "situation" would combine at once efficient and material causes. Surprisingly omitted from this cursory treatment in *Rhetoric* 1378a is the final cause of rhetorical speech: persuasion (i.e., convincing listeners of the correctness or value of the thrust of the speech), as well as the formal cause, namely, the structural character of the rhetoric itself. Of special relevance here is James Hillman's effort to discuss emotion in terms of the four causes in his *Emotion: A Comprehensive Phenomenology of Theories and Their Meanings for Therapy* (London: Routledge and Kegan Paul, 1960), part 3: "Integration."

28. Aristotle, *Art of Rhetoric*, 1378a.

29. Aristotle, *Art of Rhetoric*, 1378a; italics in original.

30. "With all anger there must be an attendant *pleasure*, that from the *prospect of revenge*. For it is pleasant to think that one will achieve what one seeks" (Aristotle, *Art of Rhetoric*, 1378a–b; italics in translation).

31. Aristotle, *Art of Rhetoric*, 1378b.

32. Aristotle, *Art of Rhetoric*, 1378b–79a.

33. Aristotle, *Art of Rhetoric*, 1379a.

34. Aristotle, *Art of Rhetoric*, 1379a; my italics.

35. Aristotle, *Art of Rhetoric*, 1380a, 1389b; my italics.

36. This is a comment by Margaret Graver in her translation of and commentary on *Cicero on the Emotions* (Chicago: University of Chicago Press, 2002), 168. The passage in question from "On the Orator" is found at 2.189–96.

37. This is not to ignore the fact that Aristotle also gives a detailed treatment of nine other emotions in the *Rhetoric* and of still other emotions in the *Ethics*.

38. Cicero, "Tusculan Disputations," in Graver, *Cicero on the Emotions*, 167.

39. The whole first line is: "Wrath—Goddess, sing the wrath of Peleus's son Achilles, murderous, doomed, that cost the Achaeans countless losses, hurling down to the house of Death so many sturdy souls" (*Iliad*, lines 1–4).

40. Leonard Muellner, *The Anger of Achilles: "Ménis" in Greek Epic* (Ithaca, NY: Cornell University Press, 1996), 180. Also at stake are two other domains: those of the priest and the people, that is, of "sovereignty and magic" and "fertility and well-being" (ibid.).

41. This is Gregory Nagy's formulation in his foreword to Muellner's book (*Anger of Achilles*, vii; italics in original).

42. Cited by Muellner, *Anger of Achilles*, 180, from Charles Malamoud's essay

"Manyúh Svayambhéh," in *Mélanges d'indianisme à la mémoire de Louis Renou* (Paris: Éditions E. de Boccard, 1908), 493–94.

43. P. Considine, "The Etymology of *Ménis*," in *Studies in Honor of T. B. L. Webster*, ed. J. H. Betts, J. T. Hooker, and J. R. Green (Bristol, UK: Cornwall, 1986), 86; cited in Harris, *Restraining Rage*, 51n5.

44. *Ménis*, the dominant theme in the *Iliad*, pertains strictly speaking to near-divine Achilles and the gods. Humans experience anger as *cholos* (bile) and, in later terminology, as *orgé* (disposition or temperament) and *thumos* (heart or chest, as in Plato's *Republic*). See Harris's discussion of all this in *Restraining Rage*, chapter 3: "The Greek and Latin Terminology."

45. Harris, *Restraining Rage*, 26. The parallel with the ego psychology of Sigmund and Anna Freud is striking: it is just because what is repressed into the unconscious is so difficult to restrain that the egological self develops an entire system of defenses against "the return of the repressed." See Sigmund Freud, *The Ego and the Id*, trans. J. Riviere and J. Strachey (New York: Norton, 1960); and Anna Freud, *The Ego and the Mechanisms of Defense*, trans. C. Baines (New York: Routledge, 2018). As Jung liked to put it, uncontrolled anger represents an "invasion" from the unconscious.

46. See Fred Evans, *The Multivoiced Body: Society and Communication in the Age of Diversity* (New York: Columbia University Press, 2009).

47. Harris, *Restraining Rage*, 200.

48. Cited by Harris, *Restraining Rage*, 186. Nevertheless, Demosthenes, whose eloquence was legendary, in his public speaking "often explicitly attempts to excite the *orgé* [temperamental anger] of his audiences in both political and judicial contexts, and he owed much of his success to his ability to stir his hearers' emotions" (ibid., 188). Similarly, despite arguing for achieving the mean between indifference and irascibility, Aristotle states in the *Rhetoric* that "one must, by means of the speech, bring the judges into the state of those who are irascible [by showing] one's opponents [in a legal case] to be responsible for those things that are the causes of anger, and that they are the sort of people against whom anger [should be] directed" (*Art of Rhetoric*, 1380a 2–5).

49. Cited in Harris, *Restraining Rage*, 186.

50. Plato, *Phaedrus* 267c–d.

51. Harris, *Restraining Rage*, 158.

52. Plato, *Republic*, book 8, 562e 5: "It breeds anarchy among the very animals"—that is, it leads to a situation in which anything goes and anything can be said.

53. Harris, *Restraining Rage*, 158. We observe here a variation of what Jacques Derrida terms the "autoimmunity" of democracy—its tendency to allow for developments that ultimately undermine itself. (See Jacques Derrida, *Rogues: Two Essays on Reason*, trans. Michael Naas and Pascale-Anne Brault [Stanford, CA: Stanford University Press, 2005], 87–88, 123–24.)

54. "The Greeks did not conceive of emotions as internal states of excitation. Rather, the emotions are elicited by our interpretation of the words, acts, and intentions of others, each in its characteristic way" (Konstan, *The Emotions of the Ancient Greeks*, xii).

Chapter 2

1. Lucius Annaeus Seneca, *Anger, Mercy, Revenge*, trans. Robert A. Kaster and Martha C. Nussbaum (Chicago: University of Chicago Press, 2010), 72–73. Hereafter in the text I refer to this treatise by its original Latin title *De ira*. Seneca's approach belongs to the Stoic tradition of "care of the self" (*cura sui*), which is thematized by Michel Foucault in his study *The Care of the Self*, vol. 3 of *The History of Sexuality*, trans. Robert Hurley (New York: Vintage, 1988).

2. "Nothing is less appropriate to [the person] meting out judgment than anger, since punishment is all the more conducive to correction if it's imposed as an act of considered judgment"; and note the further observation that a criminal judge should be "not wrathful but resolved" (Seneca, *Anger*, 27, 28).

3. Seneca, *Anger*, 31. I would add to "quickly" another adverb: "effectively." If our anger does not make a difference in a given situation, it can be turned back on ourselves with potentially negative consequences such as depression.

4. Seneca, *Anger*, 20; see also 21: "Once [anger] has begun to carry us off course, it's difficult to sail back to safety."

5. Seneca, *Anger*, 22.

6. Seneca, *Anger*, 31.

7. Seneca, *Anger*, 21.

8. Seneca, *Anger*, 14; see also 42: "anger is ugly per se."

9. Seneca, *Anger*, 15.

10. Seneca, *Anger*, 19.

11. Seneca, *Anger*, 18.

12. Seneca, *Anger*, 57; translation slightly altered.

13. By the same token, anger is antirational, since it is by way of reason that we not only recognize our deeply social bonds, but also the necessity of preserving and nurturing them whenever possible.

14. Seneca, *Anger*, 22, 23.

15. Seneca, *Anger*, 36–37; translation slightly altered.

16. Seneca, *Anger*, my italics; translation slightly modified.

17. For this concept, see Edmund Husserl, *Experience and Judgment*, trans. Karl Ameriks (Evanston, IL: Northwestern University Press, 1975); and *Analyses concerning Active and Passive Synthesis*, trans. Anthony J. Steinbock (Dordrecht: Springer, 2001).

18. Seneca, *Anger*, 37.

19. Seneca, *Anger*, 29.

20. Seneca, *Anger*, 24.

21. Seneca, *Anger*, 32.

22. Seneca, *Anger*, 22.

23. By denying "an identifiable phase of conscious deliberation" in Descartes's model of emotional genesis, I am not overlooking the role of the Cartesian method as an important ex post facto technique for understanding this genesis in principle. But unlike Seneca, Descartes does not invoke a phase of deliberative reason in the processing of a given emotion such as anger.

24. Julia Kristeva, *Tales of Love* (New York: Columbia University Press, 1987), 376–78; my italics. Here I draw from Paul Shepard's discussion of Kristeva in

"Wildness and Wilderness," in his book *Coming Home to the Pleistocene* (Washington, DC: Island, 1998), 144.

25. René Descartes, "The Passions of the Soul," trans. R. Stoothoff, in *The Philosophical Writings of Descartes*, trans. J. Cottingham, R. Stoothoff, and D. Murdoch (Cambridge: Cambridge University Press, 1985), 328; my italics.

26. Descartes, "Passions of the Soul," trans. Stoothoff, 339.

27. Descartes, "Passions of the Soul," trans. Stoothoff, 339. So, too, Kant claims that in the feeling of the sublime "the mind feels agitated" (Immanuel Kant, *Critique of Judgment*, trans. W. S. Pluhar [Indianapolis, IN: Hackett, 1987], 115). We shall return to this claim in chapter 4. Cicero already remarks on this same feature.

28. This is a phrase of the translator, Stoothoff, in a footnote, "Passions of the Soul," 338n.

29. Descartes, "Passions of the Soul," trans. Stoothoff, 328.

30. Heidegger contrasts *Sein-in* and *In-sein* in *Being and Time*, trans. MacQuarrie and Robinson, section 12, p. 79. *Sein-in* connotes being inside something else, whereas *In-sein* is "a state of Dasein's Being; it is an existentiale."

31. On Aristotle's container model of place, see Edward S. Casey, *The Fate of Place* (Berkeley: University of California Press, 1997), chapter 3.

32. Descartes, "Passions of the Soul," trans. Stoothoff, 328.

33. Archytas's own original words in the one fragment of his that survives are these: "all existing things are either in place or not without place." Cited by Simplicius and translated in S. Sambursky, ed., *The Concept of Place in Late Neoplatonism* (Jerusalem: Israel Academy of Sciences and Humanities, 1982), 37. Kant, not knowing of this fragment, reaffirmed the Archytian principle in his Inaugural Dissertation of 1770, *On the Form and Principles of the Sensible and Intelligible World*. For comments on this, see Casey, *The Fate of Place*, 204–6. See my discussion of the Archytian axiom in *Getting Back into Place: Toward a Renewed Understanding of the Place-World* (Bloomington: Indiana University Press, 2009), 14–15.

34. Descartes, "Passions of the Soul," trans. Stoothoff, 357. I have altered "fear" to "terror" in keeping with Michael Moriarty's translation: René Descartes, *The Passions of the Soul*, trans. Michael Moriarty (Oxford: Oxford University Press, 2015), 211.

35. Descartes, "Passions of the Soul," trans. Stoothoff, 342–43. Again, I have changed "fear" to "terror."

36. "In order to arouse boldness and suppress terror in ourselves, it is not sufficient to have the [mere] volition [or wish] to do so. We must apply ourselves to consider the reasons, objects, or precedents which persuade us that the danger is not great; that there is always more security in defense than in flight; that we shall gain glory and joy if we conquer [our terror], whereas we can expect nothing but regret and shame if we flee" (Descartes, "Passions of the Soul," trans. Stoothoff, 345; again, I have modified "fear" to "terror").

37. For present purposes, I take the mind (*l'esprit*) and the soul (*l'âme*) to be equivalent terms.

38. I slightly modify the phrase "internal emotions of the soul" (Descartes, "Passions of the Soul," trans. Stoothoff, 381).

39. Descartes, "Passions of the Soul," trans. Stoothoff, 399.

40. Descartes, "Passions of the Soul," trans. Stoothoff, 400.

41. For the expressions conveyed by the eyes, see Descartes, "Passions of the Soul," trans. Stoothoff, 367; for the way the face changes color when experiencing various emotions, 368–69; tears are discussed on 373.

42. By "expressivity" I do not mean literally "animated." Buster Keaton's deadpan face, though not overtly animated, is nevertheless expressive in and by itself. The expressivity of emotion can be conveyed by gestures of many kinds as well as by words (both spoken and written). If feelings need not be conveyed outwardly, emotions do—to the point where we can say that *emotionality is expressivity*. This is a virtual axiom that underlies much of what I will be saying in part 2 of this book.

43. Descartes sometimes conceives of external place as a matter of "situation," a more promising idea, but one he does not go on to develop.

44. René Descartes, *Principles of Philosophy*, trans. V. R. Miller and R. Miller (Dordrecht: Reidel, 1983), 83.

45. Deleuze and Guattari, *A Thousand Plateaus*, chapter 12.

46. Descartes, *Principles of Philosophy*, 46.

47. See Elisabeth Ströker, *Investigations in Philosophy of Space* (1965), trans. Algis Mickunas (Athens: Ohio State University Press, 1987); on "expressive totality" and "expressive fullness," see 23, 19; on the pervasiveness of attunement, see 25.

48. "*Attuned* space . . . has an appropriate mode of co-existence with the lived ego" (Ströker, *Investigations in Philosophy of Space*, 19; her italics).

49. Ströker, *Investigations in Philosophy of Space*, 20; I have replaced "ego" with "self."

50. Ströker, *Investigations in Philosophy of Space*, 20.

51. Mikel Dufrenne, *The Notion of the A Priori*, trans. Edward S. Casey (Evanston, IL: Northwestern University Press, 1966), 62, 71, 96, 119, 191, 193.

Chapter 3

1. "Many of those who have written about the emotions . . . seem to conceive the place of man in Nature as being like an empire within an empire . . . [as if] he is determined by himself alone" (Benedict Spinoza, *Ethics*, ed. and trans. G. H. R. Parkinson [Oxford: Oxford University Press, 2000], 163; preface to part 3).

2. See Deleuze and Guattari, *A Thousand Plateaus*, 253–65.

3. George Eliot, *Daniel Deronda* (Auckland, N.Z.: Floating Press, 2000), 450.

4. For more on the unconscious in Freud, see chapter 8.

5. For Spinoza, there are "representations in the mind" (that is, "ideas") of what is experienced without as "objects": "Whatever happens in the object of the idea constituting the human mind must be perceived by the human mind . . . [thus] there will necessarily arise in the human mind an idea of this thing" (*Ethics*, 123; part 2, proposition 12). But such ideas do not constitute an entire interior region, as with Descartes or, for that matter, Freud.

6. Spinoza, *Ethics*, 166; part 3, proposition 2, scholium.

7. Spinoza, *Ethics*, 173–74; part 3, proposition 11, scholium.

8. Gilles Deleuze, *Spinoza: Practical Philosophy*, trans. Robert Hurley (San Francisco: City Lights, 1988), 18. Here Deleuze references the *Ethics*, part 3, proposition 2, scholium; and proposition 13, scholium.

9. Spinoza, *Ethics*, 164; part 3, definition 3; my italics.

10. See Spinoza, *Ethics*, 164: part 3, definition 1.

11. This is not to say that inadequate ideas are not simply the *cause* of sadness, nor do they express them. Further, inadequate ideas do not always have an emotional counterpart: for example, a baby's idea of nourishment by breastfeeding is not adequate, yet the infant is intensely emotional. (Here I draw on comments by Martin Benson in an e-mail of January 20, 2020.)

12. Spinoza, *Ethics*, 164; in preface to part 3.

13. On eidetic singularity, see Edmund Husserl, *Ideas Pertaining to a Pure Phenomenology and to a Phenomenological Philosophy*, trans. Fred Kersten (Dordrecht: Kluwer, 1983), book 1, section 15, 28–30.

14. Spinoza, *Ethics*, 209; part 3, proposition 56, scholium.

15. Spinoza holds that there as many species of an affect as there are affecting objects, but this does not prohibit the further proliferation of affects in a kind of "swarming" effect (*Ethics*, part 3, proposition 56). Martin Benson comments that "there are as many affects as there are combinations, or encounters; affects are singular co-individuations of force centers" (e-mail of January 20, 2020).

16. Spinoza defines "adequate ideas" as follows: "There will be an adequate idea of the mind of that which is common to, and a property of, the human body and certain external bodies by which the human body is often affected, and which is equally in the part and in the whole of any of these" (Spinoza, *Ethics*, 146; part 2, proposition 39). An adequate idea affords a good grasp, a reliable understanding, of that of which it is the idea. It is distinguished from a "true" idea, which is verified as accurate. This is not the place to discuss Spinoza's complex model of levels of knowledge. What matters for our purposes is that adequate ideas are essential to the transition from the passivity of the affective subject to its activation in full-fledged emotion or affect.

17. Spinoza, *Ethics*, 153; part 2, proposition 44, corollary 2.

18. Spinoza, *Ethics*, 164; part 3, preface.

19. "To be a mode is to be in something else, and to be conceived through that something else" (from the glossary to Parkinson's translation of the *Ethics*, 322).

20. Deleuze, *Spinoza*, 48–49.

21. We are edging here toward what Heidegger will designate in *Being and Time* as "mood" (*Stimmung*), an affective surround that is always present for human Dasein, whatever the nuanced differences in its many modulations. But mood is by no means entirely internal, as Eugene Gendlin has argued: "A mood is not just internal, it is . . . living in the world. We sense how we find ourselves, and we find ourselves in situations" (Eugene T. Gendlin, *Saying What We Mean*, ed. Edward S. Casey and D. Schoeller [Evanston, IL: Northwestern University Press, 2017], 210). Mood is a specification of *Befindlichkeit*, to use Heidegger's term, about which Gendlin remarks: "[*Befindlichkeit* names] how we sense our-

selves in situations. Whereas feeling is usually thought of as something inward, Heidegger's concept refers to something both inward and outward, but before a split between inside and outside has been made" (ibid.). For further on mood, see chapter 11.

22. Spinoza, *Ethics*, 164; part 3, definition 3.

23. Indeed, it is arguable that affections, so understood, *are* the primary form in which modes occur: for modes can be considered as "the affections of substance or of its attributes" (this is Deleuze's formulation in his *Spinoza*, 48).

24. Spinoza, *Ethics*, 223; part 3, "General Definition of the Emotions."

25. Deleuze and Guattari, *A Thousand Plateaus*, 256: "affects are becomings." Strictly speaking, what the authors call an "affect" is what Deleuze designates as an "affection" (*affectio*) in his commentaries on Spinoza. Once again, "affect" is a direct translation of *affectus*, and it is equivalent to what I am calling "emotion"—whereas *affectio* is affiliated with what I am designating as "feeling," even though the latter is not a technical term of Spinoza's. "Affectivity" (my term) refers to the entire realm composed of affects/emotions and affections/feelings.

26. Martin Benson points out that some passions also elevate the power of acting, even if we do not understand just how this is so other than saying that they "mimic reason" (e-mail of March 10, 2020). See Spinoza, *Ethics*, part 5, proposition 10, scholium.

27. Deleuze, *Spinoza*, 49.

28. For a given mode, "its power of acting or force of existing increases or decreases" in intermodal encounters in which it joins up with other modes or fails to do so respectively (Deleuze, *Spinoza*, 50).

29. In Deleuze's way of putting this: "The power of being affected belongs to essence, plainly it is necessarily fulfilled by affects [or emotions] that come from outside. These affects come from outside, they do not come from the essence. . . . actually the outside is the law to which the extensive parts acting upon one another are submitted" (https://www.gold.ac.uk/media/images-by-section /departments/research-centres-and-units/research-centres/). I thank Lissa McCullough for this reference.

30. Wallace Stevens, "Not Ideas about the Thing but the Thing Itself," in *The Collected Poems of Wallace Stevens* (New York: Alfred Knopf, 1954), 534.

31. Both citations in this sentence are from Deleuze, *Spinoza*, 50. By saying that love "comes back upon the idea from which it follows," Spinoza appears to mean that love is self-reinforcing.

32. Spinoza, *Ethics*, 175; part 3, proposition 13, scholium. Spinoza pairs hatred with love in that both proceed from an "external cause," albeit to very different effect. See also 215: "hatred is pain, with the accompaniment of the idea of an external cause" (part 3, "Definitions of the Emotions," definition 7).

33. Spinoza, *Ethics*, 177; part 3, proposition 16. Indeed, a bare thinking of the object can suffice to induce hatred.

34. Spinoza, *Ethics*, 176; part 3, proposition 15, corollary.

35. For a discussion of the place of "ideas" in relation to ideology in Spinoza, see Hasana Sharp, *Spinoza and the Politics of Renaturalization* (Chicago: Uni-

versity of Chicago Press, 2011). I owe this reference to Oli Stephano, who made several other valuable suggestions on an earlier draft of this chapter.

36. Spinoza, *Ethics*, 196; part 3, proposition 40, corollary 2, scholium.

37. As Spinoza states the basis of this misanthropic logic: "From the fact that we imagine [something or someone] to be affected with some [hurtful] emotion . . . we are affected with a similar emotion" (Spinoza, *Ethics*, 184; part 3, proposition 27). We are reminded here of Aristotle's notion that anger is most often a form of vengeance directed at those who have belittled us. In such a circumstance, moving from anger to hatred is a short step, a point to which I return just below.

38. "Among all the emotions which are related to the mind in so far as it acts, there are none apart from those which are related to pleasure or desire" (Spinoza, *Ethics*, 211; part 3, proposition 59). For Spinoza, desire and pleasure are closely related: "the desire which arises from pleasure is, other things being equal, stronger than the desire which arises from pain" (239; part 4, proposition 18).

39. Spinoza, *Ethics*, 180; part 3, proposition 20. A slight variation of this point is found on 182; part 3, proposition 23: "Someone who imagines what he hates to be affected with pain will feel pleasure." See also part 3, proposition 26: "We endeavor to affirm about a thing which we hate everything that we imagine to affect the thing with pain, and conversely to negate that which we imagine to affect it with pleasure."

40. Spinoza, *Ethics*, 196; part 3, proposition 40, corollary 2, scholium.

41. Spinoza, *Ethics*, 199; part 3, proposition 46.

42. On genocidal logic, see Anne O'Byrne's forthcoming book, *Democracy and Generational Being: Politics, Kinships, and Genocide* (New York: Fordham University Press, 2021).

43. For Spinoza, love and hatred realize a number of combinations: such as when the person you love hates you—and thus incurs your own hatred back, even as you continue to love that same person. In that case, you are "harassed by hatred and love at the same time" (Spinoza, *Ethics*, 195; part 3, proposition 40, corollary 1).

44. Spinoza, *Ethics*, 164; part 3, definition 2.

45. Deleuze, *Spinoza*, 28. (I have changed "feelings" to "emotions" here in keeping with the nomenclature I have adopted in this chapter.)

46. Spinoza, *Ethics*, 164; part 3, definition 2; my italics.

47. Spinoza, *Ethics*, 165; part 3, postulate 2.

48. See the notion of *defizienter Modus* in Heidegger, *Being and Time*, trans. Macquarrie and Robinson, 42–43.

49. Deleuze, *Spinoza*, 28.

50. See Collingwood, *Principles of Art*, chapter 13: "Art and Truth." In corrupt consciousness we *disown* that which in fact we are experiencing emotionally, acting as if it never happened.

51. This is Deleuze's formulation in his *Expressionism in Philosophy: Spinoza*, trans. Martin Joughin (New York: Zone Books, 1992), 164.

52. I borrow the phrase "knowledge in potency" from Martin Benson (e-mail communication cited previously).

53. Concerning this transmutation of feeling or affection as passion into active emotion by way of adequate comprehension, see the detailed account given by Gilles Deleuze in *Expressionism in Philosophy: Spinoza*, 217–26, and especially at 282–88. Deleuze makes clear that joy is a special case because an emotion like active joy gives rise in turn to "desires that belong to reason," a special class of active emotions whose activity is fueled by what Aristotle would term "active intellect." The operative axiom is that "an active joy always follows from what we understand" (283). With the assistance of joyful passions, other feelings can gain the status of "active"; it is as if joy gives a boost to feelings that would otherwise bog us down in their sheer passivity, such as the extreme sadness that we would now call "depression."

54. Deleuze claims that in Spinoza there is something like an "unconscious of thought" (*Spinoza*, 18–19), though I would argue that this is more a matter of what is *nonconscious* rather than unconscious in the sense of a region that is wholly unavailable to the conscious mind.

55. I am setting aside the claim in *Ethics*, part 5, that the intellect is eternal and thus exists without the body. This cuts across—from above, as it were—what is true of the immanent life of the mind.

56. In the epilogue I return to the theme of emotional intentionality under the heading of active emotional edges that are "self-eclipsing."

57. For a persuasive account of such an environment, under the rubric of an "ecosystem of ideas," see Hasana Sharp, *Spinoza and the Politics of Renaturalization*, especially chapter 2. Similarly, Oli Stephano's dissertation, "Immanent Ecologies: Ethics, Power, and Persistence" (PhD diss., Stony Brook University, 2018), pursues the extensive environmental aspects and consequences of Spinoza's thought.

58. For a convincing demonstration of the need for a public commons in today's world, see Mary Watkins, *Mutual Accompaniment and the Creation of the Commons* (New Haven, CT: Yale University Press, 2019).

59. Gendlin, *Saying What We Mean*, 116; his italics.

60. Gendlin, *Saying What We Mean*, 293; his italics.

Chapter 4

1. Sandra Shapshay, "What Is the Sublime? (According to Kant and Schopenhauer)," Erraticus, December 4, 2018, https://erraticus.com/2018/12/04/sublime-experience-kant-schopenhauer.

2. Immanuel Kant, *Critique of Judgment*, trans. Werner S. Pluhar (Indianapolis, IN: Hackett, 1987), 113.

3. Kant, *Critique of Judgment*, 99. Notice the reference to "arousing" (*regemachen*) on the same page; the sublime "concerns only ideas of reason, which, though they cannot be exhibited adequately, are aroused and called to mind, by this very inadequacy, which can be exhibited in sensibility."

4. Kant, *Critique of Judgment*, 99.

5. Kant, *Critique of Judgment*, 120.

6. Kant, *Critique of Judgment*, 112. More completely: "that magnitude of a natural object to which the imagination fruitlessly applies its entire ability to comprehend must lead the concept of nature to a supersensible substrate . . . a substrate that is large beyond any standard of sense" (ibid.).

7. Kant, *Critique of Judgment*, 99–100.

8. Kant, *Critique of Judgment*, 115.

9. Kant, *Critique of Judgment*, 98.

10. Kant, *Critique of Judgment*, 144. The idea of subreption is first defined in the Inaugural Dissertation of 1770: "We may call *fallacy of subreption* (by analogy with the accepted meaning) the intellect's trick of slipping in a concept of sense as if it were the concept of an intellectual characteristic" (*On the Form and Principles of the Sensible and Intelligible Worlds*, sect. 24; *Kants Gesammelte Schriften* [Berlin: de Gruyter, 1902 ff], 2:412; here in the translation of Werner Pluhar, *Critique of Judgment*, 114, n22; his italics). By the time of the *Critique of Judgment*, subreption (literally, "snatching under") occurs in the opposite direction: we slip into sensible things powers that belong properly to ourselves.

11. "The proper unchangeable basic measure of nature is the absolute whole of nature. . . . This basic measure, however, is a self-contradictory concept (because an absolute totality of an endless progression is impossible [to attain in a sensible intuition])" (Kant, *Critique of Judgment*, 112). The analogy between such a totality and that which is at stake in the regulative use of reason in its dialectical employment, as described in the *Critique of Pure Reason*, is striking.

12. Kant, *Critique of Judgment*, 117. The paradoxical combinations of ability/inability, pleasure/displeasure, and other incompossible pairings (such as adequacy/inadequacy) constitute an abyssal logic that is on the agenda in section 24 of the *Critique of Judgment*. On this logic, see Jean-Francois Lyotard, *Lessons on the Analytic of the Sublime*, trans. Elizabeth Rottenberg (Stanford, CA: Stanford University Press, 1994).

13. Compare Kant, *Critique of Judgment*, 115: "If a [thing] is excessive for the imagination (and the imagination is driven to [such excess] as it apprehends [the thing] in intuition), then [the thing] is, as it were, an abyss in which the imagination is afraid to lose itself."

14. Compare Kant, *Critique of Judgment*, 100: "For the beautiful in nature we must seek a basis outside ourselves, but for the sublime a basis merely within ourselves and in the way of thinking that introduces sublimity into our presentation of nature." On the conflict (*Widerstreit*) itself, see 116. Here "imagination" is restricted to what sensibility can deliver; in Kant's own terms in the *Critique of Pure Reason*, it is "reproductive" rather than "productive."

15. Kant, *Critique of Judgment*, 113.

16. In dealing with the dynamical sublime, one "has the feeling that his imagination is inadequate for exhibiting the idea of a whole, [a feeling] in which imagination reaches its maximum, and as it strives to expand that maximum, [but fails to do so], it sinks back into itself, but consequently comes to feel a liking [that amounts to an] emotion" (Kant, *Critique of Judgment*, 109). "Consequently" refers to the satisfaction we take in activating our own powers of reason in the

wake of the frustration of never being able to catch up with the sublime in nature by means of perception and/or imagination.

17. "Hence, that magnitude of a natural object to which the imagination fruitlessly applies its entire ability to comprehend must lead the concept of nature to a supersensible substrate (which underlies both nature and our ability to think), a substrate that is large beyond any standard of sense and hence makes us judge as *sublime* not so much the object as the mental attunement in which we find ourselves when we estimate the object" (Kant, *Critique of Judgment*, 112; his italics).

18. Martin Heidegger, "The Origin of the Work of Art," in *Poetry, Language, Thought*, trans. Alfred Hofstadter (New York: Harper and Row, 1971), 17.

19. Heidegger, "Origin of the Work of Art," 55.

20. Kant, *Critique of Judgment*, 121.

21. Kant, *Critique of Judgment*, 121. In the two phases cited in this sentence, Kant plays on the verbal pairs *erhaben/erheben* and *erhaben/erhöhen*; for the latter, see 120.

22. Alfred North Whitehead, *Science and the Modern World* (Cambridge: Cambridge University Press, 1929), 72.

23. Whitehead, *Science and the Modern World*, 80. A more technical definition is this: "To say that a bit of matter has *simple location* means that, in expressing its spatiotemporal relations, it is adequate to state that it is where it is, in a definite finite region of space, and throughout a definite finite duration of time, apart from any essential reference of the relations of that bit of matter to other regions of space and to other durations of time" (ibid., 72; his italics).

24. Immanuel Kant, "First Metaphysical Principles of Phoronomy," second definition, first remark, in his *Metaphysical Principles of Natural Science*; see *Kants gesammelte Schriften*, 4:482. To compare Kant's discussions of dynamics in chapter 2 of this treatise, "Metaphysical Foundations of Dynamics," with his later conception of the dynamical sublime would be of interest, but lies beyond the scope of our discussion.

25. Kant, *Critique of Judgment*, 124; see also 115: what is "excessive for imagination" is "an abyss in which the imagination is afraid to lose itself."

26. On "absolute presuppositions," see R. G. Collingwood, *An Autobiography* (Oxford: Oxford University Press, 1939).

27. For more on this notion of *site*, see my *Getting Back into Place*, 103, 177–78, 216, 226, and 267–70. Robert Harvey points out that movement complicates both site and position, and mentions that Lyotard, in *The Differend*, writes of *agitation sur place* (e-mail correspondence of February 19, 2019). See Jean-François Lyotard, *The Differend: Phrases in Dispute*, trans. Georges van den Abbeele (Minneapolis: University of Minnesota Press, 1988). I also wish to thank Harvey for a number of constructive suggestions he made on this chapter.

28. Thus, when we require that others like the beautiful as we do, Kant remarks, we speak of it "as if it were a property of things. . . . [We say] the *thing* is beautiful" (*Critique of Judgment*, 56; his italics). Also, the judging person "will talk about the beautiful as if beauty were a characteristic of the object" (54). Kant observes that "for the beautiful in nature we must seek a basis outside ourselves, but for the sublime a basis merely within ourselves" (100). Even here, however,

the attribution is misplaced, according to Kant himself: "beauty is not a property of the flower itself" (ibid., 14; my italics). Ultimately, beauty resides somewhere between the object and the beholder: we call something beautiful "only by virtue of that characteristic in which it adapts itself to the way we apprehend it" (ibid.). Notably, there is no equivalent of the *sensus communis* for the judgment of sublimity, for this judgment is based entirely on my own feeling, not on any agreement with others' judgments: "Just as we charge someone with a lack of *taste* if he is indifferent when he judges an object of nature that we find beautiful, so we say that someone has no *feeling* if he remains unmoved in the presence of something we judge sublime" (ibid., 125; his italics).

29. Here Whitehead fails us, for it does not help to claim, as he does in *Science and the Modern World*, that "in a certain sense, everything is everywhere at all times" (114).

30. In Plato's *Timaeus* it is no accident that *chora*, the earliest Western version of "place," bears the epithet "the participant," for the binary pairs hot/cold, dry/moist, and so on reside in it regarded as a "receptacle," *hupodoché*. Notably, *hupo*- is the Greek equivalent of the Latin *sub*-, which turns up in such diverse terms as "subject" and "subversive" as well as in "sublime" itself. This is one of the more striking cases when a premodern idea has anticipated a postmodern direction. See the detailed study of this ironic twist in my book *The Fate of Place: A Philosophical History* (Berkeley: University of California Press, 1997), part 1: "From Void to Vessel," esp. chapter 2, "Mastering the Matrix: The *Enuma Elish* and Plato's *Timaeus*."

31. Wallace Stevens, "The Idea of Order at Key West," in *The Collected Poems of Wallace Stevens* (New York: Alfred Knopf, 1990).

32. Kant, *Critique of Judgment*, section 28. The "colossal" is explored in section 26, "respect" in section 27, and "humility" in section 29. "Amazement" is treated in the "General Comment on the Exposition of Aesthetic Reflective Judgments." On this topic, see Robert Doran, *The Theory of the Sublime from Longinus to Kant* (Cambridge: Cambridge University Press, 2015).

33. For treatment of this theme, see Irene Klaver, "Silent Wolves: The Howl of the Implicit," in *Wild Ideas*, ed. D. Rothenberg (Minneapolis: University of Minnesota Press, 1995), 117–33.

34. Walt Whitman, "Song of Myself." I cite this remarkable line more than once in the course of this book: it encapsulates a major leitmotif in my interpretation of emotion.

35. The phrase "a way out" occurs in Freud's essay "On Narcissism," in *Standard Edition of the Complete Psychological Works of Sigmund Freud*, ed. and trans. James Strachey (London: Hogarth, 1957), 14:94: "Sublimation is a way out, a way by which those demands [of the ego] can be met *without* involving repression."

36. Kant, *Critique of Judgment*, 124. "Expand" is also invoked in a discussion of the second maxim of wisdom, that is, under the heading of "a broadened way of thinking" (ibid., 161).

37. Kant writes: "For it is precisely nature's inadequacy to the Ideas . . . that constitutes what both repels our sensibility and yet attracts us at the same time" (*Critique of Judgment*, 124).

38. *Alles Raümliche dehnt sich aus*: Theodor Lipps as cited by Rudolf Arnheim in *The Dynamics of Architectural Form* (Berkeley: University of California Press, 1977), 86.

39. Kant writes: "It seems, then, that we must not regard a judgment of taste as *egoistic*; rather, we must regard it necessarily as *pluralistic* by its inner nature on account of itself rather than the examples that others give of their taste" (*Critique of Judgment*, 140; his italics).

40. Kant, *Critique of Judgment*, 126; his italics. See also: "*Simplicity* (artless purposiveness) is, as it were, nature's style in the sublime" (136; his italics). Judgment is for Kant the epitome of relation: for example, in its capacity to relate subject and predicate, content and object, and so on.

41. The term "superelevation" is Derrida's: "*Erhaben*, the sublime, is not only high, elevated, nor even very elevated. Very high, absolutely high, higher than any comparable height, more than comparative, a size not measurable in height, the sublime is *superelevation* beyond itself" (Jacques Derrida, "Parergon," in *The Truth in Painting*, trans. Geoff Bennington and Ian McLeod [Chicago: University of Chicago Press, 1987], 122; his italics).

42. Adapted from Wallace Stevens, "Of Mere Being," in *The Palm at the End of the Mind*.

Chapter 5

1. Maurice Merleau-Ponty, "The Film and the New Psychology" (1945), in *Sense and Non-Sense*, trans. H. L. Dreyfus and P. A. Dreyfus (Evanston, IL: Northwestern University Press, 1964), 52–53.

2. Merleau-Ponty, *The World of Perception*, 83–84. Roy Ben-Shai brought this passage to my attention.

3. Merleau-Ponty, *The World of Perception*, 84; my italics.

4. Merleau-Ponty, "The Film and the New Psychology," 52–53; his italics.

5. Merleau-Ponty, "The Film and the New Psychology," 53.

6. It is noteworthy that this section of *The World of Perception* is titled "Man Seen from the Outside."

7. Heidegger, *Being and Time*, trans. MacQuarrie and Robinson, 68; I replace the word "mine" in this citation with "ours."

8. Kant, *Critique of Judgment*, 123. We have encountered this statement before, and it is worth quoting again in full: "Hence sublimity is contained not in any thing of nature, but only in our mind, insofar as we become conscious of our superiority to nature within us, and thereby also to nature outside us (as far as it influences us)."

9. I owe this last formulation to Aaron Bernstein.

10. Brennan, *The Transmission of Affect*, especially chapters 3 and 4.

11. A preliminary version of this first half of chapter 5 was presented to the Merleau-Ponty Circle at Fordham University, September 2019.

12. Max Scheler, *The Nature of Sympathy*, trans. Peter Heath (London: Routledge, 1954). Most of the passages on which I draw are from this major text as rearranged and supplemented in Max Scheler, *On Feeling, Knowing, and Valuing*, ed. Harold J. Bershady (Chicago: University of Chicago Press, 1992). Note that Scheler employs the term "feeling" (*Fühlen*) so broadly that it is not rigorously distinguishable from my own generic use of "emotion."

13. Max Scheler, "Community of Feeling, Fellow Feeling, Vicarious Feeling, Emotional Infection," in *On Feeling, Knowing, and Valuing*, 54; his italics. (Hereafter I refer to this book as *On Feeling*.)

14. "They [the parents] are inevitably 'external' to [her] . . . inspiring only commiseration 'with' and 'upon' [their] suffering" (Scheler, *On Feeling*, 54). We can also add: *at* their suffering.

15. Scheler, *On Feeling*, 55.

16. Scheler, *On Feeling*, 69; his italics.

17. Scheler, *On Feeling*, 55; Scheler capitalizes the word "cruel."

18. In emotional contagion "there is no true appearance of fellow feeling at all" (Scheler, *On Feeling*, 56).

19. "*All* fellow feeling involves *intentional reference* of the feeling of joy or sorrow to the other's experience" (Scheler, *On Feeling*, 54; his italics). He adds that "here there is neither a *directing* of feeling toward the other's joy or suffering, nor any participation in her experience" (56; his italics).

20. I borrow the phrase "sharing common ground" from the title of Robert Harvey's book *Sharing Common Ground: A Space for Ethics* (New York: Bloomsbury, 2017).

21. Scheler, *On Feeling*, 56; his italics.

22. Scheler, *On Feeling*, 56–57; his italics. Also active here, Anthony Steinbock suggests, may be a "sympathetic" bond with others, where "sympathy" is used in Scheler's sense of "participating in others' lived lives as they are lived by these others" (e-mail of April 24, 2020).

23. Scheler, *On Feeling*, 57.

24. Caleb Crain, "City Limits: What a White-Supremacist Coup Looks Like," *The New Yorker*, April 29, 2020, 70.

25. Anthony Steinbock, e-mail of April 5, 2020. We shall look at issues of crowd behavior in greater depth in chapters 7, 8, and 9.

26. In fact, Scheler considers emotional identification to be itself a form of emotional infection, "a heightened form, a limiting case, of [such] infection" (*On Feeling*, 58). But the difference is clearly that identification is typically a long and slow process, while emotional infection is very often spontaneous and quickly moving. As Scheler himself avers, emotional identification "may be of long duration, and can even become habitual through whole phases of life" (ibid.).

27. Scheler, *On Feeling*, 59.

28. Scheler, *On Feeling*, 61, 60.

29. Scheler, *On Feeling*, 59, 64.

30. Very likely there are other such planes. Scheler himself points to one of these, "mutual coalescence," which occurs when members of a collectivity merge

emotionally to the point that they can barely distinguish themselves from one another, forming "a *single* stream of instinct and feeling, whose pulse thereafter governs the behavior of all its members" (*On Feeling*, 64; his italics).

Chapter 6

1. Sara Ahmed, *The Cultural Politics of Emotion* (Edinburgh, UK: Edinburgh University Press, 2004), 9.

2. Ahmed, *Cultural Politics of Emotion*, 12.

3. Ahmed, *Cultural Politics of Emotion*, 14.

4. Ahmed, *Cultural Politics of Emotion*, 53; my italics.

5. Such a scene is not limited to singular events such as Lorde's early experience on the subway train. It is itself a concrete expression of a larger syndrome: "it is the circulation of hate between figures that works to materialize the very 'surface' of *collective bodies*" (Ahmed, *Cultural Politics of Emotion*, 46; my italics).

6. Ahmed, *Cultural Politics of Emotion*, 53.

7. Ahmed, *Cultural Politics of Emotion*, 44.

8. Ahmed, *Cultural Politics of Emotion*, 43.

9. Ahmed, *Cultural Politics of Emotion*, 59.

10. Hurston's essay "How It Feels to Be Colored Me" was first published in 1928. Its famous line became the basis of an artwork by Glenn Ligon, *Untitled* (1992), which contrasts the title, graphed in black, against a white background in numerous repetitions, with the two colors blurring toward the bottom of the work. I owe this reference to Grant Nagai (e-mail of June 2, 2020).

11. Ahmed, *Cultural Politics of Emotion*, 43. Ahmed begins the chapter "The Organization of Hate" with a statement from the website of the Aryan Nations group. For a further analysis of hate groups, see that entire chapter.

12. On the love–hate intermixing, see Ahmed, *Cultural Politics of Emotion*, 50–51.

13. It is striking that here Ahmed uses the very term, "impression," that is featured in the first phase of Seneca's model of emotion, though she claims to pick it up from Descartes; see Ahmed, *Cultural Politics of Emotion*, 5, 7.

14. Ahmed, *Cultural Politics of Emotion*, 6.

15. The last string of words is Ahmed's citation from *Spinoza's Ethics*, trans. A. Boyle (London: Everyman's, 1959), 85.

16. Ahmed, *Cultural Politics of Emotion*, 4.

17. Ahmed, *Cultural Politics of Emotion*, 8.

18. Ahmed, *Cultural Politics of Emotion*, 12.

19. Ahmed, *Cultural Politics of Emotion*, 1.

20. Ahmed, *Cultural Politics of Emotion*, 10. By saying "as if they are objects," Ahmed hints that we have to do with *phenomena* or experienced entities or events rather than anything like physical objects or material "things."

21. On this interplay, note the statement by Marjolein Oele: "the very materiality of the interfaces . . . co-generate and co-constitute . . . living beings"

(Marjolein Oele, *E-Co-Affectivity: Exploring Pathos at Life's Material Interfaces* [Albany: State University of New York Press, 2020], 7). These interfaces are where affectivity is generated in all forms of life. I return to Oele's insights in chapter 10.

22. I analyze this incident in terms of the power of a single glance in *The World at a Glance* (Bloomington: Indiana University Press, 2007), 441, 457.

23. Stickiness is discussed in Ahmed's *Cultural Politics of Emotion* at 15–16, 45, 46, 59, and 60. An especially striking statement is on 54: "Histories are bound up with emotions precisely insofar as it is a question of *what sticks*, of what connections are lived as the most intense or intimate, as being closer to the skin" (my italics). So the skin is not only a surface of inscription, but a vulnerable region where racist attitudes and behavior are especially apt to do lasting harm. I return to the importance of skin in chapter 10.

24. Thus Ahmed tries to demonstrate "how hate works by sticking 'figures of hate' together, transforming them into a common threat, within discourses on asylum and migration" (*Cultural Politics of Emotion*, 15).

25. Ahmed, *Cultural Politics of Emotion*, 18. The last phrase reminds us that sticking is not only a matter of attraction or attachment, as the term may seem to imply, but refers to any and all ways that the interdigitation of "objects" (very much including people) with emotions may occur—ways that are endless in kind and type.

26. I add "images" to "signs" in order to fill out Ahmed's model. Images figure precisely insofar as they are literally superficial—bearing on surface features, the *superficies*.

27. Ahmed, *Cultural Politics of Emotion*, 4; my italics.

28. At one point Ahmed mentions "affective forms of reorientation" (*Cultural Politics of Emotion*, 8). Had she pursued this further, it might well have led to a more adequate notion of agency. Of course, Ahmed is not the only thinker whose work raises an issue of agency. It is also evident in Foucault, and in structuralism more generally—with which Ahmed at least tacitly affiliates herself by her emphasis on the "circulation" of signs, objects, and affects.

29. Ahmed, *Cultural Politics of Emotion*, 10.

30. For Derrida's discussion of these two phases of deconstruction, see his interview with Julia Kristeva, "Semiology and Grammatology," in *Positions*, trans. Alan Bass (Chicago: University of Chicago Press, 1981), 15–35.

31. For a more complete discussion of this difference, see Casey, *The World on Edge*, chapter 1: "Borders and Boundaries." With Mary Watkins, I have discussed the US–Mexican border wall in Edward S. Casey and Mary Watkins, *Up Against the Wall: Re-Imagining the U.S.–Mexican Border* (Austin: University of Texas Press, 2014).

32. Ahmed, *Cultural Politics of Emotion*, 54; italics in original.

33. Ahmed, *Cultural Politics of Emotion*, 44.

34. See Gloria Anzaldúa, *Borderlands/La Frontera: The New Mestiza* (San Francisco: Aunt Lute, 1987).

35. On active edges, see Casey, *The World on Edge*, 35ff. and passim.

36. J. J. Gibson, *An Ecological Approach to Visual Perception* (Hillsdale, NJ: Erlbaum, 1989), 23.

Chapter 7

1. Daniel N. Stern, *The Interpersonal World of the Infant* (New York: Basic Books, 2000), 142.

2. Stern, *Interpersonal World of the Infant*, 139.

3. Stern, *Interpersonal World of the Infant*, 140, 141.

4. Although Stern's examples involve a mother and her child, nothing excludes the father or any other caretaker from taking up the responsive role in relation to the child's behavior. If I speak more often of the "mother," this is due to the makeup of Stern's original research situation, and is not meant to exclude others who achieve affective attunement with young children.

5. Stern, *Interpersonal World of the Infant*, 141.

6. Stern, *Interpersonal World of the Infant*, 142.

7. Stern, *Interpersonal World of the Infant*, 142.

8. I say "differentially" because adults, in contrast with infants, are responding from a lifetime of individuated experiences of emotional attunement. Thus the closely "matched" interactions at stake in Stern's analysis are more rarely present among adults, although there are strong temptations in this direction in the case of intense crowd behavior—as we shall find in Le Bon's model of such behavior.

9. Stern, *Interpersonal World of the Infant*, 156. At another level, vitality affects also "correspond to the momentary changes in feeling states involved in the organic processes of being alive" (ibid.).

10. See Stern, *Interpersonal World of the Infant*, 159. The attunement is to this kind of affect rather than to what Stern calls "classical" affects; that is, anger, joy, and so on, which the infant does not experience in any full-fledged form.

11. Grant Nagai comments: "It's as if there is a sort of dyadic improvisation occurring between mother and child—but one that takes place on a very intuitive, imaginative, and felt-out plane unlike the group improvisation that often takes place between highly skilled and trained jazz musicians that make judgments—albeit split-second judgments—in order to play cohesively alongside the other members of the group" (e-mail of May 7, 2020).

12. See Stern, *Interpersonal World of the Infant*, 151; also 148.

13. Stern, *Interpersonal World of the Infant*, 145. This is not to deny that factors of social overdetermination are also at play in this situation. A caretaker in this situation is not narrowly scripted, but has a sense of what is appropriate, and what not, in responding to the infant. Her or his behavior is certainly different from that of a friend who comes to visit and also interacts with the same infant. Both persons have absorbed paradigms of what is appropriate in becoming affectively attuned with the infant—implicit models that come from social sources that long preceded any specific encounters with the infant: the caretaker's role in relation to the infant being different from that of the friend. Of course, either person can depart from these paradigms, but when they do, it is with at least a fleeting eye on what the paradigms implicitly prescribe. As Fred Evans points out, "social voices" at one level interact subtly with emotionally charged gesticular bodily

movements at a concrete level, the two levels existing in a relationship of what Deleuze and Guattari term "reciprocal presupposition" (e-mail of May 10, 2020). For an insightful analysis of voice in social and political contexts, see Ron Scapp, *A Question of Voice: Philosophy and the Search for Legitimacy* (Ann Arbor: University of Michigan Press, 2020).

14. Stern, *Interpersonal World of the Infant,* 149; his italics. By italicizing the word "process," Stern indicates that while mother and child are aware of their respective affective states, both in themselves and in relation to each other, they are not comparably aware of the very *way* in which it happens. This "way" is what Stern as a child psychologist discerns and discusses.

15. Even if no words are exchanged, this does not mean there is not a discursive factor present—here in the form of an implicit prescription for how members of a group of bodies interact. (As "social distancing" came into effect in the weeks thereafter, this prescription became a social rule.) Fred Evans comments that "the arrangement of bodies, how close or far apart, touching permitted or not, the accepted or novel ways of expressing and maintaining the resulting affective attunement as well as the continuity of the interrelated bodies, are regulated by social voices/discourses. The two levels are always in play at once" (e-mail of May 10, 2020).

16. See Edmund Husserl, *Experience and Judgment,* ed. L. Landgrebe, trans. James Churchill and Karl Ameriks (Evanston, IL: Northwestern University Press, 1973), part 2.

17. Operative intentionality "establishes the natural and pre-predicative unity of the world and of our life, the intentionality that appears in our desires, our evaluations, and our landscape more clearly than it does in objective knowledge" (Merleau-Ponty, *Phenomenology of Perception,* lxxxii). In chapter 6 I extended operative intentionality to emotion in its agential power. I return to such intentionality in the epilogue.

18. Fred Evans adds this important observation: "Is the emotionality any more passive than the discursive framing of it? . . . The latter is [also] active as guiding your way of living the emotional setting; and the emotionality is active when it demands a discursive reformulation of itself—like the reflective ones it was demanding of you in Lazy Acres" (e-mail of May 10, 2020). This is to say that there is an intricate intertwining of passive and active elements at all levels of the situation: perceptual, emotional, and discursive-verbal.

19. It is tempting to say that my *hearing* the music is the active component, and listening is the *passive* element. But something more subtle is going on, as Jean-Luc Nancy argues in his book *Listening,* trans. Charlotte Mandell (New York: Fordham University Press, 2007). Much the same subtlety occurs in the group improvisation of jazz—in which the active and passive components often enter into a very complex weave.

20. Gustav Le Bon, *The Crowd: A Study of the Popular Mind; Crowd Psychology* (San Bernardino, CA: Adansonia, 2018), 15.

21. Le Bon, *The Crowd,* 15.

22. Le Bon, *The Crowd,* 17.

23. "Transformed sentiments" is a rather too literal translation of *sentiments transformées*—where *sentiments* is a basic French word for what I have been calling "emotions," though it can also be translated as "feelings" and even as "passions."

24. Le Bon, *The Crowd*, 18.

25. Le Bon, *The Crowd*, 18. This formulation converges with Fred Evans's model of "the oracular voice" in the chapter on "The Social Unconscious," in *The Multivoiced Body: Society and Communication in the Age of Diversity* (New York: Columbia University Press, 2009).

26. Le Bon, *The Crowd*, 30.

27. Le Bon, *The Crowd*, 19.

28. See Scheler, *On Feeling*, 64. Scheler also characterizes this as "identification through coalescence" and observes that it appears "in the psychic life of the unorganized *group*, as Le Bon first described it" (ibid.).

29. See Eugène Minkowski, *Lived Time: Phenomenological and Psychopathological Studies*, trans. Nancy Metzel (Evanston, IL: Northwestern University Press, 1970), 64–78.

30. I am using "oracular" in the sense given to this word by Fred Evans in *The Multivoiced Body*. This is the voice of authority that tolerates no objections or qualifications. (See also footnote 25 above.)

31. Le Bon, *The Crowd*, 19–20.

32. Le Bon, *The Crowd*, 19; my italics. The full statement is: "I allude to that suggestibility of which, moreover . . . contagion . . . is neither more nor less than an effect."

33. Le Bon, *The Crowd*, 19.

34. William James, "The Energies of Men," a 1906 address delivered to the American Philosophical Association, in *On Vital Reserves: The Energies of Men / The Gospel of Relaxation* (New York: Andesite, 2017), 6. James adds that in situations of crowd suggestibility, a "live idea" releases untapped energies that are otherwise held back by "habit neurosis" (15). I thank Grant Nagai for this reference.

35. On fascination, see Le Bon, *The Crowd*, 19: "An individual immerged for some length of time in a crowd in action soon finds himself . . . in a special state, which much resembles the state of fascination in which the hypnotised subject finds himself in the hands of the hypnotiser."

36. The demonstrations that followed in the wake of the police murder of George Floyd in late May 2020 are an instance of crowd behavior that aimed at constructive alterations in policing practices in the United States, especially the elimination of unjustified police brutality.

37. This model may well fit a mob circumstance such as occurred in Wilmington on the fateful day I have recounted, but only in large and loose lines, telling us little about how it happened in detail. Nor does it include the role of a commonly hated or resented target of such a contagious mob: for example, the successful African American politicians of the 1890s, for whose success members of the Wilmington black community were being punished.

38. William E. Connolly, *Aspirational Fascism: The Struggle for Multifaceted Democracy under Trumpism* (Minneapolis: University of Minnesota Press, 2017), 5.

39. Connolly, *Aspirational Fascism*, 58.

40. Connolly, *Aspirational Fascism*, 52–53. He adds: "Hitler's rhetorical powers were aided by such bodily practices [as with the paramilitary practices of the street gangs in the 1920s], and the practices spurred crowds [in the early 1930s] to new heights of response. The speeches and training resonated together" (53). Note that although Connolly does not single out "suggestibility" as such in the manner of Le Bon, he does say at one point that "the effects [of hearing such speeches on these occasions] are hypnotic" (47).

41. Connolly, *Aspirational Fascism*, 42.

42. Evans, *The Multivoiced Body*, 57–60. Evans makes the case for a model of a political and social unity that is composed of differences. I take this model to be closely related to the theme of sameness-requiring-difference that I have drawn from Heidegger's late seminar "Identity and Difference."

43. This is Sarah Churchill's phrase: "'mobilizing passions' catalyze fascism, which is propelled . . . more by feelings than by thought" (Sarah Churchill, "American Fascism: It Has Happened Here," *New York Review of Books Daily*, May 20, 2020). Her essay traces out early forms of fascism in America (the KKK, for example), arguing that in various ways these forms paved the way for Trump's election in 2016.

44. At most we can say that certain emotions like hatred and shame are "proto-fascistic" in that they lend themselves to fascistic articulation (e.g., the pronouncements of the Aryan Nations group in Britain), while others such as a sense of dignity and generosity of spirit are "proto-democratic" insofar as they ally themselves with democratic discourse.

Chapter 8

1. In the post-Trump era, we can appreciate that this omission is not a trivial matter. Sigmund Freud, *Group Psychology and the Analysis of the Ego*, trans. J. Strachey (New York: Norton, 1959), 18; this quotation is the last sentence of the second chapter, which is devoted entirely to Le Bon. The book's German title is *Massenpsychologie und Ich-Analyse*. "Prestige" is Le Bon's term, and much of the credit for a leader's strength is attributed to it, but he says little more concerning the role of the leader who directs and inspires crowds.

2. Freud, *Group Psychology*, 26.

3. Freud, *Group Psychology*, 31. William McDougall was the author of *The Group Mind* (Cambridge: Cambridge University Press, 1921), a book that Freud briefly reviews in his *Group Psychology*.

4. Freud, *Group Psychology*, 31. See also *Beyond the Pleasure Principle*, trans. James Strachey (New York: Bantam Books, 1959): "the efforts of Eros" are "to combine organic substances into ever larger unities" (78).

5. Freud, *Group Psychology*, 31; the phrase in German is *ihnen zu Liebe*, literally "for love of them."

6. Freud, *Group Psychology*, 60–61; his italics.

7. Freud first introduced the ego-ideal (*Über-Ich*) in his essay "On Narcis-

sism" (1914), and it is subsequently seen as furnishing the moral standards by which the superego judges the actions of the ego.

8. Freud, *Group Psychology*, 46, 48; see also 50.

9. Freud, *Group Psychology*. "The mutual tie between members of a group is . . . based upon an important common emotional quality" (50).

10. Fred Evans adds this comment: "The saliency (audibility) of the oracularized voice/discourse of the leader is elevated as a resonance in the lead voices of the others" (e-mail of May 10, 2020). This is to emphasize the specifically *vocal* character of the leader's empowerment—embodying a rhetorical force that is transmitted to the leader's lieutenants, who bark out orders to a subordinate populace. This happened not only with Hitler's leading officers but already in the American Civil War; see Douglas Southall Freeman, *Lee's Lieutenants: A Study in Command*, abridged ed. (New York: Scribner, 2011).

11. The paradigm of Eros is sexual love, but in the case of group formation, it is a matter of "love instincts that have been diverted from their original [explicitly sexual] aims, though they do not operate with less energy on that account" (Freud, *Group Psychology*, 44). Striking here is the absence of any description of what Robert Harvey calls "sharing *common ground*"—that is, being brought together thanks to a basis in convergent beliefs and ideas, as happened, for example, in the racial justice demonstrations of summer 2020. See Robert Harvey, *Sharing Common Ground: A New Space for Ethics* (New York: Bloomsbury, 2017). Such beliefs and ideas add a cognitive dimension to the erotic dimension emphasized by Freud. They are explicitly recognized by William James under the headings of "volitional will" and "live ideas" (James, "The Energies of Men," 9, 15).

12. We are a long way from Scheler's model of love as a relationship in which one seeks out and helps to engender positive values in the person loved. What interests Freud is not any such flourishing of the beloved other, but an intense identification with that other which can be considered a condition of possibility for such flourishing.

13. On the theme of *von unten*, see Karl Jaspers, *Philosophy*, vol. 2, trans. E. B. Ashton (Chicago: University of Chicago Press, 1969).

14. A masterful text on such subjacent emotionality is Steinbock's *Moral Emotions*, which describes in detail the working of such formative emotions as hope, trust, humility, and loving, as well as such de-formative emotions as shame, guilt, pride, and despair. See Anthony J. Steinbock, *Moral Emotions: Reclaiming the Evidence of the Heart* (Evanston, IL: Northwestern University Press, 2014), especially the conclusion: "Moral Emotions, the Person, and the Social Imaginary." See also Steinbock's *Knowing by Heart: Loving as Participation and Critique* (Evanston, IL: Northwestern University Press, 2021). Despite many convergences, Steinbock and I move in different directions when it comes to the question of the basic localization of emotions: he prefers the heart or inner person as the privileged locus of major emotions, and I prefer the environing world.

15. John Protevi, *Political Affect: Connecting the Social and the Somatic* (Minneapolis: University of Minnesota Press, 2009), 27. Protevi's remarkable book pursues the thesis that "politically shaped and triggered affective cognition is the sense-making of bodies politic . . . affect is concretely the imbrication of the

social and the somatic" (33). See also Protevi, "Political Emotion," in *Collective Emotions*, ed. Christian von Scheve and Mikko Salmela (Oxford: Oxford University Press, 2013), chapter 21.

16. Protevi, *Political Affect*, 148.

17. A more extensive engagement with the themes of protoempathic identification in the context of group activity is offered in the next chapter (chapter 9).

18. Sigmund Freud, *The Interpretation of Dreams*, trans. James Strachey (New York: Avon, 1965), 651. He had not yet come up with the concept of the "preconscious" when he wrote these words in 1899.

19. Sigmund Freud, "The Unconscious," in *General Psychological Theory*, ed. and trans. Philip Rieff (New York: Collier, 1963), 126–27.

20. Freud, "The Unconscious," 128. Freud adds that "there are no unconscious affects in the sense in which there are unconscious ideas" (ibid.). For repression proper is of *ideas*, not emotions as such. But that which ideas represent may certainly be said to have the status of something unconscious, especially insofar as it is a manifestation of an instinctual impulse, which as something organic and somatic is literally non-conscious. Freud further asserts that "repression can succeed in inhibiting the transformation of an instinctual impulse into affective expression" (127), where the repression in this case is not just of an idea, but of the fate of an instinctual impulse coming from within the somatic matrix of the human subject.

21. "The affect does not as a rule arise [into conscious awareness] until it has succeeded in penetrating into the Cs [consciousness] in attachment to some new substitutive idea" (Freud, "The Unconscious," 128).

22. "The collective unconscious is identical with Nature to the extent that Nature itself, including matter, is unknown to us" (C. G. Jung, *The Earth Has a Soul: The Nature Writings of C. G. Jung*, ed. Meredith Sabini [Berkeley, CA: North Atlantic Books, 2009], 82).

23. These phrases are from the same passage of *The Interpretation of Dreams* that is cited just above, 651; they are italicized in Freud's text.

24. On resentment, see Max Scheler's essay *Ressentiment*, ed. Lewis B. Coser (Milwaukee, WI: Marquette University Press, 1994).

Chapter 9

1. On operative intentionality, see Merleau-Ponty, *Phenomenology of Perception*, lxxxii. This notion, already mentioned in part 2, is revisited in the epilogue. I hold that emotions have an intrinsic operative intentionality that sets them apart from the operative intentionality of perception, which was Merleau-Ponty's own primary concern.

2. See Evans, *The Multivoiced Body*, especially chapters 3 and 6.

3. Pertinent here is Lyotard's distinction between fully articulated voicing at the level of *logos* and the unarticulated "mixed voice" or "confused voice" which, though not spelled out in so many words, is nonetheless communicable.

Such spontaneous voicing is fully embodied—as we see in the case of an outcry such as the collective "howl" that traversed the marchers in the Women's March of 2017—even if it is not expressed in so many words, much less syntactically. It is a voicing that carries its own force, especially in crowds where voices commingle in a mass of sounds, only some of which are fully articulate. Included here as well is the role of shared silence in crowd situations. See Jean-François Lyotard, "Affect-Phrase" (from a Supplement to *The Differend*), in *The Lyotard Reader and Guide*, ed. Keith Crome and James Williams (New York: Columbia University Press, 2006), 105–10. I owe this last reference to Grant Nagai (e-mail of July 10, 2020).

4. I take this account from a diary entry I made at the time of the march.

5. Emile Durkheim remarks that "in order for a thing to be the object of common sentiments, it must necessarily be shared: that is to say, it must be present in all minds such that everyone can represent it in the same manner" (Durkheim, *Selected Writings*, ed. Anthony Giddens [Cambridge: Cambridge University Press, 1972], 137).

6. Durkheim, *Selected Writings*, 137; my italics.

7. Durkheim, *Selected Writings*, 140.

8. In the introduction and conclusion of *Political Affect*, Protevi explores various ways by which distinctively "pro-social" actions and institutions can be cultivated. The term is his own.

9. Here I employ Fred Evans's three criteria of democracy: solidarity, heterogeneity, and fecundity. These were first set forth in *The Multivoiced Body* and then expanded on in Evans's more recent book *Public Art and the Fragility of Democracy* (New York: Columbia University Press, 2018). Even though the African American Day Parade was something that unfolded temporally, in contrast with a single lasting piece of sculpture or a commemorative wall, in my view it should count as an authentic instance of public art. It exemplifies what Evans calls "a unity composed of difference," in contrast with "a unity imposed on difference" (e-mail of May 10, 2020).

10. On group improvisation, see George E. Lewis, "Improvised Music since 1950: Afrological and Eurological Perspectives," *Black Music Research Journal* 16, no. 1 (Spring 1996): 91–122. Thanks to Grant Nagai for this reference.

11. Samuel IJsseling, *Mimesis: On Appearing and Being* (Amsterdam: Kok Pharos, 1997), 27. The entire book is relevant to this discussion.

12. Sadly, however, this same commingling has been held responsible for the intense outbreak of COVID-19 in New Orleans soon after the Mardi Gras of February 2020.

13. Craig Fortier, *Unsettling the Commons: Social Movements Within, Against, and Beyond Settler Colonialism* (Winnipeg, Canada: ARP, 2017), 10–11.

14. Also effective is "call and response" chanting such as occurred in Brooklyn during the George Floyd protests: *"How do you spell racist?"* (followed by) *"NYPD!"*; *"Say his name!"* (followed by) *"George Floyd!"* and *"Say her name!"* (followed by) *"Breonna Taylor!"*

15. See "Coronavirus: Germans Sing *Bella Ciao* from Rooftops in Solidarity with Italy," *Guardian News*, https://www.youtube.com/watch?v=z5CrScIHAuE. I owe this reference to John Protevi (e-mail of April 27, 2020).

16. Barbara Ehrenreich, *Dancing in the Streets: A History of Collective Joy* (New York: Henry Holt, 2006).

17. Ricardo C. Ainslie, *No Dancin' in Anson: An American Story of Race and Social Change* (Lanham, MD: Aronson, 1995).

18. "Riot" is a highly ambiguous term. However destructive a given riot can be, it may express a deeply felt need on the part of the rioters—a need that is not being addressed by the society in which the rioters are embedded. As Martin Luther King Jr. said in 1967: "I think America must see that riots do not develop out of thin air. Certain conditions continue to exist in our society which must be condemned as vigorously as we condemn riots. But in the final analysis, a riot is the language of the unheard" (address at Stanford University; see https://www.crmvet.org/docs/otheram.htm). Many of those participating in the failed attempt to disrupt confirmation of the 2020 election results by the US Congress on January 6, 2021, considered themselves to be unheard. (I thank Grant Nagai for bringing King's statement to my attention.)

19. On place as event, see my discussions in the "Postface" to *The Fate of Place: A Philosophical History* (Berkeley: University of California Press, 1997); and my essay "How to Get from Space to Place in a Fairly Short Stretch of Time," reprinted in *Getting Back into Place: Toward a Renewed Understanding of the Place-World*, 2nd ed. (Bloomington: Indiana University Press, 2009), 317–48.

Chapter 10

1. The mutability of emotions helps make psychotherapy viable; without it there would be no prospect of alleviating a client's troubled psyche. But due to its variable manifestations, a given emotion is difficult to track over time and is full of unexpected twists and turns, often surprising the therapist as much as the client.

2. Teresa Brennan, *The Transmission of Affect* (Ithaca, NY: Cornell University Press, 2004), 73.

3. Sigmund Freud, "Project for a Scientific Psychology," in *Standard Edition*, ed. and trans. James Strachey, 1:158.

4. See Megan Craig and Edward S. Casey, "Thinking in Transit," in *Philosophy, Travel, and Place*, ed. Ron Scapp and Brian Seitz (Cham, Switz.: Palgrave Macmillan/Springer, 2018), 51–67.

5. This is not to deny that thoughts can carry affective valences of their own, or that emotions can possess cognitive dimensions.

6. Artworks as bearers of emotion are addressed in my analysis of paintings by Gerhard Richter and Anselm Kiefer that bear witness to the Holocaust; see the appendix.

7. Brennan, *Transmission of Affect*, 2, 6.

8. Brennan, *Transmission of Affect*, 15.

9. Brennan, *Transmission of Affect*, 6.

10. Brennan, *Transmission of Affect*, 3.

11. Brennan, *Transmission of Affect*, 3; my italics. This phraseology is repeated on p. 19: affect is "a vehicle connecting individuals to one another and the environment."

12. Brennan, *Transmission of Affect*, 8. Nevertheless, the environmental dimension of affects reenters her discourse from time to time, as in her phrase "environmental-inflected affects" and in the language of "atmosphere," as in "an atmosphere in a room tells us at once that the transmission of affect does not work only between two persons" (ibid., 15, 20). This last statement opens the door at least partly to affective transmission beyond the interpersonal; but Brennan does not further attempt to spell out what this would be like. My own effort is to do precisely that in this and the next chapter.

13. Brennan, *Transmission of Affect*, 17. This claim is part of her historicist account in which modernity, in its "quest for certainty" (in John Dewey's phrase), entered into a delimiting and destructive embrace of visuocentrism, valorizing sight above all the other senses. The result was that "by the nineteenth century sight was the first of the senses, and to this day the only sense, to attain objective status" (ibid.).

14. This is not to deny that vision has certain non-objectifying dimensions. George Quasha points out that vision "sees texture" and can be closely allied with other senses such as touch: "Full-body seeing is a possibly useful concept" (e-mail of January 13, 2021).

15. Brennan, *Transmission of Affect*, 9. Brennan backs this up with citations of research on hormones and pheromones (ibid., 9–10).

16. For a forceful statement of the multisensory determination of experience, see Bruce Wilshire, *The Much-at-Once: Magic, Science, Ecstasy, and the Body* (New York: Fordham University Press, 2016); as well as the breakthrough book of Glen Mazis, *Emotion and Embodiment: Fragile Ontology* (Albany: State University of New York Press, 1993). Constraints of space do not allow me to do justice to these earlier efforts, which take decisive steps in the direction of my own work.

17. Brennan, *Transmission of Affect*, 23.

18. Richard Kearney, "The Wager of Carnal Hermeneutics," in *Carnal Hermeneutics*, ed. Richard Kearney and Brian Treanor (New York: Fordham University Press, 2015), 21. For a more complete statement, see Richard Kearney, *Touch: Recovering Our Most Vital Sense* (New York: Columbia University Press, 2021). I was not able to consult this work in time to incorporate its nuanced insights into my own text.

19. Further ambiguities and nuances in the case of touch have been explored in detail by Jean-Luc Nancy in his books *Being Singular Plural* and *Corpus*, and are further refined in Jacques Derrida's book *On Touching: Jean-Luc Nancy*. These comparatively recent books both bear out Aristotle's claim that touch is the most basic of the senses in living organisms. A sign of the importance of touch is found in the fact that touch is highly coded socially, as we see in the case of inappropriate touching. George Quasha refers to this as "touch literacy" (e-mail of January 13, 2021).

20. Brennan, *Transmission of Affect*, 65.

21. Vision is a fifth, but I am bracketing its role in view of Brennan's stric-

tures and because I have treated it at length in *The World at a Glance* (Bloomington: Indiana University Press, 2007), especially in part 3: "Getting Inside the Glance."

22. Brennan attends closely to Spinoza at several places in *The Transmission of Affect* (101–2, 117, 156) and refers her reader to Susan James, *Passions and Action: The Emotions in Seventeenth-Century Philosophy* (Oxford: Oxford University Press, 1997).

23. R. P. Michael and Eric B. Keverne, "Pheromones in the Communication of Status in Primates," *Nature* 218 (1958): 746; cited by Brennan, *Transmission of Affect*, 69.

24. Brennan, *Transmission of Affect*, 69.

25. George Quasha, *Poetry in Principle* (New York: Spuyten Duyvil/Dispatches Editions, 2019), 55.

26. Quasha, *Poetry in Principle*, 78, 73.

27. George Quasha, *Not Even Rabbits Go Down This Hole* (New York: Spuyten Duyvil, 2020), xi; his italics.

28. Quasha adds: "When we're in the grip of an emotion, we react according to past patterns/habits because in part we need a familiar orientation. Emotion involves intensification in a way that competes with free awareness. It takes a special kind of mindfulness to see beyond that compelling need for stable perspective. If we can see the event beyond that Newtonian orientation, we may enter a space of further insight. Another transform is nonlocation—not just action at a distance, but interaction over distance. This tendency toward experimental orientation is part of how I understand the psychonautic. We are inside the field whose dynamic is an emotion 'we're having' or is 'having us'—but, better, is co-occurring. Made conscious, it becomes *co-performative* and *co-configurative*" (e-mail of July 4, 2020; his italics).

29. G. A. Bradshaw, *Elephants on the Edge: What Animals Teach Us about Humanity* (New Haven, CT: Yale University Press, 2009).

30. Donna J. Haraway, *When Species Meet* (New York: Columbia University Press, 2008).

31. Cynthia Willett, *Interspecies Ethics* (New York: Columbia University Press, 2014), 92. See also Evelyn B. Pluhar, *Beyond Prejudice: The Moral Significance of Human and Nonhuman Animals* (Durham, NC: Duke University Press, 1995). Willett's book, taken together with Pluhar's and Haraway's work, opens up an entire field of investigation that is deeply consequential not only for understanding the transmission of emotion but for the formation of diverse biosocial groupings, with important implications for the political dimension of human societies, as Willett demonstrates eloquently.

32. Willett, *Interspecies Ethics*, 138.

33. If "affects constitute an elementary ground for communicative ethics from infancy through adulthood" (Willett, *Interspecies Ethics*, 90), then they can serve as the ground for many forms of biosocial interaction between diverse species. On the socialized symbiosis of humans and bears, see Gay Bradshaw's account of Charlie Russell's ongoing relationships with bears: *Talking with Bears: Conversations with Charlie Russell* (Calgary, Canada: Rocky Mountain Books, 2020);

on the human–primate relation, see the striking accounts of Barbara Smuts, for example, "Encounters with Animal Minds," *Journal of Consciousness Studies* 8 (2001): 293–309; and see Frans de Waal, *The Age of Empathy: Nature's Lessons for a Kinder Society* (New York: Harmony, 2009).

34. Willett, *Interspecies Ethics*, 80–81.

35. Willett, *Interspecies Ethics*, 80.

36. The Snyder citation is found in Gary Snyder, *The Practice of the Wild* (San Francisco: Shoemaker and Hoard, 2004), 12. Snyder also refers suggestively to "the web of the wild world" (ibid., 41). The other citation is from Willett, *Interspecies Ethics*, 140.

37. Willett, *Interspecies Ethics*, 140. Here Willett joins forces with Evelyn Pluhar, who insists on a specifically moral dimension of animal behavior, a dimension that cannot be restricted to human beings (as it is by Kant and many other Western thinkers).

38. Willett, *Interspecies Ethics*, 141.

39. Brennan, *Transmission of Affect*, 65. Brennan insists that it is as social that affects have causal force: "If we have to make a distinction pro forma, the *social*, not the physical, is causative" (ibid., 71; her italics).

40. Brennan, *Transmission of Affect*, 65.

41. Brennan, *Transmission of Affect*, 77.

42. Merleau-Ponty, *Phenomenology of Perception*, 156.

43. Merleau-Ponty, *Phenomenology of Perception*, 399; my italics. I owe this reference to Adam Blair. By the phrase "natural attitude" Merleau-Ponty is not referring to Husserl's technical term that concerns what must be suspended in phenomenological investigations, but rather to what we experience in a spontaneous and unforced way.

44. Marjolein Oele, *E-Co-Affectivity: Exploring Pathos at Life's Material Interfaces* (Albany: State University of New York Press, 2020). "By drawing on a broader and deeper spectrum of affectivity in line with Aristotle's usage and as applied to multiple forms of life, I move explicitly beyond a narrow, psychological interpretation of affect as passion, mood, feeling, and emotion" (ibid., 7).

45. Michael Henry, *Material Phenomenology*, trans. Scott Davidson (New York: Fordham University Press, 2008).

46. Henry, *Material Phenomenology*, 3. By "pathetic" Henry does not intend the usual connotations of weak or pitiable. He is drawing on the Greek term *pathos*, which signifies suffering-as-undergoing.

47. Oele, *E-Co-Affectivity*, 7; italics in original. On "suffering-with," see part 3: "Pathos-With." The phrase "affective interface" is employed on p. 158. For Oele, such interfaces are also to be found in soil, for example, not only in living things per se; see 149ff., especially 153, where "soil as mediating interface" is the focus.

48. Oele, *E-Co-Affectivity*, 111; her italics. Such world-formation is also found in social and political contexts. Oele cites Walter Mignolo: "the outside [is] built from the inside in the process of building itself as inside" (Mignolo, "Decolonizing Western Epistemology: Building Decolonial Epistemologies," in *Decolonizing Epistemologies: Latina/o Theology and Philosophy*, ed. Ada Isasi-Diaz and Eduardo

Mendieta (New York: Fordham University Press, 2012), 26. Oele would likely insist that here too skin is an active formative factor as a pervasive interface.

49. Oele, *E-Co-Affectivity*, 136. Oele adds that "this dermatological interface is not merely passive, but—in a middle-voiced fashion—chooses and (re)generates our time, place, and being."

50. Michel Serres, *The Five Senses: A Philosophy of Mingled Bodies*, trans. M. Sankey and P. Cowley (London: Continuum, 2008), 80; cited by Oele in *E-Co-Affectivity*, 110. Jean-Luc Nancy says this about skin: "Truth is in the skin, it makes skin; an authentic expression exposed, entirely turned outside while also enveloping the inside" (Jean-Luc Nancy, *Corpus*, trans. Richard Rand [New York: Fordham University Press, 2008], 159).

51. Oele, *E-Co-Affectivity*, 111. This phrase sums up the position of François Dagognet in *La Peau découverte* (Le Plessis-Robinson, Fr.: Synthélabo, 1993), especially 12–13. Oele elaborates: "the skin is also allowing for the productivity of the interior. . . . What I want to highlight is the interaction of 'internally emergent and externally emergent factors coming to bear on an interface'" (e-mail of July 15, 2020, quoted with permission).

52. I am taking "ecoproprioception" in Quasha's sense as the sensing of movement in kinesthesia—a movement that situates us in the larger domain of the lived environment. This happens in considerable part by means of what Ani Albers calls "tactile sensibility." Albers writes that such sensibility involves the tactile perception of both the "surface quality of material that can be observed by touch" and "the tactile perception of material related to inner structure (pliability, sponginess, brittleness, porousness)" (Ani Albers, *On Weaving* [Mineola, NY: Dover, 1965], 63). For Albers, "grain, roughness, and smoothness" can be felt through contact with the skin (as opposed to "colors" that can be seen visually)" (ibid.). Grant Nagai comments: "A key term that Albers uses to differentiate tactile sensibility from visual sensibility is 'texture' and the experience of what Albers calls 'material . . . in the rough'" (e-mail of June 15, 2020). Such texture and material in the rough serve as effective transmitters of emotion as *felt*, that is, as we experience it when we realize for instance that a certain touch conveys another person's affection to us.

53. Another tissue of importance here is the skin of the eardrum: a skin that serves as an interface between sounds in the environment and the hearing apparatus of the inner ear. Such sounds carry emotion to us from various directions, so that the eardrum is itself an affective interface. Note also that the inner ear itself, being the source of equilibrium, is integral to ecoproprioception as discussed earlier.

54. Oele, *E-Co-Affectivity*, 77. On the subtleties of touch in the life of birds, see especially 55ff., which I draw on closely in this section.

55. On the relationship between edge and surface more generally, see Casey, *The World on Edge*, 39–45.

56. The phrase "layout of places" is inspired by the thinking of James J. Gibson in his seminal book *The Ecological Approach to Visual Perception* (Hillsdale, NJ: Erlbaum, 1986). But Gibson restricts layout to surfaces; see especially 22, 24, 33–36, 307.

57. See Gary Snyder, "The Porous World," in *A Place in Space* (New York: Counterpoint, 1995). The receptacle (*hypodoche*) for Plato is "the nurse of all becoming and change," a "neutral plastic material" that has no character of its own but reflects all that enters it (*Timaeus* 49a, 50c).

58. Scheler, *On Feeling*, 56. The phrase "dynamogenic effect" is in William James's essay "Energies of Men," 6. It is just such a directly shared emotionality as experienced in a public space that was often missing—and acutely missed!—during the pandemic of 2020–21.

59. Scheler, *On Feeling*, 56; his italics.

60. On tacit knowing, see Michael Polanyi, *The Tacit Dimension* (New York: Anchor, 1967).

Chapter 11

1. See Glenn A. Albrecht, *Earth Emotions: New Words for a New World* (Ithaca, NY: Cornell University Press, 2019). Despite its promising title, this book continues to locate emotion itself largely in human beings, as when the author states that "*human* emotions are embedded in the structure of the cosmos" (6; my italics) and that "emotional states such as jealousy and anger find their correlates in the capriciousness and violence in nature" (7).

2. John Dewey, in chapter 2 of *Art as Experience*, discusses the dynamic interaction between live creatures and their environments as constituting events that are perceivable by observers of this interaction.

3. Scheler, for example, employs "atmosphere" in this statement: "Even the objective aspects of such feelings, which attach to natural objects, or are discerned in an 'atmosphere'—such as the serenity of a spring landscape, the melancholy of a rainy day, the wretchedness of a room—can work infectiously . . . on the state of our emotions" (Scheler, *On Feeling*, 56; he italicizes "objective"). The quotation marks around "atmosphere" indicate that he is thinking of it as a metaphorical term.

4. For an account of Nature as something we can plausibly consider "wicked"—angry *at us*—see Benjamin Hale, *Nature as Wild and Wicked: On Nature and Human Nature* (Cambridge, MA: MIT Press, 2016). Hale argues that to feel that nature is "wicked"—angry enough to punish us in various concrete ways (hurricanes, tsunamis, and global pandemics, as we must now add, with the recent advent of COVID-19)—is to experience it as possessing the rough equivalent of human anger, on a much vaster scale.

5. I refer to Julia Kristeva's *Black Sun: Depression and Melancholia*, trans. L. S. Roudiez (New York: Columbia University Press, 1989). See my essay on aspects of this book, "Depression: Heading Down and Out," in *The Philosophy of Julia Kristeva*, ed. Sarah Beardsworth, Library of Living Philosophers 36 (Carbondale, IL: Open Court, 2020); this essay is paired with Alina N. Feld, "Melancholia: Passing Through and Beyond" in the same volume. See also Christopher Bol-

las, *Meaning and Melancholia: Life in the Age of Bewilderment* (New York: Routledge, 2018); and especially Alina N. Feld, *Melancholy and the Otherness of God: A Study of the Hermeneutics of Depression* (Lanham, MD: Lexington, 2011).

6. See Martin Heidegger, *Identity and Difference*, trans. Joan Stambaugh (Chicago: University of Chicago Press, 2002).

7. Plato's unwritten doctrine of the indefinite dyad is outlined in Aristotle, *Metaphysics* 987b.

8. Notice that here I do distinguish between "affect" and "emotion" to the extent that affect can be considered the impinging edge of emotion as it draws us into its ambience—just as the opening moment of a weather system draws us into its embrace. Even as this distinction fits much ongoing experience, I continue to employ "emotion" as the generic term, of which affect and feeling are variant modalities.

9. This is Kathleen Freeman's translation of Anaximenes's fragment 1, in her study *Ancilla to the Pre-Socratic Philosophers* (Cambridge, MA: Harvard University Press, 1948), 19.

10. Freeman, *Ancilla*, 19; translation slightly modified. This is fragment 3, regarded by Freeman as spurious; but spurious or not, it is of considerable interest to us for what it suggests.

11. On the difference between border and boundary, see Casey, *The World on Edge*, chapter 1.

12. Anaximander, fragments 1, 3, as translated in Freeman, *Ancilla*, 19.

13. In using the phrase "doom-to-come" I adapt Derrida's locution *a-venir*, which he invoked in his discussion of "democracy-to-come" as non-messianic, that is, not as fated to happen but felt as something that *can*, and indeed *should*, happen. See Jacques Derrida, *Rogues: Two Essays on Reason*, trans. Michael Naas and Pascale-Anne Brault (Stanford, CA: Stanford University Press, 2005).

14. By stressing air as a carrier of emotion, I do not mean to deny the role of other material elements as affective media—water, for example, as invoked in the phrase "drowning your sorrows."

15. Luce Irigaray, *The Forgetting of Air in Martin Heidegger*, trans. Mary Beth Mader (Austin: University of Texas Press, 1999), 5. "Clearing" itself, though pointing in the right direction, is not sufficient in the end for Irigaray: "Prior to any clearing, air is that medium of which [spatial] extension is built" (ibid., 19). Note that Irigaray's critique of presence rejoins that of Derrida in his early writings.

16. The various citations in the last several sentences are all from Irigaray, *The Forgetting of Air*, 8–9.

17. Irigaray, *The Forgetting of Air*, 14. As Irigaray spells out the primacy of air, it is "the arch-mediation: of *logos*, of thinking, of the world—whether physical or psychical. Air would be the substance of the copula that would permit the gathering-together and the arrangement of the whole into life and Being of man, and permit his habitation in space as a mortal" (12).

18. "The Encompassing" (*das Umgreifende*) is a major concept in Karl Jaspers's *Philosophy*, vol. 1, trans. E. B. Ashton (Chicago: University of Chicago Press, 1971).

19. Brian Massumi, *Politics of Affect* (Cambridge: Polity, 2015), 210.

20. Heidegger, *Being and Time*, trans. Macquarrie and Robinson, 176; his italics.

21. Heidegger, *Being and Time*, 173. Heidegger adds that "a state-of-mind implies a disclosive submission to the world, out of which we can encounter something that matters to us" (ibid.).

22. Heidegger, *Being and Time*, 173.

23. Heidegger, *Being and Time*, 174.

24. Heidegger, *Being and Time*, 175.

25. Heidegger, *Being and Time*, 174; my italics.

26. Heidegger, *Being and Time*, 175; his italics.

27. Heidegger, *Being and Time*, 178; my italics. Dasein "evades itself" in its own fallenness, its proclivity to thrownness.

28. But this is not to say that for Heidegger we find our fully authentic self in mood. In my reading of *Being and Time*, we find an amplified self in mood that can be said to be akin with an existentially authentic self: the latter being most completely realized in affirming one's being-toward-death.

29. For a comparable but differently expressed and argued assessment of mood, see David Abram, *Becoming Animal: An Earthly Cosmology* (New York: Pantheon, 2010), 131–58.

30. Gendlin writes that for Heidegger, mood is how we sense ourselves in situations: "Whereas feeling is usually thought of as something inward, Heidegger's concept [of mood] refers to something both inward and outward, but before a split between inside and outside has been made. . . . A mood is not just internal, it is this living in the world. We sense how we find ourselves, and we find ourselves in situations" (Gendlin, *Saying What We Mean*, 210).

31. Gendlin, *Saying What We Mean*, 131; his italics.

32. Gendlin, *Saying What We Mean*, 134, 135; his italics. The body is pivotal for Gendlin: "The body is made of environmental stuff and its organismic events happen in the environment. The body *is* environmental body-constituting. Body-environment is a single sequence of environmental events" (135–36; his italics). And "*because* an organism is environmental, therefore it happens directly into the environment" (169; his italics).

33. Gendlin, *Saying What We Mean*, 304 (his italics), 176.

34. Martin Heidegger, "The Aroundness of the Environment and Dasein's Spatiality," in *Being and Time*, 134–48. He emphasizes that "we must show how the aroundness of the environment, the specific spatiality of entities encountered in the environment, is founded upon the worldhood of the world" (135). Here I would modify "spatiality" to "placiality" in keeping with my own emphasis on places-of-presentation.

35. Massumi, *Politics of Affect*, 52. He adds, "I don't mean the body as a *thing* apart from the self or subject" (ibid.; my italics).

36. On "place-bearing" common spaces and relationships, see Fortier, *Unsettling the Commons*, 95, 104.

37. Dewey, *Art as Experience* (New York: Perigee, 2005), 193. Grant Nagai

brought to my attention this passage as well as the ones cited from Dewey's *Experience and Nature*.

38. Dewey, *Art as Experience*, 390.

Epilogue

1. Merleau-Ponty, *Phenomenology of Perception*, trans. Landes, lxxxii. I cite these words a first time in a footnote in chapter 7.

2. Deleuze writes: "All the new sports—surfing, windsurfing, hang-gliding—take the form of entering into an existing wave. There's no longer an origin as starting point, but a sort of putting-into-orbit. The key thing is how to get taken up in the motion of a big wave, a column of rising air, to 'get into something' instead of being the origin of an effort" (Gilles Deleuze, "Mediators," in *Negotiation*, trans. Martin Joughin [New York: Columbia University Press, 1995], 122). I owe this reference to Grant Nagai.

3. Here I am invoking the rhizomatic structure defined by Deleuze and Guattari: "an acentered, nonhierarchical, nonsignifying system [or multiplicity] without a General and without an organizing memory or central automation, defined solely by a circulation of states" (Deleuze and Guattari, *A Thousand Plateaus*, 21). Given that a rhizome in the botanical meaning of the term is typically under (or on) the ground, my own use of the metaphor flips it into the air or atmosphere which I have valorized as a privileged medium for the display of extrasubjective emotions. But the locution "lines of flight" as employed by Deleuze and Guattari works well with my aerial proclivity. I fully endorse the notion of a noncentered set of diverse places that cannot be mapped "from the top down," and thus with Deleuze and Guattari's critique of "topophilia" (see 12–15).

4. I would not deny, however, that there are circumstances where we should attempt to curtail certain emotions, especially those that threaten to do violence to ourselves or others. These are limit cases that must be taken seriously and understood on their own terms.

5. By referring to "primary emotionality" I am not endorsing the dubious notion of "primary emotions." I have avoided employing the term "primary emotions," as in Paul Ekman's efforts to delineate the seven basic "emotion categories." See Paul Ekman, ed., *Emotion in the Human Face* (1972; New York: Malor, 2013), 42–48. This is a futile pursuit in my view because what determines the meaning of "major" depends largely if not entirely on context, and indeed other researchers have proposed wide variants in such categories.

6. For Aristotle's account of *topos* as "the first unchangeable limit of that which surrounds," see his *Physics*, book 4, 212a 19–20, in Edward Hussey's translation in *Aristotle's Physics, Books III and IV* (Oxford: Oxford University Press, 1983), 28.

7. See Casey, *The World on Edge*, 35.

8. Henry Corbin, *Spiritual Body and Celestial Earth: From Mazdean Iran to Shi'ite*

Iran, trans. Nancy Pearson (Princeton, NJ: Princeton University Press, 1977), xiii. This passage is cited as an epigraph in Tom Cheetham's book *The World Turned Inside Out* (Putnam, CT: Spring, 2003), vi.

Appendix

1. Compresent with such emotionality and material implication is a discursive dimension that is at least tacitly present. This concerns the truth of what was happening in the Holocaust—the truth not as felt emotionally but as stateable verbally. My own textual commentary, abbreviated as it is, is a case in point. I thank Fred Evans for underlining the importance of this dimension (in conversation and in his e-mail of June 26, 2020).

2. That vestiges of such fascism were not altogether terminated in 1945 has become evident in neo-Nazi groups that have now arisen in Germany and in other parts of Europe—and in the United States (e.g., among white supremacists). William E. Connolly wrote *Aspirational Fascism* (2017) to address this recrudescence of fascism.

3. Peter Schjeldahl, "Painting History: The Dense Layers of Gerhard Richter's Work," *The New Yorker,* March 16, 2020, 94.

4. Harvey writes: "The unique power of the artwork and the unmitigated confidence that one may have in its power are testimony to its adequacy to the role of model for gratuitous and highly moral witnessing" (Robert Harvey, "Telltale at the Passage," in *Yale French Studies Number 99: Jean-Francois Lyotard, Time and Judgment* [New Haven, CT: Yale University Press, 2001], 115). Harvey argues that such testimonial art induces empathy on the part of those who take in an art image which shows or suggests suffering or its indelible traces. I am extending Harvey's model of artificial witnessing as subsequently developed in his *Témoins d'artifice* (Paris: L'Harmattan, 2003) and in *Witnessness* (New York: Continuum, 2010) by stressing the emotional bearing of the artwork as indirect witness rather than its moral force, which is Harvey's emphasis.

5. Photographs were in fact taken by a member of the *Sonderkommando*; but they were mostly empty images and show very little of what went on in the crematoria. Nevertheless, they too stand as testimony to the mass killings that happened there. As Didi-Huberman writes: "As a 'place of memory' such photography is useless because it is deprived of the referent at which it aims: one sees no one in these images. But is a clearly visible reality necessary for witnessing to take place?" (Georges Didi-Huberman, *Écorces* [Paris: Éditions du Minuit, 2011], 49; available in English as *Bark,* trans. Samuel E. Martin [Cambridge, MA: MIT Press, 2017]). Similarly, the absence of recognizable figures in Gerhard Richter's painting does not invalidate its role as a form of witnessing this phase of the Holocaust. I thank Robert Harvey for the Didi-Huberman citation.

6. This quote and the first two sentences of the epigraph at the beginning of this appendix are from *Joan Mitchell,* exhibition catalogue, ed. Marcia Tucker (New York: Whitney Museum of American Art, 1974), 6. The third sentence of

the epigraph, "I get feelings from the outside," is from an interview between Mitchell and Yves Michaud held in August 1989, as found on p. 2 of the typescript of the interview that is now held in the Joan Mitchell Archive, New York City. I owe both citations to Adam Blair.

7. In its sheer size, the painting occupies an entire wall in the Metropolitan Museum of Art. It is also extremely heavy, bearing many layers of leaded paint, a hallmark of Kiefer's work. These considerable dimensions and weight reinforce the historical gravity of the Holocaust. In contrast stands the motif of light and fragile flowers presented on the surface of the painting. Note that "Flowers of Auschwitz" is the name of a group of sketches made with India ink by Zinowij Tołkaczew (I owe this reference to Robert Harvey).

8. By "deferred" I intend the equivalent German adverb, *nachträglich*, "later" or "belatedly," literally a "bearing after" by way of a pent-up emotional intensity whose full force is delayed until later in life. This is a critical term in Freud's theory of trauma, as first fleshed out in the case of the "Wolfman."

Index

Page references in *italic* refer to images in the text.